The Status, Rights and Treatment
of Persons with Disabilities
within Customary Legal Frameworks in Uganda
A Study of Mukono District

David Brian Dennison

Globethics.net African Law No. 9

Globethics.net African Law

Series editor: Prof. Dr. Obiora Ike, Executive Director of Globethics.net in Geneva and Professor of Ethics at the Godfrey Okoye University Enugu/Nigeria.

Globethics.net African Law 9
David Brian Dennison, *The Status, Rights and Treatment of Persons with Disabilities within Customary Legal Frameworks in Uganda: A Study of Mukono District*

Geneva: Globethics.net, 2021
ISBN 978-2-88931-409-6 (online version)
ISBN 978-2-88931-410-2 (print version)
© 2021 Globethics.net

Managing Editor: Ignace Haaz
Assistant Editor: Nefti Bempong-Ahun

Globethics.net International Secretariat
150 route de Ferney
1211 Geneva 2, Switzerland
Website: *www.globethics.net/publications*
Email: *publications@globethics.net*

All web links in this text have been verified as of March 2021.

The Status, Rights and Treatment
of Persons with Disabilities
within Customary Legal Frameworks in Uganda

A Study of Mukono District

TABLE OF CONTENTS

ACKNOWLEDGEMENTS

First I must acknowledge my wife Mary Jane and my children Charlotte, David, Robert and Carol. They demonstrated tremendous patience, support and understanding during this challenging task.

I must also thank my supervisor Professor Chuma Himonga for her diligence, encouragement, expertise and insight. Those who have worked under her tutelage are thankful to call her "Ma." The nickname is well earned!

I owe additional gratitude to my former Dean at Uganda Christian University Dr. Pamela Tibihikirra Kalyegira who encouraged me to apply to the University of Cape Town and pursue graduate studies.

I am thankful to the people of Mukono District who willingly took part in the fieldwork as well as Mr. Baab, David Nangosi and Paul Agaba who offered invaluable assistance in the interview process. I am also appreciative for the Luganda translation assistance provided by Dr. Richard Watuulo, Jonathan Mwesigye and Simon Peter Ddamba Anatoli.

Special thanks should also go to Dr. Jeff McNair of Joni & Friends International and Calvary Baptist University for the provision of disability studies materials to Uganda Christian University.

Finally, I am deeply appreciative of the institutional support I received from Uganda Christian University during this process under the leadership of the Rev. Dr. Canon John Senyonyi.

To God be the Glory!

-Brian Dennison

To Zoë Reid and the Family of Joan Kagezi

1

INTRODUCTION

Introduction

This research project is motivated by two key premises. First, customary law and legal frameworks are highly consequential within lived environments in Sub-Saharan contexts. Second, human impairments have pervasive social impacts on people's lives that are likely to impact status, rights and treatment in customary legal settings.

The thesis includes the product of extensive desk research and fieldwork. The reading phase of the research provides the theoretical grounding to construct a research project at the intersection of legal anthropology, disability theory, legal content and human rights development. The fieldwork offers insights on the lived experiences and social context of persons with disabilities in Mukono District, a home to deeply pluralistic customary legal frameworks.

The foundational tenets of deep legal pluralism inform the research approach. Deep legal pluralism 'is a concomitant of social pluralism: the legal organisation of society is congruent with its social organisation'.[1] To understand the rights, status and treatment of persons with disabilities in Mukono District, we must obtain some understanding of their lived experiences, relevant social factors and the effective consequences of life events.

---

[1] J Griffiths 'What is legal pluralism?' (1986) 24 *Journal of Legal Pluralism and Unofficial Law* 1-55 at 38.

The thesis demonstrates the vital importance of customary legal scenarios to the status, rights and treatment of persons with disabilities. In these scenarios the perceived normative substance of formal and customary law can influence decisions, but the decision makers' working knowledge of this legal substance as it pertains to disability status is disparate, varied and incomplete. Under these circumstances the process and outcomes of customary scenarios are shaped by suppositions about the capacity and functionality of persons with disabilities as well as situational analysis. The flexibility of customary law combines with the diversity of human disability to generate varied legal outcomes where particular biases and an individual or group's rational thought process can play effectual roles.

The field research method shifts the focus from discerning the substance of normative customary law to appreciating the significance of various dynamics at play within informal scenarios where legal rights are meted out by family, clan and community members. It does so using the inclusive lens of Sally Falk Moore's semi-autonomous social field.[2]

In addition, the fieldwork findings offer insights into how the processes and outcomes of customary legal scenarios in Mukono District can be impacted and engaged in ways that advance disability rights. The resulting insights lead to suggestions for change strategies for those seeking to improve and advance the social and legal cause of persons with disabilities in Mukono District and similar settings.

The Research Problem

This thesis addresses a largely unstudied question: How does customary law impact the status, rights and treatment of persons with disabilities? It addresses this problem by presenting qualitative findings

---

[2] SF Moore 'Law and social change: the semi-autonomous social field as an appropriate subject of study (1973) 7(4) *Law & Society Review* 719-746.

about the rights, status and treatment of persons with disabilities within customary legal frameworks in deeply pluralistic, post-colonial contexts.

Customary law is resilient and ubiquitous.[3] Despite the proliferation of legal formalism in sub-Saharan Africa, customary legal content and practice remain impactful and dispositive in people's lives. Matters of marriage, family relations, succession, land ownership, and cultural leadership often hinge on legal determinations made within customary legal frameworks.[4]

Given the tendency of human impairments to elicit negative social responses, there is a need to assess the status, rights and treatment of persons with disabilities in highly relational customary legal frameworks. Yet unlike the extensively treated interaction between women's rights and customary law[5], the relationship between disability status and legal custom remains largely unaddressed.

---

[3] E Ehrlich *The Fundamental Principles of the Sociology of Law* (1936) at 37 ('[j]ust as we find the ordered community wherever we follow its traces . . . so we also find law everywhere, ordering and upholding every human association').

[4] International Justice Mission (IJM) *Property Grabbing from Ugandan Widows and the Justice System: A Mixed-Methods Assessment in Mukono County, Uganda* (2014).

[5] See e.g. FW Jjuuko & E Kibalama *Culture and Women: The Position of Women in Buganda* (2011); BK Twinomugisha 'African customary law and women's human rights in Uganda' in J Fenrich, P Galizzi & T Higgins (eds) *The Future of African Customary Law* (2011) 446-466; C Himonga 'Constitutional rights of women under customary law in Southern Africa' in B Baines, D Barak-Erez and T Kahana (eds) *Feminist Constitutionalism: Global Perspectives* (2012) 317-335; C Nyamu-Musembi 'Are local norms and practices fences or pathways? The example of women's property rights' in AA An-Na'im (ed) *Cultural Transformation and Human Rights in Africa* (2002) 126-150; A Claassens & S Mnisi 'Rural women redefining land rights in the context of living customary law' (2009) 25 *SAJHR* 491-516; L Khadiagala 'Negotiating law and custom: judicial doctrine and women's property rights in Uganda' (2002) 46 *Journal of African Law* 1-13.

Customary legal frameworks entail a wide-ranging assessment of agents and factors that contribute to the sourcing and application of customary law and practice. Customary frameworks include the legal substance, social relationships and cultural practices that help to generate the content, determination and application of customary law. Customary frameworks include indigenous legal content, relevant cultural beliefs, ceremonial rights, leadership structures, decision making bodies, formal laws and the affective engagement of formal institutions. The plural term 'frameworks' used in the thesis title reflects the fact that even a singular district in Uganda is home to multiple customary frameworks.

This thesis employs the analytical lens of the semi-autonomous social field for assessing and evaluating customary legal frameworks. Moore writes that

> '[t]he semi-autonomous social field has rule making capacities, and the means to induce or coerce compliance; but it is simultaneously set in a larger social matrix which can, and does, affect and invade it, sometimes at the invitation of persons inside it, sometimes at its own instance'.[6]

The semi-autonomous social field enables to consider both discrete individual transactions that reflect the lived law as well as the impact on norms resulting from legislation and legal decisions.[7]

Customary law is rightly discerned by researching its existence and application within the lived environment.[8] This thesis employs qualita-

---

[6] Moore (note 2) at 720.

[7] *Ibid* 743.

[8] Moore (note 2); SF Moore 'Certainties undone: fifty turbulent years of legal anthropology' (2001) 7 *Journal of the Royal Anthropology Institute* 95-116; SF Moore 'Changing African land tenure: reflections on the incapacities of the state' (1998) 10(2) *European Journal of Development Research* 33-49; J Grif-

tive field research guided by literature review to determine how customary legal frameworks interface with and impact persons with disabilities in Mukono District. The thesis is built on the input and narratives of 63 persons with disabilities along with interviews of 23 community members reputed as knowledgeable in cultural matters. These two cohorts of interviewees offer insights helpful to addressing the research problem.

The field research demonstrates the vital importance of customary legal scenarios to the status, rights and treatment of persons with disabilities. These scenarios are occasions where consequential decisions about people's lives and circumstances are made outside of formal legal proceedings. They need not involve juridical or quasi-juridical actors. Key scenarios where consequential decisions are made outside of formal institutions include family and clan gatherings subsequent to burial rites and meetings where young men seek permission to marry from the father of an intended bride. Non-judicial actors in these social occasions influence and determine weighty matters including clan leadership, land inheritance, martial status and custody relationships.

Customary legal scenarios are not mere exercises in recalling and applying dispositive normative rules. Decision-makers in these scenarios take various factors into consideration when determining the rights, status and treatment in customary scenarios. This is especially the case in matters involving persons with disabilities who present with unique traits and characteristics that are resistant to the formation of established precedents. Thus the research problem calls for an analysis concerning how and why determinations involving persons with disabilities are made in customary scenarios as opposed to the unearthing of established customary substantive law. Moore's semi-autonomous social field ensures the generous consideration of affective sources and influences within consequential scenarios.

---

fiths 'The social working of legal rules' (2003) 48 *Journal of Legal Pluralism and Unofficial Law* 1-84.

This thesis involves more than a descriptive catalogue of outcomes from customary legal occurrences involving persons with disabilities. It includes an assessment of cultural attitudes about persons with disabilities. It considers the influences of other legal sources and actors on customary legal scenarios including domestic law and international instruments. It assesses the viability of strategies to improve legal status, rights and treatment within customary scenarios. This ambitious scope reflects the need to account for diverse influences and the pragmatic potential of the research to improve the lives of persons with disabilities in deeply pluralistic, Majority World contexts.

Justification of the Research

There is abundant justification for this thesis. It offers insights in important and challenging contexts where research-based knowledge and guidance are limited.

First, the thesis concerns disability status, rights and treatment. Persons with disabilities make up a substantial portion of the world's population. The World Health Organization asserts that more than one billion people are disabled[9] and of these 'nearly 200 million people experience considerable disabilities in functioning'.[10] Uganda's census reports that 14 per cent of its population over five years of age has a disability.[11] The census reports that out of Mukono District's 2014 population of 501 644 there were 59 650 persons with disabilities.[12]

---

[9] UN World Health Organization (WHO) *World Report on Disabilities* (2011) s xi at 23 available at < http://www.who.int/disabilities/world_report/2011/report.pdf> last accessed 9 October 2017.

[10] *Ibid.*

[11] Uganda Bureau of Statistics, *The National Population and Housing Census* (2014) at 22.

[12] *Ibid* at 80 in table A11.

Despite the sizable population of persons with disabilities, existing research in the area of disabilities in Uganda is limited. In a 2012 case study regarding disability rights development, Norad found that '[r]esearch is one of the areas' that their evaluation of Uganda 'found least supported'.[13] Ugandan policy makers agree that research is needed in the context of disability matters.[14] For its part the World Health Organisation posits that '[c]ollecting information on knowledge, beliefs and attitudes about disability can help identify gaps in public understanding that can be bridged through education and public information'.[15]

The relationship between poverty and disability heightens the importance of this research. Poverty is endemic to much of sub-Saharan Africa including Uganda.[16] Poverty and disability promote each other in a reciprocal cycle.[17] There is a 'bidirectional link' between poverty and disability whereby disability increases the risk of poverty and poverty increases the risk of disability.[18] Persons with disabilities in low-income

---

[13] Norwegian Agency for Development Cooperation *Mainstreaming Disability in the New Development Paradigm, Evaluation of Norwegian Support to Promote the Rights of Persons with Disabilities: Uganda Country Study—summary* (2012) 6.

[14] Ministry of Gender, Labour and Social Development, *National Policy on Disability in Uganda* (2006) at 20-21.

[15] WHO (note 9) at 267.

[16] According to the World Bank in 2014 19 of the 20 nations with the lowest GDP per person were in sub-Saharan Africa with Uganda ranking as the 16th poorest nation in the world. Data available at <http://data.worldbank.org/indicator/NY.GDP.PCAP.CD?order=wbapi_data_value_2013+wbapi_data_value&sort=asc> last accessed on 27 October 2015.

[17] Although richer nations have a higher percentage of persons with disabilities, this is largely attributable to having a higher life expectancy and a higher percentage of older citizens. WHO Report (note 9) at 27 (reporting that the prevalence rate for disability for adults in higher income countries is 11.8 per cent and the rate in lower income countries is 18 per cent).

[18] WHO (note 9) at 10.

countries are typically overrepresented among the poor[19], and personal poverty is linked to disability in developing nations.[20]

Developing nations have fewer financial resources to allocate towards empowering and improving the lives of persons with disabilities. Funding is often restricted to those experiencing the 'most significant difficulties in functioning'.[21] In developing nations only one to two per cent of gross domestic product goes to social safety-net programmes.[22] The burden of dealing with these challenges falls on individuals with disabilities and kinship groups[23], thus raising the importance of the customary legal frameworks which often govern and influence personal law and familial relations.[24]

In addition, customary legal frameworks remain operative and vital in the lives of people in Mukono District. A recent study by International Justice Mission found that only 1.3 per cent of widows engage in the mandatory formal court-based probate process after the death of their husbands.[25] Given the prevalence of customary legal scenarios it is important to understand how persons with disabilities are treated in those scenarios.

---

[19] WHO (note 9).

[20] S Mitra, A Posarac & B Vick 'Disability and poverty in developing countries: a multidimensional study'(2012) 41 *World Development* 1-18; United Nations Commission for Social Development *Mainstreaming Disability in the Development Agenda* (2008) available at <www.un.org/disabilities/default.asp?id=708> last accessed on 27 October 2015.

[21] Ibid at 165 citing A Marriott & K Gooding *Social* Assistance and Disability in Developing Countries (2007).

[22] Ibid at 144 citing C Weigand & M Grosh Levels and Patterns of Safety N*et* Spending in Developing and T*ransition* Countries (2008) available at <http://siteresources.worldbank.org/SOCIALPROTECTION/Resources/SP-Discussion-papers/Safety-Nets-DP/0817.pdf > last accessed 27 October 2015.

[23] Ibid at 157.

[24] Twinomugisha (note 5) at 452.

[25] IJM (note 4) at 16-17.

This study also touches on the crucial area of land rights. Persons with disabilities 'are prone to the loss of land rights and are threatened by landlessness due to poverty-induced asset transfers, distress land sales, evictions, land grabbing and abuse of land inheritance procedures'.[26] Customary legal scenarios often determine land rights. Given the importance of customary legal scenarios in the determination and establishment of land rights, this study offers vital insights.

Customary law is living law.[27] It is the law that people apply in their lives. Customary legal traditions are flexible, diverse and dynamic.[28] Customary legal systems have the capacity to adapt to unique situations and new developments.[29] Thus customary law has the capacity for progressive engagement. It changes over time. It can incorporate emergent norms and values and presents a means for community-based adoption of human rights principles. This thesis shines a light on the process and possibility of human rights-based change within customary legal frameworks.

Another strategy for human rights-based change is aligning existing customs and values with human rights. Many indigenous customs and cultures are reputed to foster general communitarian principles that appear to offer the promise of potential benefits to persons with disabilities. In particular, Bantu cultures in Africa are known for the practice and veneration of the social ethos known as 'ubuntu'. The Baganda, the predominant group of people in Mukono District, are a Bantu people. I assess the potential for leveraging an indigenous communitarian ethos for the advancement of the human rights of persons with disabilities.

---

[26] Uganda Land Policy s 72.

[27] Ehrlich (note 3).

[28] L Cotula 'Introduction' in L Cotula (ed) Changes in "Customary" Land Tenure Systems in Africa (2007) at 10.

[29] United States Institute of Peace & the Rift Valley Institute Local Justice in Southern Sudan (2010) at 5.

In sum, the potential benefits of this thesis are substantial and expansive. It provides information on the treatment, status and rights of persons with disabilities in Mukono District. It can also serve as a model for those in the disability rights movement seeking to engage indigenous communities in bottom-up social and legal reform. Furthermore, the thesis offers insight opportunities for constructive engagement with customary law and practice.

Objectives of the Thesis

This thesis qualitatively assesses the rights, status and treatment of persons with disabilities as experienced within situations governed and impacted by customary legal frameworks. It presents salient information about the way persons with disabilities experience customary legal scenarios in Mukono District. The thesis offers instructive and beneficial insights to those devising legal and social strategies for meeting and preserving human rights standards for persons with disabilities in deeply pluralistic majority world settings.

Scope of the Thesis

The subject matter of this thesis largely defines its scope. It concerns: 1) persons with disabilities 2) in customary legal frameworks 3) in Mukono District. In addition, because of the geographic scope the study is dominated by a specific people group the cultural scope centres on 4) the Buganda. These four subjects are treated below in order to better establish and define the scope of the thesis.

Persons with Disabilities

Disability is a complex and politically charged term.[30] The challenge of categorically defining disability is exhibited in the Convention on the Rights of Persons with Disabilities (CRPD). Instead of defining the term, the CRPD frames disability as follows:

> Recognizing that disability is an evolving concept and that disability results from the interaction between persons with impairments and attitudinal and environmental barriers that hinders their full and effective participation in society on an equal basis with others, . . . [31]

This thesis adopts the CRPD's framing of disability.

The term 'persons with disabilities' is the most widely preferred term of reference in the English language for those experiencing disability.[32] This phrase is aligned with the social model of disability because it

---

[30] 'Disability: Who Counts? Defining disability is tricky—and measuring it is even harder' The Economist (14 December 2013) 56.

[31] Convention on the Rights of Persons with Disabilities (CRPD), adopted 13 December 2006 by GA Res 61/106 Annex I UN GAOR 61st Sess Supp No 49 at 65 UN Doc A/61/49 (2006) entered into force 3 May 2008 UN Doc A/61/61; signed by Uganda on 30 March 2007 and ratified by Uganda on 25 September 2008 pre.

[32] While 'persons with disabilities' is presently predominant, its use and acceptance is not universal. According to Clark and Marsh the British civil rights movement has rejected the term because it disabilities refers to a medical condition and thus confuses disability with impairment. Moreover, they note that the phrase diminishes political identity by separating the person from the identifying marker. L Clark & S Marsh 'Patriarchy in the UK: The language of disability' (2002) 2nd Draft <http://pf7d7vi404s1dxh27mla5569.wpengine.netdna-cdn.com/files/library/Clark-Laurence-language.pdf> last accessed on 25 September 2017.

expresses that disablement is not an inherent aspect of the person.[33] Notably the CRPD uses the phrase. It inclusively classifies 'persons with disabilities' which it describes as:

> including those who have long-term physical, mental, intellectual or sensory impairments which in interaction with various barriers may hinder their full and effective participation in society with an equal basis with others.[34]

This thesis also takes up the CRPD's classification of persons with disabilities.

Another key term included in the CPRD classification is 'impairment'. The term impairment adopted by the World Health Organization entails problems with body function and body structure.[35] This is consistent with Uganda's formal definition of impairment as 'any loss or abnormality[36] of psychological, physical, neurological or anatomic func-

---

[33] M Wickenden, D Mulligan et al 'Stakeholder consultations on community-based rehabilitation guidelines in Ghana and Uganda' (2012) 1(1) African Journal of Disability 1-10 at 2. However, there are some adherents of the social model who find the phrase lacking. See for example C Ngwena 'The new disability convention: Implications for disability equality norms in the South African workplace in OC Dupper & C Garbers (eds) Equality in the workplace: Reflections from South Africa and beyond (2010).

[34] CRPD art 1.

[35] World Health Organization, The International Classification of Functioning, Disability and Health (2014) defines 'impairments' as problems in bodily function or alterations in body structure.

[36] When using the word 'abnormality' it is important that the term should only be used in its scientific sense and should not be used to refer to a person as being 'not normal' or somehow less than a 'normal' person. National Center on Disability and Journalism Disability Language Style Guide definition of 'Abnormal/abnormality' available at http://ncdj.org/style-guide/ last accessed on 20 August 2017. This thesis uses the term impairment in the scientific and medical sense of the term to refer to an actual physical or bodily condition.

tion or structure'.[37] Impairment is a component of the CRPD classification of person with a disability as adopted by this thesis.

I use the term 'impairment' to place an emphasis on the anatomical and mental conditions that present themselves scientifically as opposed to the term 'disability' which entails the role and impact of social factors. This approach to terminology runs the risk of both marginalising the role society plays in disablement and in objectifying persons with disabilities as objects requiring a cure.[38] However, despite its problematic connotations and associations, the term impairment remains helpful when there is a need to distinguish the physical presentation of biological conditions from the impact of social forces and cultural systems. Thus for the purpose of this thesis, 'disability' includes the social context while 'impairment' only concerns physical and mental conditions.

Customary Legal Frameworks

This study concerns customary legal frameworks. The adjective 'customary' refers to something that is indigenous to a place that it rooted in the traditions of the people.[39] Customary law has certain traditional attributes such as being oral, mutable, situational and naturally occurring without formal legislation.[40] For the purpose of this thesis these qualities are treated as common characteristics of customary law rather than mandatory requirements. Prior codified versions of customary law or

---

[37] Ministry of Gender, Labour and Social Development, National Policy on Disability in Uganda (2006) at 26.

[38] V Perju 'Impairment, discrimination, and the legal construction of disability in the European Union and the United States' (2011) 44 Cornell Int'l L J 279.

[39] World Intellectual Property Organization Customary Law, Traditional Knowledge and Intellectual Property: An Outline of the Issues (2013) at 2.

[40] GR Woodman 'A survey of customary laws in Africa in search of lessons for the future' in J Fenrich, P Galizzi & T Higgins (Eds), The Future of African Customary Law (2011) 9-30.

pronouncements by customary monarchs are not disqualified as sources of customary law under this approach.

The title refers to 'customary legal frameworks' as opposed to 'customary law' in order to reflect the fact that customary law operates in systems and it is not monolithic even in the context of a single district. In addition, this term allows for the consideration of various elements within semi-autonomous social fields as opposed to limiting consideration to purely official legal phenomena. Given the limited findings regarding normative customary laws with partcularised relevance to persons with disabilities it was important for the research to gather information about actual customary legal scenarios.

Mukono District

Mukono District is a one of Uganda's 111 districts. It is located in Central Uganda east of the capital city of Kampala and north of Lake Victoria. Mukono is a traditional indigenous home to the Buganda although other tribal groups now inhabit the District as well due to increased mobility within Uganda. Mukono District is located in a transitional area that includes semi-urban towns within the suburban expansion of greater Kampala as well as rural areas.

The Buganda

The people group at the cultural centre of this study are the Baganda. They are the largest of the 65 ethnic groups recognised under the Constitution[41] comprising almost 17 per cent of Uganda's population.[42] They are considered to be part of a larger ethnic category known as Bantu. Bantu peoples are found largely in the southern half of Uganda while

---

[41] Constitution of Uganda 1995 (as amended in 2005) sch 3.

[42] World Fact Book of the United States Central Intelligence Agency (2015).

people in the other broad ethnic categories are primarily indigenous to the northern half.[43]

In terms of nomenclature, the people group is called the Baganda and their kingdom and historic territory is referred to as Buganda. For the purposes of this thesis the word Baganda is also used as an adjective to refer to things attributable to the Baganda people[44] and Buganda is an adjective that refers things attributable to the Buganda Kingdom. The language of the Baganda people is Luganda.

The traditional social structure of Buganda is monarchical and feudalistic. The Buganda king is the Kabaka.[45] Historically the Kabaka had the power to rule, tax, judge, wage war and bestow chieftainships.[46] He enjoyed power over the life and death of his subjects and the use of their labour.[47]

The British partnered with Buganda to achieve political hegemony in the Protectorate of Uganda.[48] The British treated the Baganda more favourably than other people groups in the Protectorate and granted Buganda significant legal authority and autonomy including the right to legislate in consultation with, and approval of, the colonial regime.[49]

---

[43] J Tumusiime & CO Bichachi (Eds), The People and Culture of Uganda 4th Ed (2011) at 3.

[44] Kiganda is a Luganda word that can also be used as an adjective used to refer cultural aspects of the Baganda. However, for stylistic purposes the term Kiganda is not used in this thesis.

[45] Tumusiime & Bichachi (note 43) at 4.

[46] Ibid at 4.

[47] ES Haydon Law and Justice in Buganda (1960) at 5.

[48] GH McKnight 'Land, politics, and Buganda's "indigenous" colonial state' (2000) 28(1) The Journal of Imperial and Commonwealth History 65-89.

[49] Haydon (note 47) at 21 quoting the decision of Nasanairi Kibuka v. A.E. Bertie 1 U.L.R. 41 (1908) which held in part: 'the native Government of Uganda has power to legislate for the subjects of the Kabaka after consultation with and following the advice of the Governor . . .'

The colonial regime kept the customary law of the Baganda operative[50] and colonial authorities did not dispense with Buganda's traditional court system.[51] During British rule the Kabaka remained especially active and involved in the administration of legal matters including the appointment and oversight of customary heirs.[52]

Despite British respect for Buganda's customary justice system[53], non-indigenous people were excluded.[54] The Buganda Agreement provided that '[t]he Jurisdiction of the native court of the Kabaka of Uganda, however, shall not extend to any person not a native of the Uganda province.'[55]

The end of colonial rule resulted in a significant diminishing of the Buganda Kingdom. The power vacuum brought about by the British departure in 1962 left Buganda's formal institutions vulnerable. Although Kabaka Mutesa II was named as the first president after Ugandan independence, his time in office was short. In 1966 Prime Minister Milton Obote, a Langi from Northern Uganda, took control of the national government by force and Mutesa II fled to the United Kingdom to live in exile until his death in 1969.[56]

Under Obote, and later Amin, the Buganda government and court structures dissipated, leaving Baganda customary law bereft of legitimising formal institutions. Today, despite the presence of a Kabaka and the formal recognition of traditional leaders, customary law remains 'trun-

---

[50] Ibid at 25 quoting s 20 of the Order of Council and at xxxvii quoting s 10(b) of the Buganda Courts Ordinance.

[51] Ibid at 11 and 30 citing HR Horne 'The native of Uganda and the criminal law' (1938-39) Uganda Journal 1 at 6.

[52] Ibid at 195, 208-214.

[53] Ibid at 11, 47.

[54] Ibid at 8.

[55] Buganda Agreement of 1900 s 6.

[56] R First 'Uganda: The latest coup d'état in Africa' (1971) 27(3) The World Today 131-138.

cated because, although the substantive customary law exists, its courts and procedures do not'.[57]

Research Question and Argument of the Thesis

An appreciation of the history and heritage of the Buganda Kingdom helps us understand the place of Baganda cultural institutions and customary law in contemporary Uganda. This thesis answers the specific research question: How does customary law impact the status, rights and treatment of persons with disabilities in Mukono District, Uganda? It does so through qualitative data generated in interviews conducted in Mukono District and the study of relevant literature.

The field research is an exploratory study.[58] Exploratory research does not set out to prove a specific hypothesis.[59] Instead, the value of exploratory research is rooted in the utility; knowledge that might lead to the generation of particular hypotheses.[60] Exploratory research is particularly useful in contexts where little or nothing is known about a certain subject matter. The purpose of this thesis is to learn about the rights, status and treatment of persons with disabilities under customary legal frameworks.

This study traverses a number of theoretical disputation. Disability is a highly politicised subject with a diverse array of theoretical schools. Customary law is the subject of a rich debate between legal anthropologists who seek to describe things the way they are and legal formalists who prefer to talk about what the formal law says things are or should be. The interface of aspects of indigenous culture—which includes customary law—with human rights is a contested zone pitting normative universalists against cultural relativists. Despite these controversies, this

---

[57] Jjuuko & Kibalama (note 5).

[58] RA Stebbins Exploratory Research in the Social Sciences (2001).

[59] Ibid at 25.

[60] Ibid at 54.

thesis commends a generous approach to theory. In the challenging context of this research, strident adherence to one theoretical approach to the exclusion of others fails to address the layers of challenges and needs.

Certain foundational premises undergird and direct the field research. First, customary law is highly relevant to lived environments in Mukono District. Second, customary law is rightly discerned by researching its existence and application within the lived environment. Third, the attributes and application of customary law can be place-specific and situation-specific. The basis and support for these foundational premises is presented in Chapter 3 of the thesis.

Building on those premises, the argument of this thesis is that disability status is a relevant factor in customary legal scenarios in Mukono District and that the thesis' fieldwork will provide relevant and useful information as to the rights, status and treatment of persons with disabilities in customary legal frameworks.

Literature Review

The literature review for this thesis was broad and multifaceted. Addressing the research problem requires knowledge of several content areas. For example the literature review required a theoretical understanding of disability, customary law, legal pluralism and proposed strategies for effecting socio-legal change. It also required a cultural and historic appreciation of the Baganda people and the reported content of Baganda customary law. Because the thesis employs Moore's semi-autonomous social field as an analytical lens, I needed to appreciate the domestic and international formal law that speaks to disability and customary matters in Uganda. Finally, because this thesis entails fieldwork, there was foundational literature that informed the research design.

To a great extent Chapters 2, 3, 4 and 5 of the thesis present expanded topical literature reviews on the subject matter assigned to those chapters. This literature review locates this thesis within the existing scholarship without exhausting the literature explored in subsequent chapters.

Customary Law and Legal Pluralism

The thesis requires a working understanding of traits and tendencies of customary law. Woodman[61] writes about the dominant attributes of customary law such as its mutability, flexibility and diversity. Oba[62], Ochich[63] and Ubink[64] provide useful analysis on the present status and future of African customary law in the context of increasing legal formalisation.

Many authors address the challenge of customary law to adapt to modern human rights requirements.[65] Often times these articles address the tension between customary laws and modern conceptions regarding women's rights and gender equality. Himonga[66] writes about the capacity of customary legal systems to align with universal rights standards through change and transformation. This possibility of human rights alignment informed the research design which investigated the openness

---

[61] Woodman (note 40).

[62] AA Oba 'The future of customary law in Africa' in J Fenrich, P Galizzi & T Higgins (Eds) The Future of African Customary Law (2011) 58-82.

[63] GO Ochich 'The withering province of customary law in Kenya' in J Fenrich, P Galizzi & T Higgins (Eds) The Future of African Customary Law (2011) 103-128.

[64] J Ubink 'The quest for customary law in African state courts' in J Fenrich, P Galizzi & T Higgins (Eds) The Future of African Customary Law (2011) 83-128.

[65] AM Banks 'CEDAW, compliance, and custom: human rights enforcement in Sub-Saharan Africa' (2009) 32 Fordham International Law Journal 781-845; M Ssenyonjo 'Culture and the human rights of women in Africa: between light and shadow' (2007) 51(01) Journal of African Law 39-67; Claassens & Mnisi (note 5); Khadiagala (note 5); Twinomugisha (note 5).

[66] Himonga (note 5).

of local customary knowledge bearers to human rights treaties and external change agents. In addition, those who denounce cultural practices in the name of human rights must appreciate that there is also a right to practice culture[67] and this right has particular resonance in the context of post-colonial indigenous people.[68]

Legal Attributions and Condition of Customary Law

The right to culture is proclaimed by the formal law of Uganda. The Constitution[69] provides for the right to practise culture and custom. However Ugandan formal law places limitations on the right to practice one's culture, including customary legal practice. For example, the Judicature Act includes a 'repugnancy clause' that limits the enforcement of customary law to instances where the custom is 'not repugnant to natural justice, equity and good conscience and not incompatible either directly or by necessary implication with any written law.'[70]

Theoretical Justification for Developmental Engagement with Customary Law

This thesis addresses customary law despite the fact that the state law has largely displaced customary law on a formal basis. The thesis design is informed by the reality of 'deep legal pluralism' and is thereby appreciates that customary law as a 'feature of the social field' that is not dependent on official legal recognition.[71]

---

[67] E Grant 'Human rights, cultural diversity and customary Law in South Africa' (2006) 50(01) Journal of African Law 2-23.

[68] A Afadameh-Adeyemi Indigenous Peoples and the Right to Culture: An International Law Analysis (2009) PhD Dissertation University of Cape Town.

[69] Uganda Constitution art 37, national objectives and directives principle XXIV.

[70] The Judicature Act of 1996 (cap 13) s 15.

[71] JC Bekker, C Rautenbach & N Goolam (Eds) Introduction to Legal Pluralism in South Africa 3 ed. (2010) at 4.

Corradi[72] makes a thorough case for the use of 'bottom-up' approaches for legal reform in deeply pluralistic legal settings in the developing world. Kane, Oloka-Onyango and Tejan-Cole[73] address the evolving nature of customary law and challenge biases about the incapacity of customary systems to embrace norms that are compliant with modern human rights standards.

This thesis places an emphasis on the actual experiences of persons with disabilities. Cornwall and Nyamu-Musembi[74] bring out the necessity of direct engagement and struggle in the realization of meaningful rights advancement in African contexts. They also note the difficulty in bringing about tangible human rights reform through outside actors and the formal justice sector. Noting these challenges, Nyamu-Musembi[75] discusses the impediments to bringing about broad-based meaningful change through formal legal institutions and emphasises the need to adopt 'actor-oriented' perspectives for effecting social and legal change. Her work speaks to the importance of bottom-up approaches and why such approaches have special currency in the African context. This thesis' research makes inquiries that are relevant to the effectiveness and potential of bottom-up disability empowerment strategies.

---

[72] G Corradi 'Advancing human rights in legally plural Africa: the role of development actors in the justice sector' (2013) 26(1) Afrika Focus 89-98.

[73] M Kane, J Oloka-Onyango & A Tejan-Cole 'Reassessing customary law systems as a vehicle for providing equitable access to justice for the poor' (2005) Arusha Conference 'New Frontiers of Social Policy' at 12.

[74] A Cornwall & C Nyamu-Musembi 'Why rights, why now? Reflections on the rise of rights in international development' (2005) 36(1) IDS Bulletin 9.

[75] C Nyamu-Musembi 'Review of experiences in engaging with 'nonstate' justice systems in East Africa' (2003) Department for International Development (DfID) UK; C Nyamu-Musembi 'Towards an actor-oriented perspective on human rights' in N Kabeer (ed) Inclusive citizenship: Meanings and expressions (2005) 31-49.

Customary law in Mukono District

The field research and the resulting analysis was informed by background reading about the content and practice of Baganda customary law[76] including materials generated in Uganda's colonial era.[77] A recent study published by International Justice Mission speaks to the persistence and extent of customary practice in the context of succession in Mukono District.[78]

Disability

The key international human rights instrument concerning disabilities is the CRPD. Uganda ratified the CRPD in September of 2008. The prominent domestic laws concerning disabilities issues in Uganda are the Constitution[79] and the Persons with Disabilities Act.[80] These sources of formal disability law are unpacked in greater detail in Chapter 5.

Weber[81] and Doyle[82] present the rise of the disabilities rights movement in the West. Herr, Gostin and others[83] produced a wide-ranging collection of articles concerning the legal trajectory of the international disabilities movement leading up to the adoption of the CRPD. The articles combine to portray the rapid ascension of disability rights to international prominence.

When it comes to scholarship on the CRPD, Lord and Stein are prodigious in reporting on the scope, content and potential of the treaty.[84]

---

[76] Jjuuko & Kibalama (note 5).

[77] Haydon (note 47).

[78] IJM (note 4).

[79] Constitution of Uganda art 35, 21, 24 and nat obj and dir pr XVI and VI.

[80] The Persons with Disabilities Act of 2006 (Uganda).

[81] MC Weber Understanding Disability Law (2007).

[82] BJ Doyle Disability Discrimination: Law and Practice (6 Ed 2008).

[83] SS Herr, LO Gostin & HH Koh (Eds) The Human Rights of Persons with Intellectual Disabilities: Different but Equal (2003).

[84] See e.g. JE Lord & MA Stein 'The domestic incorporation of human rights law and the United Nations Convention on the Rights of Persons with Disabili-

Harpur[85] discusses the potential of the CRPD to promote societal change through legal action. Van Reenen and Combrinck[86] discuss the possibility of the communitarian ethos in Africa to inform and enliven the implementation of the CRPD. The work of these authors covers many of the foundational aspects of the CRPD and allowed me to move towards a finer applied assessment of the CRPD through the field research.

The disabilities studies movement has generated a large body of literature on the social context facing persons with disabilities. Key foundational works on the social context of persons with disabilities include those by Goffman[87] on 'stigma', Wolfensberger[88] on 'normalization' and 'social role valorization' and Oliver[89] on the 'politics of disablement'. Flynn and Nitsch[90] address normalisation in the context of social integration. Link and others[91] label and outline the ways that persons with disabilities are marginalised and discriminated against. Engel[92]

---

ties' (2008) 83 Washington LR 449-479; JE Lord & MA Stein 'Prospects and practices for CRPD implementation in Africa' (2013) 1 ADRY 97-114, at 111.

[85] P Harpur 'Time to be heard: how advocates can use the Convention on the Rights of Persons with Disabilities to drive change (2011) 45(3) Valparaiso Univ LR 1271-1296.

[86] T Van Reenen & H Combrinck 'The UN Convention on the Rights of Persons with Disabilities in Africa: Progress after 5 years' (2011) 14 SUR-Int'l Journal on Human Rights 133-165.

[87] E Goffman Stigma: Notes on the Management of Spoiled Identity (1963).

[88] W Wolfensberger A Brief Introduction to Social Role Valorization: a High-Order Concept for Addressing the Plight of Societally Devalued People, and for Structuring Human Services (1998); Wolfensberger, WP, Nirje, B, Olshansky, S et al The Principle of Normalization in Human Services (1972).

[89] M Oliver, The Politics of Disablement: A Sociological Approach (1990).

[90] RJ Flynn & KE Nitch Normalization, Social Integration, and Community Services (1980).

[91] BG Link, LH Yang & PY Collins 'Measuring mental illness stigma' (2004) 30(3) Schizophrenia Bulletin 511-541.

[92] DM Engel 'Vertical and horizontal perspectives on rights consciousness' (2012) 19(2) Indiana Journal of Global Legal Studies 423-455.

describes and contrasts vertical and horizontal perspectives on transmitting rights consciousness. These works alerted me to social causes and consequences of disability in Western contexts as well as proposed means of addressing discrimination and social displacement.

Stone-MacDonald and Butera[93] produced an extensive literature review of writings on cultural beliefs and attitudes about disability in East Africa. It offers a thorough and relatively current assessment of the scope and breadth of disability oriented research in East Africa.

Devlielger[94] writes extensively on the topic of language and cultural meaning in the context of disabilities. Similarly Ogechi and Ruto[95] discuss the portrayal of disability though personal names and proverbs in Kenya. Bickenbach[96] addresses the negative role of cultural beliefs in the social status and treatment of persons with disabilities in developing societies. These studies inform the research with respect to social factors relevant to the status, rights and treatment of persons with disabilities in the East African context.

Research in Uganda on the legal rights and status of persons with disabilities is limited. Oyaro wrote a helpful report providing statistical

---

[93] A Stone-MacDonald & G Butera, 'Cultural beliefs and attitudes about disability in East Africa' (2012) 8(1) Review of Disability Studies: An International Journal 62-77.

[94] PJ Devlieger 'Physical "disability" in Bantu languages: understanding the relativity of classification and meaning' (1998) 21(1) International Journal of Rehabilitation Research 51-62; PJ Devlieger 'From handicap to disability: language use and cultural meaning in the United States' (1999) 21(7) Disability and Rehabilitation 346-354; PJ Devlieger 'Persons with a physical disability at the interstices of classification: examples from Africa and the United States' (1998) 2 Zeitschrift Behinderung und Dritte Welt 45-49.

[95] NO Ogechi & SJ Ruto 'Portrayal of disability through personal names and proverbs in Kenya; evidence from Ekegusii and Nandi' (2002) 2(3) Vienna Journal of African Studies 63-82.

[96] JE Bickenbach Physical Disability and Social Policy (1993).

information and an overview of the relevant legal content as well as the key disability policy initiatives, activities, actors and challenges in Uganda.[97] There are also reports and papers addressing overall international rights compliance with an emphasis on the CRPD.[98] There is material from the United Nations[99] outlining written law regarding persons with disabilities in Uganda. Uganda's Ministry of Gender[100] issued the National Policy on Disability that catalogues the disabilities law and policies in Uganda prior to ratification of the CRPD.

However, none of the existing disabilities-based literature originating from Uganda places specific emphasis on their legal rights and status in customary legal contexts. Katsui and Kumpuvuori[101] discuss the implementation of disability rights within Uganda's political space contrasted with the lack of disability rights development in Uganda's social space. Mulumba[102] writes about persons with disabilities in the context of pro-poor initiatives in Uganda from rights-based approach. Legal Action People with Disabilities[103] (LAPD) has a draft report regarding research on the challenges faced by women with disabilities. There are

---

[97] LO Oyaro 'Country report: Uganda' (2014) 2 ADRY 247-266.

[98] Office of the High Commissioner for Human Rights 'Working paper, a review of the Ugandan legal framework relevant to persons with disabilities: comparative analysis to the Convention on the Rights of Persons with Disabilities' (2008).

[99] United Nations, 'From exclusion to equality: realizing the rights of persons with disabilities' (2007).

[100] Ministry of Gender, Labour and Social Development (note 37).

[101] H Katsui & J Kumpuvuori 'Human rights based approach to disability in development in Uganda: a way to fill the gap between political and social spaces?' (2008) 10(4) Scandinavian Journal of Disability Research 227-236.

[102] M Mulumba Mainstreaming Disability into the Poverty Reduction Processes in Uganda: The Role of the Human Rights-Based Approach to the National Development Plan (2011) unpublished LLM thesis Stellenbosch University.

[103] Legal Action for People with Disabilities 'Violation of rights for the disabled woman: draft baseline study report' (2011).

also Ugandan case studies regarding the discriminatory treatment in the context of microcredit and the relationship between poverty and disability.[104]

Research Methodology

Arksey and Knight[105] provide guidance on social science research through interviews. Ewick and Silbey[106] discuss the value of individual stories from individuals facing socio-legal challenges in the context of legal studies and provide examples of the effective use of narrative research methodology. Griffiths notes that personal stories are particularly valuable in demonstrating how people see the law and how the law applies to their lives.[107] Benda-Beckmann writes that customary law in pluralist legal frameworks is discerned through the lived experiences of individuals.[108] Baffoe recommends placing persons with disabilities at the centre of research initiatives because they are 'expert knowers' of their own lived experiences and should be consulted as knowing authori-

---

[104] PG Méon, R Mersland, A Szafarz & M Labie 'Discrimination by microcredit officers: theory and evidence on disability in Uganda' (2011) 11(06) ULB--Universite Libre de Bruxelles; C Lwanga-Ntale 'Chronic poverty and disability in Uganda' paper presented at Staying Poor Chronic Poverty and Disability Policy Manchester, United Kingdom (April 2003) at 4 available at <http://digitalcommons.ilr.cornell.edu/gladnetcollect/320> last accessed 28 October 2015.

[105] H Arksey & PT Knight (Eds) Interviewing for Social Scientists: An Introductory Resource with Examples (1999).

[106] P Ewick & SP Silbey, The Common Place of Law: Stories from Everyday Life (1998).

[107] A Griffiths 'Using ethnography as a tool in legal research: an anthropological perspective' in R Banakar & M Travers (eds) *Theory and Method in Socio-Legal Research* (2005) 113-131, at 115.

[108] F von Benda-Beckmann 'Who's afraid of legal pluralism' (2002) 47, *Journal of Legal Pluralism and Unofficial Law* 37 at 71.

ties.[109] The first phase of the field research for this thesis bore out the wisdom of Baffoe as the interviews offered instructive qualitative content about the rights, status and treatment of persons with disabilities in customary scenarios.

Scheyvens and Storey[110] write about fieldwork in the context of development-related efforts and settings. Knight[111] provides insights on small-scale research design. Behling and Law[112] offer insights on the translation of questionnaires and other research instruments. Liamputtong[113] writes about the special challenges a researcher faces when researching vulnerable subjects. For Liamputtong the research of vulnerable people calls for researcher sensitivity, robust collaboration with members of the vulnerable group, and an overriding need to give people who are discouraged from speaking the ability to tell their stories through qualitative research. I incorporated this guidance into the research design, my approach to interviewee engagement and my interview technique.

Both the University of Cape Town and the Ugandan Government issued ethical pre-clearance for the fieldwork.[114] The actual fieldwork process ran quite smoothly and no complaints were lodged by any of the interviewees or any other individual or official.

---

[109] M Baffoe 'Stigma, discrimination & marginalization: gateways to oppression of persons with disabilities in Ghana, West Africa' (2013) 3(1) *Journal of Educational and Social Research* 187-198 at 191.

[110] R Scheyvens & D Storey (Eds) Development Fieldwork (2003).

[111] P Knight (Ed) Small Scale Research Design (2002).

[112] O Behling & KS Law Translating Questionnaires and Other Research Instruments (2000).

[113] P Liamputtong Researching the Vulnerable Moral and Ethical Issues in Researching Vulnerable People (2006).

[114] The University of Cape Town Faculty of Law's Research Ethics Committee granted a 24 month ethical clearance for the proposed field work involving human participants on 20 June 2014. The Uganda National Council for Science and Technology granted clearance in 2014 for application SS 3538

Gaps in the Literature

It is evident from the discussion of the literature that disability law and related socio-legal aspects are vibrant areas of research. In the African setting this research tends to emphasise the implementation of international human rights standards, the compliance of domestic law and policy with international standards, and the impact of the formal legal system and the modern human rights regime on the social and economic welfare of persons with disabilities.

The interface and interaction of customary law and disability status has been point of emphasis in literature encountered by this researcher. Certain catalogues of customary law touch on disabilities issues, but these issues tend to be on the periphery and are not the focus of any prior work. Moreover, even if these large general gaps did not exist, there would still be a gap in the research regarding the specific state of customary law concerning the status, rights and treatment of persons with disabilities within Uganda generally and within Mukono District specifically.

Research Methodology

Overview of the Research Methodology

Mukono District was an appropriate situs for the field research. As my home for seven years, Mukono offered ease of access and a wealth of contacts and relationships. Second, as an indigenous home to the well-studied Baganda people, the research could benefit from ample prior studies describing the customary laws and practices of the Baganda. Third, Mukono District offers a wide variety of settings because it is in an area that encompasses both secluded villages and transitional urban and semi-urban zones within the ever expanding reach of metropolitan Kampala. Thus Mukono District is home to the transitional dynamics that are pervasive in sub-Saharan Africa.

The field research was qualitative, exploratory and empirical. It sought descriptions, and narratives about the actual customary law and practices that specially concern the rights, status and treatment of persons with disabilities in Mukono District. The research was grounded in the understanding that customary legal content is discoverable in the knowledge of people, the status of persons and social interactions.[115]

I endeavoured to avoid imposing responses on the interviewees. The first phase of the field research interviews consisted of open-ended questions and narrative opportunities that gave the interviewees with disabilities the opportunity to speak about their own observations and experiences. t. Thus, the field research was not specifically calibrated to prove or disprove a theory. Instead it sought, in the tradition of Sally Falk Moore, primarily to discern and describe what is real, relevant and influential in the lived environment.[116]

Post-interview coding and the inclusion of direct questions in the second and third phases of the field research provided the opportunity to cross check the validity of the findings drawn from the open-ended and narrative inquiries comprising the majority of first stage of field interviews.

The field research also uncovered beliefs about the heritage of current customary practices relevant to matters of trajectory and legal legitimacy of customary law and practices within formal legal forums in Uganda.

The field research comprised three stages of interviews: 1) interviews of persons with disabilities; 2) interviews of people with actual and locally respected knowledge regarding Baganda customary law and practice; and 3) follow-up interviews with persons with disabilities concerning the results of the second stage of interviews.

---

[115] Benda-Beckmann (note 108) at 65-67.
[116] Moore (note 2) at 730.

In the first phase, I identified interview participants through the use of key contacts who had relationships with persons with disabilities throughout Mukono District. I implemented selective sampling to locate willing interviewees with disabilities.[117] Two persons with disabilities who reside in Mukono District assisted in identifying willing interviewees.

I conducted the first phase of interviews from January through March of 2015. Interviews were conducted in eight locations in Mukono District: Mukono Town, Seeta, Kalagi, Kyabakadde, Kimenyedde, Nakifuma, Nagojje, Kitimbwa and Nabbaale. Of these locations Mukono Town and Seeta are semi-urban transitional areas. The other interview locations are rural.

The interviewees came from a broad range of backgrounds in terms of age, employment status, religious affiliation and lived environment. The interview cohort was somewhat imbalanced in terms of gender and impairment type.

I obtained informed consent from all of the research participants. The consent protocol and materials met the core criteria of disclosure, understanding, voluntariness and competence.[118]

Interviews were conducted in private. I used semi-structured interview templates.[119] The semi-structured interview templates were modified and supplemented over the course of the interviews to address relevant and recurrent issues brought out in preceding interviews.[120] Interview templates and consent forms were translated into Luganda to facili-

---

[117] RL Miller Researching Life Stories and Family Histories, Analysing Life Histories (2000) 76 citing L Schatzman & AL Strauss Strategies for a Natural Sociology (1973) (Selective sampling is recognised as an appropriate methodology in light of the inability of random sampling to generate relevant interviewees).

[118] Liamputtong (note 113) at 15.

[119] Arksey & Knight (note 114) at 7.

[120] Miller (note 116) at 96.

tate the interview process and ease the work of the translator. The initial templates for each phase of the interviews as well as the informed consent form are included in the appendix II of this thesis.

There are a few specific points on language worth noting. Luganda does not use a multi-word phrase to express the concept 'person with a disability'. Instead Luganda speakers use the single word 'obulema' which means a person who has a limp or limb-based disability as well as the more general meaning of person who has a disability. To make sure interviewees applied the expansive use of obulema interviewees were asked to talk about different types of obulema. This also ensured that interviewees had the opportunity to brainstorm and think expansively about disability before proceeding further with the interviews. During the interviews it was clear that people appreciated the broad meaning of obulema to be a class of people that include people experiencing a wide range of impairments with some people's conception being broader and more nuanced than others as will be discussed in Chapter 6.

One could critique the use of the term 'obulema' because it connects a person more directly to disability both grammatically and in terms of association than the phrase 'person with a disability'. However, the prefix and root combination we see in obulema entrenched in the language and Uganda's disability community does not condemn the use of the term. Moreover, the fact that the personal preface 'obu' in obulema places that word in a lexical category of nouns associated with humans is a positive feature. If obulema was a term that connotes a non-human lexical status then arguably some other Luganda word choice would have been necessary.

The interview templates encouraged the interviewees to think expansively and inclusively about disability and human impairment. This increased the scope of subject matter for relevant stories and knowledge about the status, rights and treatment of persons with disabilities.

Most interviews were conducted in Luganda with the assistance of a translator. Participants with hearing impairments were interviewed with the assistance of sign language interpreters. Interviews typically lasted between one to two hours.

The researcher, translator and participants collaboratively developed written responses in English that fairly and accurately reflected the substance of the answers and stories provided in Luganda. This included a review of answers at the conclusion of the interview. I made and preserved audio recordings of the interviews that were referenced as needed. This was the procedure for all three phases of fieldwork interviews.

The interviewees received a stipend of 25 000 Uganda Shillings for participating in the interview as well as a soda or water. The amount paid was roughly equivalent to $8 to $9 US Dollars at the time of the interviews. This amount is consistent with current cultural expectations and necessary to advance the research. The interviewees received payment before they gave their interview to ensure that the interviewee did not think payment was dependent on the content or quality of the answers provided. This protocol involving both procedures and amounts was approved with directed inquiry in the Faculty of Law Research Ethics Committee ethical review process.

The interviews of persons with disabilities sought information regarding indigenous beliefs and perceptions relevant to the rights, status and treatment of persons with disabilities under customary law and practices. Semi-structured interviews and prompts for narrative responses allowed for the collection of stories arising out of lived experiences.[121] This facilitated a grounded approach to the research by enabling interviewees to discuss complex matters in their own words and by limiting my ability to manipulate responses. I adopted a saturation-based approach whereby collection of data ended after the interviews were no

---

[121] A Griffiths (note 107).

longer producing 'genuinely "new" material'.[122] I modified the interview template over the course of the stage one as interviewees alerted me to the importance of issues that were not included in the initial template.

The second phase of field interviews were semi-structured interviews of individuals who could be considered as having heightened knowledge about Baganda customary law and practices.[123] The interview template for the second set of interviews was revised after the conclusion of the first set of interviews. These interviews were largely conducted in Luganda with a translator. The second phase of interviews had the same protocols as the first. The second phase consisted of 23 interviews.

The 23 customary knowledge bearer interviews were reviewed and an additional questionnaire was developed for the purpose of validating the results of those interviews by persons with disabilities.[124] The questionnaire asked persons with disabilities to determine whether assertions extrapolated out of the apparent findings from stage two of the interviewee process were consistent with the beliefs and perspectives of persons with disabilities.

The third stage of interviews consisted of six short interviews of persons with disabilities.[125] These short interview scripts were translated directly into Luganda by the translator assisting with the interview sessions. These interviews checked the validity of the responses given by the customary knowledge bearers by running the apparent findings from those interviews by persons with disabilities. This third stage of inter-

---

[122] Miller (note 116) at 124.

[123] Per s 46 of the Evidence Act of 1909 (cap 6) customary rights and customs can be proven in court by the testimony of those deemed likely to know of the existence of customs and rights.

[124] See appendix II of the thesis for a combined interview script English Luganda.

[125] See appendix II of the thesis for interview script in English.

viewees confirmed the findings generated in the customary knowledge bearer interviews.

At the conclusion of the fieldwork the interview content was logged and analysed. This process entailed a review of the interview responses to identify recurring themes and trends. Prominent issues were coded and highlighted on the interview sheets. Due to the complexity of responses and the variety of demographic traits in the first stage of interviewees, I compiled two matrices to better analyze the results.. A redacted version of one these matrices appear in Appendix IV. This matrix includes demographic information and responses to more direct prompts concerning the existence and general performance and various customary practices. The redacted version of this matrix excludes names, occupations and other information about the interviewees with disabilities that could enable someone to discern the identity of the interviewee. I organised the second matrix by various topics such as 'stories that reflect the characterisation of disability by society' and 'notable legal stories'. The second matrix is not included in Appendix IV because it contains detailed narrative content that could potentially compromise the confidentiality of interviewee identity.

I analysed the data to check for connections between responses and certain demographic characteristics such as sex, age, disability, and people group affiliation, educational background and vocation. Highly and moderately negative responses (e.g. 'people with disabilities cannot inherit property') in terms of the social or legal treatment of persons with disabilities were highlighted on the grid sheets to determine if there was a correlation between the frequency of negative responses and any particular demographic quality. This review did not result in any noteworthy correlations in this regard. Negative results were fairly evenly distributed across all of the tracked demographic attributes.

The findings of this research are reported in a manner that preserves the confidentiality of the interviewees while retaining the value of the qualitative research.[126]

Demographic Breakdown of Interview Phases

Persons with disabilities exploratory interviews

The first phase of fieldwork consisted of 63 interviews of persons with disabilities residing in Mukono District. Nineteen of these interviewees were women and 44 were men (Appendix III, table A). The ages of the interviewees ranged from 19 to 73. The average age was between 39 and 40 years of age.

While persons experiencing a variety of impairments were interviewed, persons with physical disabilities were the dominant cohort in terms of impairment type. (Appendix III, table B) A total of 51 interviewees self-identified as persons with physical disabilities that impact movement, mobility and/or limbs; and 27 of these interviews cited polio as the cause of their physical disability. Others sources of physical disabilities included malaria, accidents, amputations, bone diseases, and cerebral palsy. One interviewee stated that the cause of his physical disability was witchcraft.

Six interviewees had vision impairments. Two of those with vision impairments also had physical limb-based impairments. Four interviewees self-identified as deaf. One interviewee had a speech impediment. One of the interviewees has albinism. One interviewee was a little person and one was the survivor of a severe acid burn. Due to concerns over ethical complications and methodology the field work did not entail the purposeful interviewing of persons with mental disabilities or their caregivers.[127] Future research that directly investigates the lives and

---

[126] Liamputtong (note 113) at 20.

[127] I use the term 'mental disabilities' collectively to include both intellectual (cognitive) disabilities and psychosocial disabilities.

experiences of persons with mental disabilities in customary legal scenarios would be helpful in supplementing the research findings.

Although the Baganda people are the dominant indigenous tribe in Mukono District there was considerable ethnic diversity among the interviewees (Appendix III, table C). Thirty-nine interviewees self-identified as Baganda; 12 of the interviewees identified as members of other Bantu people groups (three Basoga, three Bugisu, two Batoro, one Byanyankole, one Bahima, and two Rwandese); 12 self-identified as members of non-Bantu people groups (four Samia; four Eteso, one Japadohla, one Acholi, one Langi, and one Lugbara).

In terms of religious background 30 self-identified as protestant (including six expressly identifying as Anglican and four expressly identifying as Pentecostal); 17 self-identified as Catholic; 14 self-identified as Muslim; one self-identified as Latter Day Saints (Mormon); and one self-identified as Jehovah's Witness (Appendix III, table D).

The educational background of the interviewees was varied (Appendix III, table E). Three had no formal educational background. One interviewee had some education in Islamic studies and 19 attended school without advancing beyond primary level. 23 interviewees ended their education at the secondary level. 17 interviewees attended tertiary institutions with some earning degrees and certificates.

The interviewees constituted a diverse spectrum in terms of employment status. (Appendix III, table F) Nineteen of the interview pool was involved primarily in agriculture; 21 were involved in small scale trade and services; five were involved in disability advocacy and support. There were three who self-identified as home-makers, three as teachers and counsellors, four as administrative workers, three as students, one electrical engineer and four who self-identified as unemployed or retired.

Customary Knowledge Bearer Interviews

This second stage of the research consisted of interviews of individuals who are reputed to be knowledgeable about Baganda customary practices and who have significant life experiences in Baganda custom. This phase of the research was intentionally limited to Baganda-based cultural expertise because the Baganda are the dominant people group in Mukono District. Although there are many non-Baganda people in the district, the variety of other people groups represented is too extensive to sufficiently investigate within the limitations of this research project. For example, the 24 non-Baganda persons with disabilities interviewed in the first phase of the research self-identified with 12 different people groups.

This second stage of interviews took place in small towns and rural areas in Mukono District. Interview locations included Kalagi, Nakifuma, Kitovu, Kasana, Kimenyedde and Mukono Town. I utilised the connections of one particularly active and widely connected community member in Mukono District to identify a number of the stage two interview subjects. Additional participants were identified through the interviews conducted in stage one and through other connections and relationships. During the interviews the participants were asked whether they were considered to be experts in customary matters in their communities and whether they were actually knowledgeable about local customary law and practices. They were also asked to provide the basis of their heightened knowledge of customary laws and practices.

The level of cultural knowledge and expertise varied among the interviewees. However, most of the participants supposed that others perceived them as experts and indicated they had a solid level of knowledge in matters of local custom and culture. Three of these interviewees held noteworthy positions of leadership and status within the Buganda Kingdom and several others claimed to be leaders within their clans.

Age is an important factor within Baganda society in order to be considered an expert in cultural matters. Thus the second stage interviewees were relatively advanced in age. The average age of these participants was 68 years. The oldest individual interviewed was 94 and the youngest was 43.

Baganda culture views men as the primary bearers of cultural knowledge and the administrators of customary practices. However, I interviewed eight women in this phase of the research despite that existing gendered preference (Appendix III, table G). All but one of the female interviewees demonstrated significant knowledge of cultural and customary matters. Similarly all but two of the male interviewees demonstrated significant knowledge of local cultural and customary matters. A comparative analysis revealed no notable discrepancies in the responses by male and female interviewees.

The participants were diverse in terms of religious background. (Appendix III, table H) Ten interviewees self-identified as Muslim and 13 self-identified as Christians. Of the Christian interviewees eight were Protestant and five were Catholic. There were no notable discrepancies in the responses that were associated with religious affiliation.

Although one of the participants in the second phase of interviews described herself as a 'herbalist', no self-identified traditional healers (often referred to by community members as 'witch doctors') were interviewed. On three occasions reputed traditional healers did not appear for scheduled interviews. Other traditional healers demanded relatively substantial financial payments to participate in interviews in line with the amounts they charge for spiritual assistance. Thus these individuals could not be interviewed in accordance with the ethical guidelines established for the allowable amount for a stipend to interview participants.

Despite the lack of interviews with traditional healers, many participants had extensive knowledge about traditional religious beliefs relevant to disability. Moreover, matters of customary law pertinent to the status, rights and treatment of persons with disabilities were not directly linked to indigenous religious beliefs or practices. The only indication of a direct connection was one interviewee's isolated comment that traditional healers can play a role in divorce proceedings.

Two of the 23 customary knowledge bearer interviewees self-identified as having physical disabilities. Any concern over the number of interviewees with disabilities in this customary expert stage was addressed through the perspectives of persons with disabilities collected in interview stages one and three.

Validation Interviews by Persons with Disabilities

Much of the interview content concerning the impact of other legal sources came from the customary knowledge bearers. This is because the question sets in stage one were open-ended and sought stories about actual life experiences. In contrast, the customary knowledge bearer interview questions in stage two were more pointed about specific issues and covered certain areas that we left largely unexplored in the stage one interviews. In order to check the answers of the stage two interviewees against the beliefs and experiences of persons with disabilities, I conducted a set of follow up interviews in stage three. The stage three interview participants were individuals who had been interviewed during the first stage of interviews. There were six interviews in this third phase of the field research—three women and three men. There was a high level of agreement with the findings generated from the customary knowledge bearer interviews. Thus additional validation interviews were not deemed necessary.

Limitation of the Study

There were several limitations of this study. First there were limitations in terms of time and resources. This was a single researcher project performed with minimal financial support. Thus there was a practical limit on the number of interviews that could be conducted.

This study was limited in geographic and cultural scope. It concerned one district in Uganda and focuses on the customs and culture of one people group. This limited scope cautions against overly generalised findings. This is especially the case given the situational and idiosyncratic qualities of customary law and process.

I am not fluent in Luganda, and had to rely on interpreters for the information I received in almost all of the interviews.[128]

I am Caucasian American. The social dynamics resulting from my identity could have had an impact on the findings. For example, it is possible that some interviewees may have provided answers they thought someone with my background would like to hear. This is particularly the case when it comes to interview responses concerning opinions about outside actors and international human rights.

I made the strategic choice not to pursue information from persons with mental disabilities or their caretakers. This was done to simplify matters ethically and logistically. Yet the study's findings indicate that mental disability can be a highly determinative trait in customary legal matters. Thus, the stories and input of persons with mental disabilities would have added depth and insight to the research.

Only 30 per cent of the persons with disabilities who were interviewed were women. Given the significance of gender the research would have benefitted from a higher percentage of female interviewees with disabilities.

---

[128] There are techniques that can be used to ensure greater fidelity in the translation process such as written reverse translation. Instead the research utilised what I considered to be a more efficient and direct form of oral reverse translation where at the conclusion of the interviews the interviewee's answers were read out in English and translated back into Lugnada by the translator for confirmation from the interviewee.

The percentage of persons with limb-based impairments far exceeded their relative percentage of the population among persons with disabilities in Uganda. However, despite the disparity in percentages the interview pool included interviewees who presented with a wide range of physical impairments including vision, hearing, speech-related and albinism.

The cultural diversity encountered in Mukono District presented a research challenge. Approximately one third of the persons with disabilities who were interviewed self-identified with an ethnic group other than Baganda. These interviewees self-identified with a total of 12 other people groups. It was not possible to make thorough research-based and literature-based inquiries as the unique culture and customs of each of the people groups represented by the interviewees with disability. Other than a few isolated comments as to the special features of the customs of other people groups, the study does not seek to present findings about the special features, traditions or customs of people groups other than the Baganda.

Due to the exploratory nature of the research, certain issues suitable for detailed inquiry did not come into focus until the end of the fieldwork. One example of a late identified issue was the use of customary guardianship as a mechanism for taking children away from widows with disabilities.

I obtained information about the functioning of Buganda Kingdom institutions from interviews and literature. Although the research included interviews of two high ranking individuals in the Buganda Kingdom, Baganda cultural institutions were not directly investigated as part of the research design.

Structure and Outline of the Thesis

The thesis begins with this introductory chapter. The introduction is followed by four foundational chapters setting the stage for the fieldwork by laying out the theoretical and legal framework underlying this thesis.

Chapter 2 presents relevant aspects of disability, including the history and trajectory of the disability movement, a survey of disability theory and a discussion of societal features with particular salience to disability in sub-Saharan settings.

Chapter 3 concerns relevant descriptive and anthropological legal theory. It includes a treatment of legal pluralism and an examination of customary law with an emphasis on contextual aspects relevant to Mukono District.

Chapter 4 offers a critical survey of various approaches to effecting legal change in postcolonial developing world settings. It includes descriptions of various top-down and bottom-up strategies for effecting desired changes.

Chapter 5 consists of legal and policy descriptions and analysis. It sets forth the layered legal context relevant to the status, rights and treatment of persons with disabilities in Mukono District. It includes a treatment of international legal instruments with an emphasis on the CRPD, a presentation of the domestic law and policy of Uganda that specially concerns persons with disabilities and a survey of the customary law and practices of the Baganda people with particular relevance to the rights, status and treatment of persons with disabilities.

Chapter 6 presents findings from the research about disability and society in Mukono District. These findings provide fodder for the critical assessment of theoretical approaches to disability presented in Chapter 2.

Chapter 7 presents fieldwork findings concerning the status, rights and treatment of persons with disabilities in Mukono District in customary legal scenarios. The findings demonstrate that customary scenarios are highly consequential events in the contexts of marriage, guardianship, cultural leadership, succession and land rights. While decisions made in customary scenarios do not adhere to clear normative rules based on disability status, customary actors affect the rights and status of persons with disabilities based on those actors' beliefs about disability and the capabilities of persons with disabilities.

Chapter 8 builds on the findings in Chapter 7 and considers the legal plight of persons with disabilities in Mukono District through the analytical lens of Moore's semi-autonomous social field. Chapter 8 includes a topical treatment on the impact and influence of various sources within customary legal frameworks relevant to disability status, rights and treatment including formal law, state institutions, religions and cultural values. It also includes assessments of the change strategies covered in Chapter 4 as well as an applied critique of the substance of the CRPD and a discussion of the relationship between gender and disability in customary contexts.

The thesis concludes with Chapter 9 which restates the major findings of the research and posits practical ways for going forward in light of the research including suggestions for further study.

2

DISABILITY:
MOVEMENT, THEORY
AND CULTURAL CONTEXT

Introduction

This chapter offers background on aspects of disability relevant to this thesis. It introduces the disabilities movement and predominant approaches to disability theory. It canvasses prevalent social-economic issues and cultural phenomena in Sub-Saharan contexts germane to the lives of persons with disabilities.

The Disability Movement

To understand the rights, status and treatment of persons with disabilities, it is helpful to have some appreciation of the disability movement. This section presents a brief survey of the disability movement by highlighting its emergence from a global, continental and national standpoint.

Global Emergence

Although the disability movement represents a massive number of people, the movement's ascent to global prominence is a relatively recent development. This brief historic treatment begins in the mid-19th Century when organisations championing the interests of persons with disabilities achieved recognition in Western Europe and North America.[129] Such initiatives maintained an ongoing presence but failed to make substantial political headway until the latter half of the 20th Century. Significant moments from that time include the launch of the Special Olympics in 1968[130] and the passing of the Americans with Disabilities Act in 1990.[131]

The United Nations publicly embraced the disabilities movement in 1970s. It issued the Declaration on the Rights of Mentally Retarded Persons in 1971[132] and the United Nations Declaration of the Rights of Disabled Persons in 1975.[133] Later the United Nations gave disability matters a global platform when it proclaimed 1981 the International Year of Disabled Persons.[134] It followed that pronouncement by declaring the ten year period beginning in 1983 the United Nations Decade of Disabled Persons.[135]

The United Nations Convention on the Rights of Persons with Disabilities (CRPD)[136] is the watershed accomplishment of the global disa-

---

[129] D Pfeiffer 'Overview of the disability movement: history, legislative record, and political implications' (1993) 21 Policy Studies Journal 724-734.

[130] Special Olympics Press Release 'Anniversary of first Special Olympics celebrates legacy of recent World Games in Greece' available at <http://www.specialolympics.org/RegionsPages/content.aspx?id=17727&LangType=1036> accessed on 26 October 2015.

[131] Americans with Disabilities Act of 1990, Pub L No 101-336, 104 Stat 328 (1990).

[132] <http://www.ohchr.org/EN/ProfessionalInterest/Pages/RightsOfMentallyRetardedPersons.aspx> accessed on 26 October 2015.

[133] Ibid.

[134] A Stone-MacDonald & G Butera 'Cultural beliefs and attitudes about disability in East Africa' (2012) 8(1) Review of Disabilities Studies 62-77.

[135] <http://www.un.org/esa/socdev/enable/disunddp.htm> accessed on 26 October 2015.

[136] Convention on the Rights of Persons with Disabilities (CRPD), adopted December 13, 2006 by GA Res 61/106, Annex I, UN GAOR, 61st Sess, Supp No 49 at 65, UN Doc A/61/49 (2006), entered into force 3 May 3 2008, UN Doc

bilities movement. It was adopted by the United Nations General Assembly on 13 December 2013. Less than two years after adoption, 159 nations had ratified or acceded to the CRPD.[137] Although the CRPD is not the exclusive international treaty addressing disability[138], it is so comprehensive that it is difficult to find gaps other human rights instruments fill in the context of disability rights.[139] Thus, although the CRPD references prior instruments that address disability rights in its Preamble[140], these other instruments have diminished significance in disability matters in the wake of the CRPD. A more extensive legal treatment of the CRPD appears in Chapter 5, Section II.

Disability Movement in Africa

Africa was home to regional pre-CRPD developments in disability rights. Article 18(4) of African Charter on Human and Peoples' Rights of 1981 provides that '[t]he aged and the disabled shall also have the right to special measures of protection in keeping with their physical or

---

A/61/61, signed by Uganda on 30 March 2007 and ratified by Uganda on 25 September 2008.

[137] <http://www.un.org/disabilities/> accessed on 26 October 2015.

[138] R de Silva de Alwis 'Mining the intersections: advancing the rights of women and children with disabilities within an interrelated web of human rights' (2009) 18 Pacific Rim Law. & Policy J 293.

[139] JE Lord & MA Stein 'The domestic incorporation of human rights law and the United Nations Convention on the Rights of Persons with Disabilities' (2008) 83 Washington LR 449-479, at 467.

[140] CRPD pre (d) 'Recalling the International Covenant on Economic, Social and Cultural Rights, the International Covenant on Civil and Political Rights, the International Convention on the Elimination of All Forms of Racial Discrimination, the Convention on the Elimination of All Forms of Discrimination against Women, the Convention against Torture and Other Cruel, Inhuman or Degrading Treatment or Punishment, the Convention on the Rights of the Child, and the International Convention on the Protection of the Rights of All Migrant Workers and Members of Their Families.'

moral needs.'[141] Other regional developments include the establishment of the African Rehabilitation Institute in 1985[142], the specific reference to children with disabilities in the African Charter on the Rights and Welfare of the Child[143], and Organization for African Unity resolutions establishing both 1999-2009 and 2010-2019 as African Decades of Persons with Disabilities[144].

African nations have been quick to adopt the CRPD.[145] Lord and Stein credit Africa with being 'innovative and resourceful' in implementing the CRPD.[146] Presently, the CRPD has assumed centre stage in disability rights matters throughout Africa, including Uganda.

There are ongoing efforts to answer calls for an Africa-specific disabilities rights treaty.[147] In February 2016, the African Commission of Human and Peoples' Rights adopted a Draft Protocol on the Rights of Persons with Disabilities in Africa.[148] The Draft Protocol builds on the

---

[141] African [Banjul] Charter on Human and Peoples' Rights, adopted 27 June 1981, OAU Doc. CAB/LEG/67/3 rev 5, 21 ILM 58 (1982), entered into force 21 October 1986, ratified by Uganda 10 May 1986.

[142] H Combrinck 'Regional developments: disability rights in the African regional human rights system during 2011 and 2012' (2013) 1 ADRY 361-368, at 363.

[143] Organization of African Unity (OAU), African Charter on the Rights and Welfare of the Child, 11 July 1990, CAB/LEG/24.9/49 (1990).

[144] OAU Doc CAB LEG/24.9/49 adopted on 11 July 1990 and entered into force on 29 November 1999; AU Executive Council Resolution EX.CL/477 (XIV), adopted during the 14th ordinary session of the African Heads of State and Government, 26–30 January 2009.

[145] JE Lord & MA Stein 'Prospects and practices for CRPD implementation in Africa' (2013) 1 ADRY 97-114, at 111.

[146] Ibid.

[147] J Mureriwa 'Some reflections on the draft African Disability Protocol and socio-economic justice for persons with disability' (2011) 12:3 ESR Rev 3-6, at 5.

[148] Draft Protocol to the African Charter on Human and Peoples' Rights on the Rights of Persons with Disabilities in Africa, adopted at the 19th Extra-Ordinary

CRPD by including points of emphasis on issues commonly encountered by persons with disabilities in Africa. For example, it addresses the abuse of persons with albinism, recognises the essential role of families, guardians and caregivers, and includes damaging attitudes and practices based on tradition, culture, religion and superstition as harmful practices.[149]

Disabilities Movement in Uganda

The disabilities movement in Uganda largely emerged during the United Nations Decade of Disabled Persons of 1983 to 1992.[150] This global initiative provided a platform for persons with disabilities in Uganda.[151] Increased awareness and support for the cause of persons with disabilities led to the launch of national initiatives and organisations. Today, the disability movement in Uganda is regarded as one of the most vibrant in Africa.[152]

Uganda is home to a number of disability rights bodies and organisations. The National Council on Disability (NCD) serves as a communicative agent and as a watchdog for persons with disabilities.[153] Other prominent groups include the National Union of Disabled Persons of

---

Session of the African Commission on Human and Peoples' Rights, 16-25 February 2016, in the Islamic Republic of the Gambia.

[149] Ibid at pre and art 1.

[150] DS Moyo Ensuring Sexual and Reproductive Health Rights of Women with Disabilities: A Study of Policies, Actions and Commitments in Uganda and Zimbabwe (2010) unpublished dissertation, Reading University at 38.

[151] Ibid at 38.

[152] AK Dube Participation of Disabled People in the PRSP/PEAP Process in Uganda (2005) available at <http://r4d.dfid.gov.uk/PDF/Outputs/Disability/PolicyProject_uganda_prsp.pdf> accessed on 26 October 2015.

[153] Norwegian Agency for Development Cooperation (Nored) Mainstreaming Disability in the New Development Paradigm, Evaluation of Norwegian Support to Promote the Rights of Persons with Disabilities: Uganda Country Study (2012) at 3.

Uganda (NUDIPU), Uganda National Action on Physical Disability (UNAPD) and Handicap International. Many of these groups are involved in legal advocacy and empowerment initiatives.

Uganda was an early ratifier of the CRPD and its Optional Protocol. Its prompt actions concerning the CRPD reflect the ruling government's willingness to promote disability rights at the formal level. Uganda is also party to other international[154] and regional[155] instruments that ostensibly address disability rights. However, the practical relevance of these other treaties is limited in light of the scope and depth CRPD.

A Primer on Disability Theory

Disability theory shapes and informs the disability rights movement. An appreciation of the influential strands of disability theory offers

---

[154] International Covenant on Civil and Political Rights (ICCPR), adopted 16 December 1996, GA Res 2200A (XX1), 21 UN GAOR Supp (No. 16) at 52, UN Doc A/6316 (1966), 999 UNTS 171, entered into force 23 March 1976, acceded to by Uganda 21 June 1995; International Covenant on Economic, Social and Cultural Rights, GA res 2200A (XXI), UN Doc A/6316 (1966), entered into force 3 January 1976, acceded to by Uganda 21 January 1987; International Covenant on Economic, Social and Cultural Rights, GA res 2200A (XXI), UN Doc A/6316 (1966), entered into force 3 January 3 1976, acceded to by Uganda, 21 January 1987; Convention on the Elimination of Discrimination Against Women (CEDAW), adopted 18 December 1979 by GA resolution 34/180, entered into force on 3 September 1981, ratified by Uganda 22 July 22 1985; Convention on the Rights of the Child, GA res 44/25, annex, 44 UN GAOR Supp (No. 49) at 167, UN Doc.= A/44/49 (1989), entered into force 2 September 1990, ratified by Uganda 17 August 1990.

[155] See treaties and instruments referenced in notes 13, 15 and 16; Protocol to the African Charter on Human and Peoples' Rights on the Rights of Women in Africa (the Maputo Protocol), adopted 11 July 2003, entered into force November 2005, signed by Uganda, 18 December 2003, ratified by Uganda, 22 July 2010.

perspective regarding the challenges facing persons with disabilities as well as strategies for improving their status, rights and treatment.

The Medical and the Welfare Models of Disability

Traditional approaches to disability seek to address disabilities through treatment and care.[156] Adherents to the medical model view disabilities primarily as problems that need to be cured or managed.[157] The goal of the medical model is to enable someone with a disability to approach 'general normality' to the greatest extent that a person's capabilities and the available services can achieve.[158] Similarly, the welfare model focuses on the maintenance of persons with disabilities through charity and government support.[159]

The Rise of 'Integrationism' and Functionalism

In the latter half of the 20th Century the vanguard of the disabilities movement shifted from the 'custodianism' of the medical and treatment models to 'integrationism'.[160] This spurred an increasing emphasis on accommodating persons with disabilities through enabling and enhancing functionality.

Disability as non-functionality is at the core of the Americans with Disabilities Act (ADA).[161] The ADA defines disability as 'a physical or

---

[156] I Grobbelaar-du Plessis & T van Reenen Aspects of Disability Law in Africa (2011) at xxiii.

[157] Ibid at xxiii.

[158] Ibid at xxiv.

[159] G Quinn 'Disability and human rights: a new field in the United Nations' in C Krause & M Scheinin (eds) International Protection of Human Rights, *A Textbook* (2009) 247-271.

[160] J TenBroek & F Matson 'The disabled and the law of welfare' (1966) 54 *California* L Rev 809-840.

[161] Sutton v United Airlines Inc [1999] 527 US 471 (SCOTUS) (holding that determination of disability under the ADA should be made in reference to an

mental impairment that substantially limits one or more major life activities of such individual; a record of such an impairment; or being regarded as having such an impairment'.[162] Uganda's Persons with Disabilities Act of 2006 (PDA) similarly defines a 'person with disability' as 'a person having physical, intellectual, sensory or mental impairment which substantially limits one or more of the major life activities of that person'.[163] Because the PDA predates the CRPD, the PDA's language is not reflective of the CRPD.

The Social Model of Disability

The past four decades have witnessed the rise of the social model of disability. This model attributes disability to societal factors.[164] The social movement is rooted in materialist conceptions and the Marxist tradition.[165] Thus many social theorists seek to deconstruct exploitive structures and critique systems that oppress persons with disabilities.[166]

According to the social model, impairment can be intrinsic to an individual but effective disability is extrinsically derived.[167] Thus, what

---

individual's ability to mitigate his or her impairment through corrective measures).

[162] 42 U.S. Code § 12102(1).

[163] Persons with Disabilities Act of 2006 (Uganda) s 2.

[164] P Harpur 'Embracing the new disability rights paradigm: the importance of the Convention on the Rights of Persons with Disabilities' (2012) 27(1) Disability & Society 1-14.

[165] M Oliver, 'Capitalism, disability and ideology: Materialist critique of the normalization principal' (1999) in R Flynn & R Lemay, A Quarterly, A Quarter-Century of Normalization and Social Role Valorization: Evolution and Impact available at <http://www.independentliving.org/docs3/oliver99.pdf> last accessed on 24 September 2017.

[166] P Abberley 'The Concept of oppression and the development of a social theory of disability' (1987) 2(1) Disability, Handicap & Society 5.

[167] Union of the Physically Impaired against Segregation *Fundamental* Principles of Disability (1976); M Priestley Disability Politics and Community Care (1999); M Oliver Understanding Disability: From Theory to Practice (1996).

makes someone experience life with a disability is the social response to the impairment? Under this model, the structure and attitudes of society are considered to be the primary disabling forces in people's lives.[168] Social model theorists seek to identify and eradicate disabling social barriers.[169]

Social theorists have traditionally critiqued the welfare and medical approaches to disability.[170] They condemn the objectification of persons with disabilities that results from treating such persons as problems to be fixed.[171] They assert that such treatment reinforces 'the perception that persons with disabilities (are) of inferior worth'[172] and contend that medical and welfare models foster dependence on services while neglecting the creation of opportunities for productive contributions to society by persons with disabilities.[173]

Social model reformers target the lived community.[174] They see the 're-arrangement of communities' as the solution to the problem of disability.[175] They hope to engender 'mind shifts' among community members who are impeding persons with disabilities.[176]

This thesis' field research demonstrates how community beliefs and attitudes concerning persons with disabilities can impact their rights,

---

[168] L Mute 'Moving from the norm to practice: Towards ensuring legal capacity for persons with disabilities in Kenya' (2012) 9 *Equal Rights Rev* 138-148, at 139.

[169] Grobbelaar-du Plessis and van Reenen (note 28) at xxv.

[170] M Oliver The Politics of Disablement (2000).

[171] Harpur (note 38) at 2-3.

[172] G Muller 'On considering alternative accommodation and the rights and needs of vulnerable people' (2014) 30 SAJHR 41-62, at 54.

[173] T Shakespeare Disability Rights and Wrongs (2006) 28; BA Areheart 'When disability isn't "just right": the entrenchment of the medical model of disability and the Goldilocks dilemma' (2008) 83 Indiana Law Journal 181-232.

[174] Grobbelaar-du Plessis & van Reenen (note 28) at xxv.

[175] Ibid at xxvi.

[176] Ibid at xxv.

status and treatment in customary contexts. This is especially the case when it comes to attitudes about the abilities and usefulness of persons with disabilities as discussed in Chapter 6, Section II and further demonstrated throughout Chapter 7.

Social theorists often look to the state as an engine for reform. They see law as a means for changing social attitudes and call upon the state to obviate structural barriers.[177] This thesis' field research indicates that both persons with disabilities and respected community members credit the government for improving the lives of persons with disabilities. Many interviewees gave Uganda's long-ruling government credit for improving the lives of persons with disabilities. However, when it comes to specifically identifying the government action that has led to improvements, interviewees tended to reference symbolic acts. For example multiple interviewees noted that the President recognizes persons with disabilities at public functions.

The social model has incurred pragmatic push-back in recent decades.[178] Its tendency to marginalise non-social challenges to persons with disabilities is the target of critiques.[179] Meanwhile proponents of the social model now present the social model as non-exclusivist.[180] For example, social movement pioneer Michael Oliver affirms the continu-

---

[177] *Ibid* at xxvi citing G Quinn & T Degener *Human* Rights and Disability: the Current Use and Future Potential of United Nations Human Rights Instruments in the Context of Disability (2002) at 10.

[178] S Gabel & S Peters 'Presage of a paradigm shift? Beyond the social model of disability toward resistance theories of disability' (2004) 19(6) Disability & Society 585-600; T Shakespeare and N Watson 'The social model of disability: an outdated ideology?' in (2001) Exploring Theories and Expanding Methodologies: Where We Are and Where We Need to Go 9-28.

[179] Gabel & Peters *Ibid.*

[180] B Albert 'Briefing note: the social model of disability, human rights and development' (2004) Disability KaR Research Project 1-8.

ing need for medical interventions to address impairments[181] and Priestly posits an overlapping four fold conception of disability typologies that includes a medical model along with three variations of social models.[182]

The social model of disability certainly has limits.[183] Creating an 'accessible environment minimises the inconvenience of impairment, but it does not equalise disabled people with non-disabled people'.[184] Impairments persist even in the absence of barriers.

Yet this thesis' fieldwork confirms the potency of social phenomena in shaping and establishing the status, rights and treatment of persons with disabilities in customary legal frameworks. The norms, values and beliefs of family and community members impact the way that customary legal scenarios play out. When it comes to access to land rights through inheritance and other significant customary occurrences, social forces are highly influential and consequential in Mukono District. Research findings affirming the relevance of the social model to the customary legal experience of persons with disabilities are presented in Section III(2) of Chapter 6, and throughout Chapter 7 of this thesis.

---

[181] M Oliver 'Defining impairment and disability: issues at stake' in C Barnes & G Mercer (Eds) Exploring the Divide (1996) 29-54.

[182] M Priestley 'Constructions and creations: Idealism, materialism and disability theory' (1998) 13 (1) Disability and Society 79. Priestly's four typologies consist of (1) a medical model, (2) an individualist model that focuses on the negotiation of social roles between individuals, (3) a materialist social model associated with Oliver, and (4) an idealist social model whose starting point is that disability is a culturally specific and requires cultural specific cultural responses.

[183] See for example T Degener 'Disability in a Human Rights Context' (2016) 5(3) Laws 35 which discusses how the CRPD and the human rights approach to disability provides for a more comprehensive approach to addressing disability and its challenges.

[184] Shakespeare (note 45) at 51.

The Minority Group Model of Disability

Other disability advocates endorse a minority group approach to disability. Adherents to this approach see possibilities for progress by constructing disability as a self-defined and self-affiliated social status.[185] This model mirrors identity politics used in the contexts of race, ethnicity, gender and sexuality.[186]

Proponents of this approach seek to mobilise persons with disabilities as a minority group that builds political capital based on their political affinity and self-identification. They call for non-discrimination and affirmative action and view litigation as an effective means for bringing about social change.[187]

However, the diversity and fluidity of disability presents challenges in terms of identity[188], and consequently solidarity This thesis' fieldwork presented in Chapter 6, Section III(4) denotes a lack of solidarity among persons with disabilities in Mukono District due to their differences in terms of impairment types and perceived political inequities.

The Human Rights Based Approach to Disability

The minority group model shares political and theoretical space with the human rights approach. Under the human rights approach persons with disabilities are seen as subjects rather than objects.[189] They are

---

[185] SR Bagenstos 'Justice Ginsburg and the judicial role in expanding "We the People": the disability rights cases' (2004) 104 Columbia Law Review 49-59, at 54 (discussing the minority view approach to disability theory as espoused by Justice Ginsberg of the US Supreme Court).

[186] H Hahn 'The political implications of disability definitions and data' (1993) 4(2) Journal of Disability Policy Studies 41-52; M Putnam 'Conceptualizing disability developing a framework for political disability identity' (2005) 16(3) Journal of Disability Policy Studies 188-198.

[187] Bagenstros (note 57) at 56.

[188] LJ Davis 'The end of identity politics: On disability as an unstable category' in (2013) The Disability *Studies* Reader 263-277.

[189] Quinn & Degener (note 49).

rights bearers as opposed to problems. Human rights advocates believe the recognition and enforcement of universally pronounced rights can provide practical assistance and empowerment to persons with disabilities.[190] Human rights proclaimed in international treaties are the normative cornerstones for the rights based approach.[191] Such rights are declared for all humans and endorsed by the consent of nations.[192] Key rights include the right to freedom from discrimination, the right to dignity, and the right to reasonable accommodation.[193]

Degener presents the CRPD as the dominant embodiment of the human rights approach.[194] She writes that while the CRPD is notable for marking a paradigm shift from the medical model to the social model, it charts a more expansive course. It encompasses civil and political rights as well as economic, social and cultural rights. Thus it responds to the social theorist demand that 'we want rights not charity' with a framework that classifies matters of provision as matters of right.[195] Moreover, the human rights model reflected in the CRPD places a greater emphasis on human dignity than the social model.

---

[190] H Katsui & J Kumpuvuori 'Human rights based approach to disability in development in Uganda: A way to fill the gap between political and social spaces?' (2008) 10(4) Scandinavian Journal of Disability Research 227-236.

[191] M Rioux & A Carbert 'Human rights and disability: The international context' (2003) 10(2) Journal on Developmental Disabilities 1-13; S Seppänen Possibilities and challenges of the human rights-based approach to development (2005).

[192] SF Moore 'Changing African land tenure: reflections on the incapacities of the state' (1998) 10(2) European Journal of Development Research 33-49, at 44.

[193] UN World Health Organisation (WHO) World Report on Disabilities (2011) at 9 available at <http://www.who.int/disabilities/world_report/2011/report.pdf> last accessed 9 October 2017.

[194] T Degener (note 55).

[195] See for example CPRD arts 24 and 25 addressing the rights to education and health.

There is little indication of an awareness of the CRPD in Mukono District. The only international instrument referenced by interviewees without disabilities was the Universal Declaration of Human Rights and that instrument was merely mentioned by two persons with no discussion of its content. Yet, many interviewees stated that they know it is wrong to discriminate against persons with disabilities. There is a general sense that Uganda Constitution prohibits discrimination against persons with disabilities.

Some of the critiques against human rights based approaches reflect anti-Western and localised viewpoints.[196] For example, some scholars question the utility and global appropriateness of the individual-centric Western approach to disability theory.[197] Often there are anti-imperialist sentiments in these critiques.[198] Yet Bickenbach and Bickenbach argue that this tension only arises when these positions are expressed in an extreme and stilted fashion.[199] They contend that when rights are considered situationally in terms of progressive realisation, the conflict between these schools of thought dissipates.[200]

Regardless of any objections to moral imperialism, Grech notes that Western disability discourse often remains at the periphery of development initiatives in the Majority World.[201] Significant contextualisation

---

[196] R Lang 'A critique of the disability movement' (1998) 9(1) Asia Pacific Disability Rehabilitation Journal 1-9.

[197] A Mollow 'Identity politics and disability studies: a critique of recent theory (2004) 43(2) Michigan Quarterly Review 269-296.

[198] M Mutua Human Rights: A Political and Cultural Critique (2013).

[199] JE Bickenbach & JE Bickenbach 'Disability, culture and the UN convention' (2009) 31(14) Disability and Rehabilitation 1111-1124.

[200] Ibid.

[201] S Grech 'Disability, poverty and development: Critical reflections on the majority world debate' (2009) 24(6) Disability & Society 771-784.

can be necessary for the successful exportation of Western disability models to settings such as Mukono District.[202]

Chapters 6 and 8[203] include research findings indicating that people in Mukono District are open to acknowledging and honoring the human rights of persons with disabilities. However, interview participants often expressed a belief that it is the role of the government to carry out the realisation of these rights through financial assistance and the allocation of resources. Moreover, there is minimal awareness concerning the substantive content of disabilities rights.

Other social theorists point to the necessity of a first-person struggle in any meaningful advancement of human rights.[204] They contend that human rights must be earned by the rights bearers for those rights to be relevant and operative.[205] This actor-based approach to human rights reflects Marxist ideology about the essentiality of struggle in achieving genuine social and political change.[206] In the context of disabilities that would mean that persons with disabilities must play an active role in the establishment of their rights in order for their rights to be real and effective.

The field research confirms the need for self-championing of disability rights. The contexts where customary law and process are functionally operative in Mukono District tend to put persons with disabilities,

---

[202] Ibid; B Ibhawoh 'Between culture and constitution: Evaluating the cultural legitimacy of human rights in the African State' 22(3) Human Rights Quarterly 838–860.

[203] See specifically ch 6, s II(5) and ch 8, s II(1)(c) for reports from the field work that tend to show an cultural openness and willingness to accept international human rights standards.

[204] IK Zola 'Developing new self images and interdependence' in NM Crewe & IK Zola (Eds) Independent Living for Physically Disabled People (1993) 49-59.

[205] T Shakespeare 'Disabled people's self-organisation: a new social movement' (1993) 8(3) Disability, Handicap and Society 249-264, at 254.

[206] LJ Macfarlane 'Marxist theory and human rights' (1982) 17(4) Government and Opposition 414-428.

whether they like it or not, in the centre of the struggle for the realisation of rights and privileges. Chapter 7 reports how persons with disabilities are often required to stand up for their right to inherit land or prove themselves capable of serving as customary guardians.[207]

Ableist Approaches to Disability

Some approaches to disability emphasise the impairments and inabilities of persons with disabilities as opposed to their capacities and abilities. This tendency has spurred a countervailing movement which stresses what persons with disabilities can do rather than what they cannot. Harpur refers to this approach as 'ableist'.[208]

The need for an encouraging and non-tragic approach to disability is endorsed by Swain and French in their affirmation model which 'addresses the limitations of the social model through the realisation of positive identity encompassing impairment, as well as disability'.[209] The capabilities framework similarly stresses the abilities and capacities of persons with impairments as opposed to their limitations.[210] This thesis' fieldwork speaks to the importance of engendering positive community attitudes about the capabilities of persons with disabilities. People's conceptions and presuppositions about what persons with disabilities can and cannot do is a major cause of discrimination against persons with disabilities in customary legal scenarios as well as other important contexts such as employment and dating. The findings presented in Chapter 7 place the beliefs of community members about the ability of

---

[207] Ch 7, secs IV, V and VI.

[208] P Harpur 'From disability to ability: changing the phrasing of the debate' (2012) 27(3) Disability & Society 325-337.

[209] J Swain & S French 'Towards an affirmation model of disability' (2000) 15(4) Disability & Society 569-582.

[210] T Burchardt 'Capabilities and disability: the capabilities framework and the social model of disability' (2004) 19(7) Disability & Society 735-751 (crediting Amartya Sen and others for spearheading the development of this approach).

persons with disabilities at the center of customary disablement in Mukono District.

The Politics of Ideology: Purity v Pragmatism

The theoretical pedigree of legislation and reform initiatives can spawn ideological discontent.[211] For example, Grobbelaar-du Plessis and van Reenen lament the continued 'trace' presence of the medical model of disability in Africa.[212] However, critiques of the continued legacy of the medical model can be difficult to appreciate in places where medical services are inadequate or nonexistent.[213]

This thesis' fieldwork found several interviewees who complained about the government's failure to deliver resources for the benefit of persons with disabilities. Conversely, no one complained about the government merely treating persons with disabilities as people who need to be cared for or cured. In fact several women with disabilities complained that they were denied pre-natal care by public hospitals on the purported ground that persons with disabilities should not bear children. When a man with a disability who works as medical clinic staffer was confronted about this alleged practice, he confirmed it and personally submitted that such women should not be provided any care. Certainly concerns about the prevalence of a medical model can fail to resonate in such a context.

---

[211] Arguably the medial/social distinction is an outdated controversy among disability theorists, but the echo of this controversy persists in legal discourse. T Degener (note 55) at page 2 of pdf version of article.

[212] Grobbelaar-du Plessis & van Reenen (note 28) at xxiv.

[213] H Meekosha 'Decolonising disability: thinking and acting globally' (2011) 26(6) Disability and Society 667-682, at 670; D Werner Nothing About Us Without Us: Developing Innovative Technologies for, by and with Disabled Persons (1998) at 6; but see Albert (note 52) at 5 (challenging the common critique that the social model is of limited relevance in nations with limited resources and capacities to reduce the functional impact of impairment).

For its part the World Health Organization (WHO) adopts a pragmatic and blended view. It observes:

> The medical model and the social model are often presented as dichotomous, but disability should be viewed neither as purely medical nor as purely social: persons with disabilities can often experience problems arising from their health condition. A balanced approach is needed, giving appropriate weight to the different aspects of disability[214]

There is wisdom in the WHO's non-exclusivist approach. The challenges of living with physical impairment in high-poverty environments call for expansive, as opposed to exclusive, approaches to improving the lives of persons with disabilities.

This study is informed by the social model in a non-exclusive way. It is not necessary to disregard the value of other theoretical approaches to disability in order to benefit from the insights of the social model. The broad spectrum of theoretical approaches to disability presents diverse insights regarding status, rights and treatment of persons with disabilities. The value of these varied perspectives outweighs any benefit of clarity or ideological purity that could come from a singular theoretical allegiance.

This study is not alone in adopting a generous and non-exclusive approach to theoretical engagement in the context of disability.[215] Harpur notes that singular approaches to disability are incapable of fully addressing the challenges that persons with disabilities encounter in

---

[214] WHO (note 58) at 4.

[215] See e.g. B Hughes & K Patterson 'The social model of disability and the disappearing body: towards a sociology of impairment' (1997) 12(3) Disability & Society 325-340; Shakespeare & Watson (note 46); T Burchardt 'Capabilities and disability: the capabilities framework and the social model of disability' (2004) 19(7) Disability & Society 735-751.

achieving equal citizenship.[216] Research commissioned by Britain's National Institute of Health Research endorses a non-exclusive approach to disability in the context of public health research design.[217] Moreover, other approaches to disability theory, including the vulnerability theory[218] and the resistance theory[219], purposefully engage both social and bodily aspects of disability.

Culture and Disability in Sub-Saharan Africa

This section offers relevant content on culture and disability in sub-Saharan Africa. Culture is a famously broad subject. It has been defined as the 'totality of values, institutions and forms of behaviour transmitted within a society as well as the material goods produced by man (and woman)'.[220] Culture includes the 'inherited ideas, beliefs, and knowledge which constitute the shared bases of social action'[221] and envelops matters such as law[222], religion, language, art and politics.[223]

Given the breadth of culture, it is not possible to fully address the relationship between culture and disability. Moreover, this challenge is

---

[216] Harpur (note 80).

[217] MJ Berghs et al 'Implications for public health research of models and theories of disability: a scoping study and evidence synthesis' (2016).

[218] M Keogh, N Fox and E Flynn 'How far towards equality, a vulnerabilities approach to the rights of disabled people' Research Paper No 29/2010 (5 July 2010) UCD Working Papers in Law, Criminology & Socio-Legal Studies available at <http://dx.doi.org/10.2139/ssrn.1634806> last visited on 12 December 2016.

[219] Gabel & Peters (note 50).

[220] R Preiswerk 'The place of intercultural relations in the study of international relations' in D Hunt (ed) (1978) The Yearbook of World Affairs 251-67.

[221] Collins English Dictionary, (4 ed 1998) at 385.

[222] TW Bennett Human Rights and African Customary Law (1995) at 24.

[223] F Raday 'Culture, religion and gender' (2004) 1(4) International Journal of Constitutional Law 663-715, at 665-66.

especially daunting in a context as large and diverse as sub-Saharan Africa. Yet it is instructive to address some prevalent cultural features that significantly impact the status, rights and treatment of persons with disabilities. This subsection addresses five key areas of cultural content: (1) collective beliefs about sources and causes of disability; (2) cultural beliefs and attitudes about persons with disabilities; (3) ubuntu and sub-Saharan communitarianism; (4) language and disability; and (5) customary law and disability.

Collective Beliefs about Sources and Causes of Disability

To appreciate the way a society treats persons with disabilities, it is helpful to understand that society's beliefs about the sources and causes of disabilities. African disability discourse is complex, combining historic and cultural beliefs with input from colonial and postcolonial sources.[224] In the context of causation theories, this plurality of sources can result in a mix of animistic beliefs attributing disability to witchcraft and curses[225], Christian and Islamic beliefs about the will, sovereignty and power of the Deity, and beliefs that are based on or built from scientific theories and findings.[226]

Religious and cultural beliefs regarding disabilities can be detrimental to persons with disabilities. Many sub-Saharan cultures attribute disabilities to supernatural causes.[227] Bickenbach observes the tendency

---

[224] PJ Devlieger 'Persons with a physical disability at the interstices of classification: examples from Africa and the United States (1998) 2 *Zeitschrift Behinderung und Dritte Weit* 45-49, at 46.

[225] M wa-Mungai '"For I name thee...": disability onomastics in Kenyan folklore and popular music' (2009) 29(4) Disabilities Studies Quarterly (noting the tendency in Kenya to see curses as a cause of disability).

[226] SG Harknett 'Cultural factors in the definition of disability: a community study in Nyankunde, Zaire' 1 African Journal of Special Needs Education 18-24.

[227] PJ Devlieger 'Why disabled? The cultural understanding of physical disability in an African society' in SR Whyte & B Ingstad (eds) *Disability and Culture* (1995) 94-106; EG Parrinder *African Traditional Religion* (1962).

of pre-industrial cultures to attribute the etiology of disability to divine retribution.[228] In Ghana there are cultural myths that attribute disabilities to spiritual offences.[229] Conversely, other African cultures associate disability with special spiritual status.[230]

The fieldwork conducted for this thesis repeatedly ran across a belief among the Baganda that a 'small god' named Wanema is responsible for physical disabilities. The presence of a family member with a limp or some other limb-related problems necessitates the building of a small shrine to Wanema and the household presence of a special stick also called Wanema which is purported to ward off further manifestations of physical disabilities. Disability is viewed as a spiritual curse that manifests itself in other family members if Wanema is not appeased.

Many people in sub-Saharan Africa obtain physical impairments from physical injuries.[231] The WHO notes '[r]oad traffic injury, occupational injury, violence, and humanitarian crises have long been recognized as contributors to disability.'[232] The high prevalence of external causation can reinforce the view that disability is the product of an event as opposed to a social context. Uganda's National Policy on Disability reflects this conception of disability when it officially lists health problems and accidents as the cause of disabilities.[233]

---

[228] JE Bickenbach *Physical Disability and Social Policy* (1993).

[229] M Baffoe 'Stigma, discrimination & marginalisation: gateways to oppression of persons with disabilities in Ghana, West Africa' 3(1) *Journal of Educational and Social Research* 187-198 at 188-89.

[230] E Mpofu 'Enhancing social acceptance of early adolescents with physical disabilities: effects of role salience, peer interaction, and academic support interventions' (2003) 50(4) *International Journal of Disability, Development and Education* 435-454.

[231] United Nations *World Youth Report 2007: Young People's Transition to Adulthood: Progress and Challenges* at 101.

[232] WHO (note 58) at 34.

[233] Ministry of Gender, Labour and Social Development, *National Policy on Disability in Uganda* (2006) at 7.

Cultural Beliefs and Attitudes about Persons with Disabilities

Society's beliefs regarding disability impact the lives of persons with disabilities. The World Health Organization lists 'negative attitudes' as one of the key disabling barriers facing people with disabilities.[234] As noted by the CPRD, the attitudes of others can hinder 'full participation in society on an equal basis with others'.[235]

Persons with disabilities have qualities that run counter to attributes that many sub-Saharan cultures value. The physical health and the absence of physical maladies is a crucial concern for Bantu people.[236] Stigma can result from conflict between cultural values and personal attributes. Stigma against persons with disabilities can lead to 'prejudice, discrimination and ultimately to the denial of rights and resources'.[237]

This thesis' fieldwork indicates that social attitudes concerning disability present formidable obstacles to persons with disabilities in Mukono District. Interviewees with disabilities consistently reported that other people often consider them to be useless and incapable, and that these unfavorable attitudes negatively impact their rights, status and treatment. This is particularly true in the contexts of employment, dating, and customary succession rights. Chapter 6 presents findings about community attitudes towards disability in Mukono District and the impact of those attitudes on employment and social interaction. Chapter 7 demonstrates the impact of those attitudes on customary succession and other areas of customary law.

---

[234] WHO (note 65) at 262.

[235] CPRD at pre (e).

[236] JV Taylor in Primal Vision 2d ed (2001) at 45 referencing PF Tempels La Philosophie Bantoue (1959).

[237] Baffoe (note 101); See also MP Mostert 'Stigma as barrier to the implementation of the Convention on the Rights of Persons with Disabilities in Africa' (2016) 4 ADRY 3-24.

Prejudices create substantial barriers for persons with disabilities.[238] A study in Cameroon notes that women with disabilities are excluded from decision-making and deemed to be unfit for marriage.[239] The study found that young girls with disabilities are often not sent to school by families with limited financial resources.[240] A study in Northern Uganda reports severe social stigma towards women with disabilities resulting in prohibitions to speak in community forums, hurtful comments, and the denial of food, clothing and shelter.[241]

There are mixed accounts about how families in sub-Saharan Africa support members with disabilities. Some reports commend families for caring for their children regardless of a child's physical condition.[242] On the other hand, a study of hearing impaired people in Uganda found that families considered their deaf children to be burdens and often hide them to avoid public shame.[243] This thesis' field research offers a mixed picture including many stories of exclusion and harsh discrimination and some reports of considerate and equitable treatment. Chapter 6 presents some of the more poignant instances of inhumane treatment including

---

[238] G VanRooy, E Amadhila, H Mannan et al 'Core concepts of human rights and inclusion of vulnerable groups in the disability and rehabilitation policies of Malawi, Namibia, Sudan, and South Africa' (2012) 23 *Journal of Disability Policy Studies* 67-81.

[239] S Kiani 'Women with disabilities in the North West province of Cameroon: resilient and deserving of greater attention' (2009) 24(4) Disability & Society 517-531, at 522.

[240] Ibid at 522.

[241] Human Rights Watch 'As if We Weren't *Human*': Discrimination and Violence against Women with Disabilities in Northern Uganda (2010) at 24-25, 29.

[242] Stone-MacDonald & Butera (note 6) at 69 citing T Masasa, S Irwin-Carruthers & M Faure 'Knowledge of, beliefs about and attitudes to disability: implications for health professionals' (2005) 47(7) *South African Family Practice* 40-44.

[243] *Ibid* at 69 citing NB Kiyaga & DF Moores 'Deafness in sub-Saharan Africa' (2003) 18 *American Annals of the Deaf* 18-24.

the story of one interviewee with polio who was abandoned in a garbage dump by her mother when she was an infant.[244]

Another important cultural factor is the social emphasis placed on usefulness. Stone-McDonald and Butera note 'the functional capacity of an individual to complete life's daily tasks without help' is 'especially salient' within East African cultures.[245] The ability to contribute economically or otherwise is a key element in being valued within many sub-Saharan communities.[246] In this thesis' fieldwork interviewees with disabilities linked family and clan perceptions about their inability to poor marketability for employment and relatively dim prospects in dating and marriage, along with diminished rights, status and treatment in customary legal contexts. Understanding the social value placed on usefulness is also important to appreciating the collectivist Bantu ethos known as ubuntu discussed in the next subsection.

Ubuntu and Sub-Saharan Communitarianism

Generalised beliefs about sub-Saharan cultures often entail some aspect of communitarianism. Sayings like 'it takes a village' and various African stories and aphorisms about the need to work together exemplify this stereotype. Given the limited government resources in most sub-Saharan nations, the idea that communities are culturally inclined to offer substantial and self-generated support to their members can be a cause for optimism.

The most prominent sub-Saharan communitarian ethos is ubuntu. Originating among Bantu peoples in Southern Africa, ubuntu is an ex-

---

[244] See ch 6, s II(2).

[245] Ibid at 69.

[246] ST Tesemma 'Economic discourses of disability in Africa: An overview of lay and legislative narratives' (2014) 2 *ADRY* 121-147; A Talle 'A child is a child: disability and equality among the Kenya Maasai' in Benedicte Ingstad & Susan Reynolds Whyte (eds) *Disability and Culture* (1995) 56-72.

pansive and flexible concept that is not easily defined in English.[247] Justice Langa, the now deceased former Justice of Constitutional Court of South Africa, observed that ubuntu 'places emphasis on communality and on the interdependence of the members of community'[248] and promotes 'unconditional respect, dignity, value and acceptance'[249] within communities. Langa asserted that ubuntu is built on the understanding that community people are not 'islands unto ourselves'.[250] For Langa, this concept is well expressed through the Zulu phrase 'umuntu ngumuntu ngabantu' which has been roughly translated as 'a person is a person through other people'. Langa posited that ubuntu fosters an appreciation for the human dignity of all people.[251]

Ubuntu has a tendency to be cast in a humanitarian light. However, collectivism in sub-Saharan contexts can be more about survival and pragmatism than an idealistic manifestation of love and generosity for one's fellow person.[252] The idea that without you I am nothing is intertwined with the pressing awareness that communities must work collectively to meet the necessities and challenges of life.

Ubuntu can be seen as communal reciprocity: *I am because you are—because you are helping me to live well (or perhaps survive) in community*. Thus the usefulness of someone towards the good of a community is at the core of ubuntu and other commensurate versions of

---

[247] C Himonga, M Taylor & A Pope 'Reflections on judicial views of ubuntu' (2013) 16(5) PER/PELJ 1-61 at fn 21 quoting JY Mokgoro 'Ubuntu and the law in South Africa' (1998) PELJ at 2-3.

[248] S v Makwanyane 1995 3 SA 391 (CC) opinion of Justice Mokgoro at para 224 (Because the African world-view cannot be neatly categorised and defined, any definition [of ubuntu] would only be a simplification of a more expansive, flexible and philosophically accommodative idea).

[249] Ibid para 224.

[250] MEC for Education: Kwazulu-Natal v Pillay 2008 1 SA 474 (CC) para 53.

[251] Makwanyane (supra note 120) para 225.

[252] P Ikuenobe Philosophical Perspectives on Communalism and Morality in African Traditions (2006).

African communitarianism. If persons with disabilities are seen as useless they are unlikely to be valued in societies that value usefulness. Therefore it is important to appreciate the centrality of usefulness and the detrimental impact of perceived uselessness when considering the potential benefits of an indigenous communitarian ethos to persons with disabilities.

The thesis' fieldwork confirms that beliefs about the usefulness or uselessness of a person with disabilities impact their rights, status and treatment in contexts where customary law is applied by family and clan members. On the other hand, as discussed in Section II(6) of Chapter 8, the fieldwork indicates that the communitarian concept of ubuntu has limited social currency and is seen by many as a non-indigenous concept.

Language and Disability in Africa

Another aspect of culture that warrants consideration is language. Language can both reflect and influence cultural attitudes regarding disability.[253] Terms for disability 'can have very different meanings and connotations depending on the cultural background and social environment'.[254] Disparaging terminology describing disability is in all human cultures[255]; cultures in Sub-Saharan Africa are no exception.[256] In re-

---

[253] J Smart Disability, Society and the Individual (2000) at 56 ('Language is a mirror that reflects a society's views toward certain groups').

[254] NO Ogechi & SJ Ruta 'Portrayal of disability through personal names and proverbs in Kenya; evidence from Ekegusii and Nandi' (2002) 2(3) Vienna Journal of African Studies 63-82, at 64 quoting BI Bruhns, A Murray, T Kanguehi et al *NEPRU Research Project No. 9: Disability and Rehabilitation in Namibia; A National Survey* (1995) at 5.

[255] Smart (note 125) at 60 (discussing disparaging terminology in Latin America and China).

[256] Baffoe (note 101) at 190 (noting that 'language used in reference to intellectual disabilities in Ghanaian society perpetuates negative societal perceptions and attitudes toward children with disabilities').

sponse to such practices, the Draft Protocol to the African Charter on Human and People's Rights on the Rights of Persons with Disabilities in Africa requires state parties to take measures to prohibit the use of derogatory language against persons with disabilities.[257]

Language that identifies people by their disability can be damaging. Smart lists five negative impacts of such language: 1) offending and demeaning people; 2) setting people apart from the rest of society; 3) imposing language on groups instead of letting groups determine what language should be used to describe them; 4) lumping people together despite differences and diversity; and 5) reducing people to one single characteristic.[258] Persons with disabilities in Uganda are often labeled with identifying language.[259]

Many languages in East Africa do not have an indigenous lexical root that stands for all disabilities or all persons with disabilities. Instead these languages tend to have various terms for persons with disabilities based largely on the body part that is impaired.[260] In Luganda the root word now used to generally cover all disabilities is 'lema'. This is the root used specifically to describe limps and other limb-based impairments.

As discussed in Section II of Chapter 6, those interviewed for this thesis indicated that hurtful and objectifying names for persons with disabilities are still in use in Mukono District. As one interviewee with

---

[257] Draft Protocol at 6.2.

[258] Smart (note 125) at 56.

[259] C Lwanga-Ntale 'Chronic poverty and disability in Uganda' paper presented at Staying Poor Chronic Poverty and Disability Policy Manchester, United Kingdom (April 2003) at 4 available at <http://digitalcommons.ilr. cornell.edu/gladnetcollect/320> last accessed 28 October 2015 (observing that persons with disabilities in Uganda are given names directly associated with their disability instead of names that refer to them as people experiencing a disability).

[260] Ogechi & Ruta (note 126) at 64.

disabilities remarked, 'they are called by their disabilities and not by their names'. One name that interviewees consider particularly harsh is 'kasiru' which is the common label for persons who are unable to hear and speak. In Luganda 'kasiru' roughly means a 'host of stupid ideas'. Another example is the name is 'kaddu wanema' which means the slave of the 'small god' who causes physical disabilities.

The common Bantu root 'lema' or 'rema' means to 'become heavy, fail, or experience difficulty'.[261] Thus this root creates an linguistic link between disability and burdens as well as incapability.[262] Similarly in Botswana, the Setswana word for a person with a disability is 'segole' which means someone who is incapable of doing what is considered normal by the community.[263] The fieldwork encountered Luganda words and names associated with persons with disabilities that reflect incapacity, dependency and uselessness. Examples include 'kateyamba' which means someone who cannot help themselves and 'omubogo' which means helpless child. Such terms, along with 'the definitions and symbols that attach to societal lexicon, can be social disablers'.[264]

Changes in syntax can reflect changing cultural attitudes.[265] A study by Stone and McDonald reported a lexical shift in Tanzania from the use

---

[261] PJ Devlieger 'Physical "disability" in Bantu languages: understanding the relativity of classification and meaning' 21 *International Journal of Rehabilitation Research* 51-62.

[262] Ibid.

[263] BR Dinokopila 'The rights of persons with disabilities in Botswana: policy and institutional framework' in Grobbelaar-du Plessis & van Reenen (note 28) 261-280, at 263.

[264] Baffoe (note 101) at 190 quoting M Kress-White The Quest of Inclusion: Understandings of Albeism, Pedagogy and the Right to Belong (2009) thesis University of Saskatchewan.

[265] PJ Devlieger 'From handicap to disability, language use and cultural meaning in the United States' (1999) 21(7) Disability and Rehabilitation 346-354 (presenting the cultural shift reflecting in the changing discourse regarding disability terminology in the United States).

of earlier indigenous words which grammatically included people with disabilities in a class of nouns that typically refer to objects as opposed to people.[266] This field research found that the present terms used for people with disabilities fall within a grammatical category of words used for humans.

African Customary Laws and Practices with Special Application and Relevance to Disability

Colonial era African legal ethnographic studies largely ignore the specific status, rights and treatment of persons with disabilities. References to the legal implications of physical impairment are limited. One example comes from Ghana where the ethnographer noted that land could not be alienated to 'a person of unsound mind' under the customary law.[267] The use of the legalistic terminology 'unsound mind' denotes some syncretism with colonial law. In his study of the Pedi, Mönning writes that Pedi men who are living with a cognitive disability remain permanent minors under the tutelage of the closest male relative.[268]

Fertility is another area where physical limitations traditionally impact customary rights and status. One example comes from the Xhosa Law of Persons which deemed those incapable of procreating children as incompetent to marry.[269] Other ethnographic studies also discussed the customary implications of barrenness and impotency.[270]

Seymour's survey of customary law in South Africa has considerable content concerning disability, but this text is more of an overview of

---

[266] Stone-McDonald & Butera (note 6).

[267] N Ollenuu Principles of Customary Land Law in Ghana (1962).

[268] HO Mönning The Pedi (1967).

[269] J Van Tromp Xhosa Law of Persons (1947).

[270] JF Holleman Shona Customary Law (1952) at 72, 273; GD Gibson, TJ Larson & CR McGurk The Kavango Peoples (1981) at 53, 188; BA Marwick The Swazi (1966) at 133-35; Y Elam The Social and Sexual Roles of Hima Women (1973).

codified indigenous hybrid law as opposed to a collection of ethnographic studies.[271] Other significant legal ethnographies merely touch on the cultural significance of disability status, but offer negligible content about the customary legal implications of disability.[272] I did not come across any ethnographic content that discussed the impact of disability on succession and land inheritance which the fieldwork identifies as the most significant customary impact on persons with disabilities in Mukono District. Instead sections on succession in customary legal systems were silent on the issue of disability in terms of heirs (customary administrators) and beneficiaries.[273]

Disability can be a negative factor within culture and custom.[274] McDonald and Butera report that in some African cultures persons with disabilities are excluded from cultural practices and this negatively impacts social acceptance.[275] However, not all customary practices pertaining to disability are negative.[276] The Maasai in Kenya allow for special pro-disability cultural concessions. They permit women with disabilities to remain in their parents' home when they bear children instead of forcing such women to move to their husband's home as is the standard

---

[271] JC Bekker Seymour's Customary Law in Southern Africa (1989) 59, 61, 178, 211.

[272] I Schapera The Tswana (1984) at 36-37 (discussing disability as a relevant factor in Tswana social status); I Schapera A Handbook of Tswana Law and Custom 2nd ed reissue (1970).

[273] See further Ibid Schapera (1984) at 42-43; Holleman (note 142) at 318-368.

[274] Ibid Schapera (1984); Mönning (note 144) at 66-67.

[275] Stone-McDonald & Butera (note 6) at 69.

[276] See further D Selway & AF Ashman 'Disability, religion and health: A literature review in search of the spiritual dimensions of disability' 13(3) (1998) Disability & Society 429-439; J Kisanji 'Interface between culture and disability in the Tanzanian context: Part II' (1995) 42(2) International Journal Of Disability, Development and Education 109-118.

practice.[277] These mothers with disabilities that remain in the home can inherit their family's property.[278]

This thesis' field research discerned little in terms of settled customary substantive law that specifically addresses persons with disabilities in distinctive ways. Instead it identifies zones where customary processes occur in which community members are able to act in a manner that negatively impacts the rights, status and treatment of persons with disabilities. Examples include not allowing persons with disabilities to inherit real property and not permitting a person with disabilities to serve as a customary heir of an estate. Zones of customary discretion can also give customary legal actors the opportunity to offer more favorable treatment to persons with disabilities. For example some interviewees indicated fathers may require a lower payment of bride wealth from a male suitor with a disability. This same freedom to set the bride wealth is used by other fathers to make the marriage process more onerous for a male suitor with a disability.

The specific customary law of the Baganda with special significance to the status, rights and treatment of persons with disabilities is addressed in Section IV of Chapter 5 of this thesis and further details regarding the findings of the fieldwork concerning customary legal content in Mukono District are reported and discussed in Chapter 7.

Conclusion

This chapter presents context. It provides an understanding of the history and theory behind the disabilities movement along with a survey of predominant Sub-Saharan cultural content relevant to the rights, status and treatment of persons with disabilities.

---

[277] A Talle (note 118) at 56.

[278] Ibid.

Globally, persons with disabilities have achieved significant political and legal advances over the last half century. Their rights have been widely recognised through the rapid and extensive adoption of the CPRD and through other legislative and policy initiatives. Yet, the actualisation of proclaimed rights and legal mandates often proves difficult to achieve in deeply pluralistic settings where resources and governmental reach are limited.

The legal and socio-economic context in Mukono District presents considerable challenges and opportunities to those seeking to improve the lives of persons with disabilities. It is a place where various approaches to disability are put to the test in terms of relevance and functionality. The fieldwork indicates that such context is best served by an inclusive approach to disability theory with the social theory assuming a predominant role.

Where formal law is ineffectual, inaccessible or largely aspirational, the substance and operation of customary law takes on heightened importance. The customary context is where disability rights are worked out at the most elemental and relevant level.

The next chapter presents the theoretical grounding behind customary law and legal pluralism that further justifies and substantiates the utility, relevance and soundness of this thesis and its field research. It provides another layer of theoretical grounding that enables instructive analysis of the status, rights and treatment of persons with disabilities in customary legal frameworks in Mukono District.

3

DISCERNING A THEORETICAL APPROACH FOR THE CUSTOMARY LAW AND PROCESS RELEVANT TO PERSONS WITH DISABILITIES IN MUKONO DISTRICT

Introduction

If one simply looked at the laws of Uganda as they are written and applied by courts one would have a false conception of the operation and relevance of customary law. There are vibrant—-and in some instances dominant—-customary legal frameworks that are officially nullified by the formal statutory law.

The persistence of formally illegitimate customary law has been observed and assessed by others with expertise in the area of legal anthropology. Their contributions help to direct the fieldwork and rightly frame expectations about the limitations of the formal law and the significance of customary legal practices.

In order to understand the status, rights and treatment of persons with disabilities within customary legal frameworks it is necessary to appreciate customary law and process. In particular it is important to grasp the characteristics of customary law and how this law interacts with formal law in post-colonial contexts.

This chapter begins with a treatment of legal pluralism. It discusses the tension between strong and weak conceptions of legal pluralism and notes the particular soundness of strong legal pluralism as a beneficial perspective for scholarly engagement with customary legal frameworks.

Next the chapter turns to customary law. It presents a general discussion of customary law and then considers the British colonial imprint on customary law. This is followed by descriptions of the formal place and persistence of customary law in Uganda. It concludes by surveying newly emergent conceptions of customary law and a treatment of challenges relevant to strategic engagement with customary law.

Legal Pluralism

Legal pluralism arises from the 'observation that individual and social behaviour is regulated by more than one normative order'.[279] It is the common phenomenon that results when there are overlapping layers of legal obligations and enforceable norms.

Approaches to legal pluralism are presented along a spectrum. At one end are formalists who have a 'weak' conception of legal pluralism. At the other end are those who have a 'strong' or 'deep' conception of legal pluralism.

Weak pluralism describes a context where formal law predominates and the government establishes and maintains a normative ordering of the administration of law and courts.[280] In weak pluralism 'the norma-

---

[279] G Corradi *Advancing Human Rights in Legally Plural Africa: The Role of Development Actors in the Justice Sector* (2013) unpublished PhD thesis Ghent University at 158 citing J Griffiths 'What is legal pluralism?' (1986) 24 Journal of Legal Pluralism and Unofficial Law 1-55; GR Woodman 'Legal pluralism and the search for justice' (1996) 40(2) Journal of African Law 152-167; J Vanderlinden 'Le Pluralisme Juridique: Essai de Synthèse' in J Gilissen ed *Le Pluralisme Juridique* (1971) 19-56.

[280] Y Sezgin 'Theorizing formal pluralism: quantification of legal pluralism for spatio-temporal analysis' (2004) 50 Journal of Legal Pluralism and Unofficial Law 101-118, at 102.

tive existence of non-state norms (such as customary law) depends upon their recognition by the central administration'.[281] On the other hand, strong pluralism 'resembles an inexorable state of affairs in which all normative orderings regardless of their origin and mutual recognition by one another co-exist side by side within a normative universe'.[282] Under strong pluralism normative standards persist despite the fact that they are not established, recognized or even allowed by the government.

Those who lean towards weak legal pluralism tend to be legal centrists. Centrists adhere to a view that 'law is and should be the law of the state, uniform for all persons, exclusive of all other law, and administered by a single set of state institutions'.[283] For legal centrists the persistence of legal pluralism is a failure of the state as opposed to an inescapable reality.

On the other hand, strong legal pluralism appreciates the unpredictability and complexity of human society and the inability of a single law-making source to exert control over human interactions and exchanges.[284] Griffiths observes that the most significant legal marketplace for most people is 'the ground floor' of society.[285] This is a place where the formal law might have minimal impact and influence.

While there are some with reservations[286], anthropologically versed legal scholars generally agree that strong legal pluralism offers a more accurate account of the workings of legal orders in people's lives. Grif-

---

[281] Ibid.

[282] Ibid.

[283] Griffiths (note 1) at 3.

[284] Ibid at 39.

[285] Ibid.

[286] Sezgin (note 2) at 102 citing F von Benda-Beckmann 'Citizens, strangers and indigenous peoples: conceptual politics and legal pluralism' (1997) 9 Law and Anthropology 1-42; K von Benda-Beckmann 'Legal pluralism' (2001) 6 Thai Culture 18-40; BZ Tamanaha 'The folly of the "social scientific" concept of legal pluralism (1993) 20 Journal of Law and Society 192-217.

fiths flatly asserts that '[l]egal pluralism is the fact. Legal centralism is the myth.'[287] Woodman similarly contends that strong pluralism is a socially observable fact.[288] These bold assertions have particular currency in Uganda which has been singled out for its highly pluralistic legal settings.[289]

Twining notes the tendency of some to view law from non-indigenous sources as filling legal vacuums.[290] Yet modern scholarship demonstrates that the importation of law necessarily involves 'interaction with pre-existing normative orders'.[291] This interaction typically results in significant changes in the imported law.[292] Thus in order to understand how non-indigenous formal law will function, it is helpful to be cognizant of pre-existing customs and practices.

Human rights actors increasingly appreciate the need to account for the reality of strong legal pluralism. Recently insights from the wider field of legal pluralism have begun to affect rule-of-law programming'.[293] The broader recognition of the reality of legal pluralism is

---

[287] Ibid at 4.

[288] GR Woodman 'Ideological combat and social observation: recent debate about legal pluralism' (1998) 42 Journal of Legal Pluralism and Unofficial Law 21-59.

[289] DN Kobusingye, M Van Leeuwen & H Van Dijk 'Where do I report my land dispute? The impact of institutional proliferation on land governance in post-conflict Northern Uganda' (2016) 48(2) The Journal of Legal Pluralism and Unofficial Law 238-255.

[290] W Twining 'Diffusion of law: a global perspective' (2004) 49 Journal of Legal Pluralism and Unofficial Law 1-45, at 25.

[291] Ibid at 25.

[292] *Ibid* at 35.

[293] United States Institute of Peace & the Rift Valley Institute Local Justice in Southern Sudan (2010) at 17 citing BZ Tamanaha 'Understanding legal pluralism: past to present, local to global' (2008) 30 *Sydney Law* Review 375-411; W Menski Comparative Law in a Global Context: The Legal Systems of Asia and *Africa* 2nd ed (2006).

causing rights-based development initiatives to adopt pragmatic strategies that seek to understand and engage customary legal frameworks.[294] Increased appreciation of customary law and the complex interaction of legal sources offer valuable insights for those seeking to engender legal reform through customary engagement.

Appreciating the fact of deep legal pluralism is not the same as praising it. Those confirming the existence of strong legal pluralism recognise that it presents problems in the context of the human rights of traditionally marginalised people. Benda-Beckmann notes that legal pluralism can reinforce inequality by weakening the power of courts and legal officers to hold the rich and powerful accountable for exploitive behavior.[295] However, the complexities of layered law can also be exploited by the poor as well.[296]

This research is guided by the fact of strong legal pluralism and motivated by the need for descriptive realism in complex legal settings. It offers a baseline of understanding about consequential relationships between customary frameworks and disability. The research does so through the lens of the semi-autonomous social field[297] in order to account for the various influences and sources that contribute to the 'ground floor' legal environment where people with disabilities live their lives.

---

[294] Ibid.

[295] C Leonardi, LD Isser, N Moro et al 'The politics of customary law ascertainment in South Sudan' (2011) 63 Journal of Legal Pluralism 111-142, at 123 citing generally F von Benda-Beckmann, K von Benda-Beckmann & J Eckert 'Rules of law and laws of ruling; law and government between past and future' in F von Benda-Beckmann, K von Benda-Beckmann & J Eckert (Eds) Rules of Law and Laws of Ruling; On Governance and Law (2009) 1-30.

[296] Ibid (von Benda-Beckmann, von Benda-Beckmann & Eckert) at 12.

[297] SF Moore 'Law and social change: the semi-autonomous social field as an appropriate field of study' (1973) 7(4) Law & Society Review 719-746.

The substance and characteristics of the operative customary law is the evolving product of a series of influences and interactions. Those that view customary law as something pure and uncorrupted from ages past suffer from a similar misconception as those that believe that the law is whatever is written in the law books. Thus to understand customary law in Mukono District it is necessary to appreciate content from the indigenous culture along with historic influences, existing formal law and other cultural forces. Chapter 8[298] includes a broad and inclusive accounting of legal sources and their interactions which shape customary legal scenarios in Mukono District.

Customary Law

Customary law is integrative and wide-ranging. It 'is not simply a set of rules and sanctions, but a contextually defined process, involving flexibility, negotiation, and reinterpretation of a dynamic body of knowledge to reflect what is considered reasonable under the circumstances'.[299] Classically, it is unwritten and rooted in actual practice and history.[300] Per Woodman '[a] customary law may be defined as a normative order observed by a population having been formed by regular social behaviour and the development of an accompanying sense of obligation.'[301] It is often described as 'living' because it exists within socie-

---

[298] See especially ch 8, secs II(1), III and IV.

[299] United States Institute of Peace & the Rift Valley Institute (note 15) at 5.

[300] L Cotula 'Introduction' in L Cotula (Ed) Changes in 'Customary' Land Tenure Systems in Africa (2007) at 10 citing TW Bennett 1985 The Application of Customary Law in Southern Africa – The Conflict of Personal Laws (1985).

[301] GR Woodman 'A survey of customary laws in Africa in search of lessons for the future' in J Fenrich, P Galizzi & T Higgins (eds) The Future of African Customary law (2011) 9-30, at 10 (Woodman prefers to use the plural term 'customary laws' as opposed to 'customary law' to 'avoid any possible implication of a denial of the variety of customary laws on the [African] continent.').

ty without the necessity of state action or support[302] and because it has the ability to adapt to changing circumstances.[303]

Customary law is not an exotic phenomena limited to African villages and Oceanic islands. Glendon observes that custom is 'a source of law present in every legal tradition'.[304] However, custom is more legally potent and pervasive in certain contexts. In particular, many post-colonial settings are home to active and effectual customary legal frameworks. This is the case in many sub-Saharan nations.[305]

Customary law is diverse. This diversity 'is the result of a range of cultural, ecological, social, economic and political factors'.[306] It may exist on its own, or beside, or complementarily to other law.[307] Legal customs may be relatively uniform within a number of societies or they might vary significantly from village to village.[308] Observers have noted

---

[302] E Ehrlich The Fundamental Principles of the Sociology of Law 4th ed (2009) (on the concept of living law generally without specific application to customary law or customary living law).

[303] C Himonga 'The future of living customary law in African legal systems in the twenty-first century and beyond, with special reference to South Africa' in J Fenrich, P Galizzi & T Higgins (eds) The Future of African Customary Law (2011) 31-53, at 34-35.

[304] MA Glendon Comparative Legal Traditions in a Nutshell (1982).

[305] OC Ruppel & K Ruppel-Schilichting 'Legal and judicial pluralism in Namibia and beyond: A modern approach to African legal architecture' (2011) 64 Journal of Legal Pluralism and Unofficial Law 33-63, at 64 (discussing the persistence of customary law in Namibia); AC Rawls Policy Proposals for Justice in Liberia: Opportunities Under the Current Legal Framework to Expand Access to Justice (2011) (noting the preference among Liberians for customary legal systems); J Fenrich, P Galizzi & T Higgins 'Introduction' in J Fenrich, P Galizzi & T Higgins (eds) The Future of African Customary Law (2011) 1-8.

[306] Cotula (note 22) at 1.

[307] Ibid at 12-14.

[308] Ibid at 10.

customary diversity within different clans, lineages and households.[309] Nyamu-Musembi quips that anything said about the substance of customary law tends to be a partial truth at best.[310]

Indigenous legal content is not self-contained nor is it immune from non-indigenous influences. While it primarily 'derives from the mores, values and traditions of indigenous ethnic groups', legal custom in contemporary Africa is influenced by other sources including monotheistic religious values[311], government policies and judicial decisions.[312] In addition, non-indigenous colonial heritages engender ongoing impacts. In Uganda the influence and impact of the British colonial heritage on customary law and practice warrants examination.

The British Colonial Approach to Indigenous Customary Law

During colonial rule, the British Empire espoused a formalist conception of customary law. Osborn's Concise Law Dictionary provides a representative formalist definition of customary law:

Custom is a rule of conduct obligatory to those within its scope, established by long usage. A valid custom has the force of law. Custom to the society is what law is to the State. A valid custom must be of imme-

---

[309] Woodman (note 23) at 17 citing NC Obi The Customary Law Manueal: A Manual of Customary Laws Obtaining in the Anambra and Imo States in Nigeria (1977).

[310] C Nyamu-Musembi 'Local norms, institutions, and women's property rights in rural Kenya' (2003) 9(2) East African Journal of Peace & Human Rights 255-289, at 265.

[311] Pew Forum on Religion and Public Life Tolerance and Tension: Islam and Christianity in Sub-Saharan Africa (2010) at 152 (Reporting that in Uganda roughly 86 per cent of people self-identify as Christian and 13 per cent self-identify as Muslim).

[312] M Kane, J Oloka-Onyango & A Tejan-Cole 'Reassessing customary law systems as a vehicle for providing equitable access to justice for the poor' a paper presented at New Frontiers of Social Policy, Arusha (2005).

morial antiquity, certain, reasonable, obligatory and not repugnant to statute law, though it may derogate from the common law.[313]

The requisite element of 'not repugnant' took on legal force in the 'repugnancy test'. This test allowed British colonial regimes to distance themselves from any indigenous legal practices offensive to British sensibilities. Customary laws found to be repugnant were stripped of any formal legal force.[314]

The British Empire developed formal rules of engagement for indigenous customary law. In order to establish a legally binding custom under British rule it was necessary to prove that the custom existed from 'immemorial antiquity', was 'certain and precise', had been 'enjoyed continuously' and was 'reasonable'.[315]

The British imprint on customary law persists in Uganda. Its continued prominence is affirmed in modern court opinions such as former Chief Justice Odoki's judgement in the *Kampala District Land Board and George Mitala v Venansio Babweyaka et al* where he characterised the rigid colonial requirements for establishing customary law as clearly established 'trite law'.[316]

---

[313] AA Jok, R Leitch & C Vandewint A Study of Customary Law in Contemporary Southern Sudan (2004) at 5.1 quoting J Burke *Osborn*'s Concise Law Dictionary at 108 (edition and publication date not provided).

[314] TW Bennett 'The compatibility of African customary law and human rights' (1991) Acta Juridica 18.

[315] Jok, Leitch & Vandewint (note 35) at s 5.2.1 (paraphrasing Dias's explanation of the origination of customary law).

[316] *Kampala District Land Board and George Mitala v. Venansio Babweyaka et al* UCSC App 2 of 2007 [2008].

The Treatment, Persistence and Place of Customary Law in Contemporary Uganda

In contemporary Uganda the formal law offers general support for customary law and recognises the legitimate domain of customary law within certain spheres.

Customary law receives general support from the 1995 Constitution.[317] Article 37 provides that '[e]very person has a right as applicable to belong to, enjoy, practise, profess, maintain and promote any culture, cultural institution, language, tradition, creed or religion in community with others.' The Constitution also announces a national objective for developing and incorporating cultural and customary values[318], provides for the institution of cultural leaders[319], and offers legal recognition for customary land tenure.[320]

There are designated zones within the national legislative framework where customary law is formally observed and applied. For example, customary marriage is a formally recognised form of marriage under the Marriage Act[321] and customary tenure is an official form of land tenure under the Land Act.[322]

British colonial standards and approaches for formal engagement with customary law endure in Uganda. Uganda's Magistrates Act defines customary law as 'the rules of conduct which govern legal relationships as established by custom and usage and not forming part of the common law nor formally enacted by Parliament'.[323] Custom is defined in the Hindu Marriage and Divorce Act as

---

[317] Constitution of Uganda 1995 (as amended in 2005) arts 33(6) and 32(1) and obj XXIV.

[318] Ibid obj XXIV.

[319] Ibid art 246.

[320] Ibid art 237.

[321] The Marriage Act of 1904 (cap 251) (Uganda).

[322] The Land Act of 1998 (cap 227) (Uganda).

[323] Magistrates Courts Act of 1971 (cap 16) (Uganda) s 1(a).

'a rule which, having been continuously observed for a long time, has attained the force of law among a community, group or family, being a rule that is certain and not unreasonable or opposed to public policy, and in the case of a rule applicable only to a family, has not been discontinued by the family'.[324]

Similarly, a contemporary Ugandan High Court[325] explains that for a local practice to qualify as customary law 'it must be reasonable in nature and it must have been followed continuously, and as if it were a right, since the beginning of legal memory'.[326]

Ugandan courts typically construe legal memory as stretching back to the time preceding colonialisation in the late 1800s.[327] This requirement is contrary to the prevailing scholarly view that 'customary law, like statutory law, is fluid and responds to political, social and economic events occurring within society'.[328]

Significantly, the British 'time immemorial' test fails to account for customary rules of recognition that include the power to create and change law. For the Baganda people their king (the Kabaka) has the power to make and change law.[329] This thesis' field research confirms that the Kabaka is still considered the ultimate law giver and legal authority among Baganda people. Thus, there is dissonance between the

---

[324] Hindu Marriage and Divorce Act of 1961 (cap 250) (Uganda) s 1(a).

[325] High Courts in Uganda are Uganda's third highest court of record after the Supreme Court of Uganda and the Court of Appeals/Constitutional Court. High Courts issue opinions that can be published and have the ability to render legal opinions that contribute to the common law of Uganda. See the Judicature Act of 1996 (cap 13) (Uganda) s 14.

[326] *Bruno Kiwuwa v Ivan Serunkuma & Juliet Namazzi* HCUg Suit No. 52 of 2006 quoting EA Martin ed Dictionary of Law 4th ed (2006) at 122.

[327] Ibid.

[328] AM Banks 'CEDAW, compliance, and custom: human rights enforcement in Sub-Saharan Africa' (2009) 32 *Fordham Int'l LJ* 781-845, at 822, 839.

[329] This power is addressed in ch 4, s IV of this thesis.

'time immemorial' requirement and the Baganda conception concerning the sourcing of customary law.

Uganda preserves the legacy of the British repugnancy test. The Constitution provides that '[l]aws, cultures, customs or traditions which are against the dignity, welfare or interest of women or which undermine their status, are prohibited'.[330] Uganda's Judicature Act only allows courts to observe and enforce customary law that 'is not repugnant to natural justice, equity and good conscience and not incompatible either directly or by necessary implication with any written law'.[331] This limitation led Justice Kasule to observe that from a formal standpoint customary law is 'primarily applied where the written law is silent'.[332]

The Uganda Constitution prevails over all customs that are inconsistent with the Constitution.[333] The effective result is a constitutional repugnancy test that can strike down any custom or cultural norm contrary to a constitutional right or standard. Significantly in the context of this research, express constitutional rights include the right of persons with disabilities to be free from discrimination[334] and their right to respect and human dignity.[335]

Vestiges of the persisting colonial conception of customary law can pose evidentiary challenges. In accordance with the evidentiary requirement established during British rule, Ugandan judges must base

---

[330] Constitution of Uganda 1995 art 33(6).

[331] Judicature Act of 1996 (cap 13) (Uganda) s 15; See also Mustafa Kadala Nsubuga v Mawandu Balumu and Others HCUg Civil Suit No. 1086 [2000](where Justice Mukiibi held that 'the requirement for the Mailo land owner's consent and the customary practice of giving a Kanzu in order to obtain such consent could not be enforced by the courts because it had become incompatible with written law').

[332] Kiwuwa (supra note 48).

[333] Constitution of Uganda 1995 art 2.

[334] Ibid art 21(2).

[335] Ibid art 35(1).

their opinions as to the existence and substance of customary law on the expert testimony of a knowledgeable person as opposed to the court's 'own experience or imagination, unless the culture or custom has gained such notoriety as to be taken judicial notice of'.[336]

The challenge of proof can keep the substance of customary law cordoned off from formal legal application and review. Here recent litigation challenging the constitutionality of bride wealth in Uganda based on the practice's discriminatory character is instructive. In *Mifumi*[337], the Constitutional Court avoided substantive issues on the grounds that the petitioners failed to present adequate proof to establish the content of the challenged bride wealth practices. Although the Supreme Court of Uganda[338] side-stepped this evidentiary hurdle on appeal and engaged the substantive issues[339], the *Mifumi* litigation illustrates the challenges posed by the formal law to both the proof and application of customary law in formal courts.

Formal law is not always the antagonist of custom in Uganda. The *Kiwuwa* case is a high water mark for the place of custom law within Ugandan courts.[340] In *Kiwuwa,* High Court Justice Remmy Kasule prevented a man and women who were members of the same Baganda clan to enter into a Christian marriage on the ground that Kiganda custom prohibits marriage between clan mates. Justice Kasule held that the

---

[336] Opinion of J Obura in Yawe v Asaba HCUg Misc. App. No. 128 [2013].

[337] Mifumi (U) Ltd and 12 Others v Attorney General UGCC 2 Const Petition No. 12/07 [2010].

[338] The Supreme Court of Uganda has appellate jurisdiction over the Constitutional Court. The Court of Appeals and the Constitutional Court are the same judicial organ in terms of personal with the Constitutional Court having jurisdiction, in some gases original jurisdiction, over certain constitutional matters.

[339] Mifumi (U) Ltd and 12 Others v Attorney General UgSC Const App No. 2/14 [2015].

[340] Kiwuwa (supra note 48).

custom preventing the marriage of clan members was not repugnant and applied to non-customary forms of marriage. Thus the communal right to uphold the customs of the clan prevailed over two individuals' right to marry the person of their choice. However, it should be noted that Justice Tumwesigye of the Supreme Court of Uganda recently opined that *Kiwuwa* was wrongly decided because it applied customary standards to non-customary law.[341]

Despite the formal challenges outlined above, customary law is pervasive and resilient in Uganda.[342] Far from a mere legal ghost whose potency is contingent on courts and government, customary law is widely practiced and applied at the grassroots level. This is especially the case in the context of succession and probate where Ugandan formal law officially displaces customary law.[343]

According to an International Justice Mission (IJM) study conducted from 2010 to 2013, out of 2,068 relationships in Mukono District where husbands predeceased their wives only 27 widows engaged in the formal (and legally required) estate administration process.[344] This amounts to 1.3 per cent usage rate of the mandated formal system. Clearly customary ways persist despite formal invalidity in Mukono District. The IJM study quotes a Magistrate Judge in Mukono District who observes that the people of Mukono District follow Uganda's Succession Act 'very

---

[341] Mifumi *(U) Ltd and 12 Others v Attorney General* UgSC Const App No. 2/14 [2015] in the opinion of Tumweigye at p 35; This position was also taken prior to this case by BK Twinomugisha in 'African customary law and women's human rights in Uganda' in J Fenrich, P Galizzi & T Higgins The Future of African Customary Law (2011) 446-466, at 452.

[342] International Justice Mission (IJM) Property Grabbing from Ugandan Widows and the Justice System: A Mixed-Methods Assessment in Mukono County, Uganda (2015) at 16-17.

[343] Ibid at 68; JMN Kakooza 'The application of customary law in Uganda' (2003) 1(1) The Uganda Living Law Journal 23-42, at 37.

[344] Ibid (IJM) at 65.

rarely, if at all'.[345] The Judge observes that '[o]rdinary people don't follow the Succession Act; they do the distribution of property according to their traditions and customs. The girls get less and the boys get more.'[346] According to IJM, communities, clans and local leaders in Mukono District uphold the cultural norms regarding the distribution of family property instead of following the formal law.[347]

The resilience of customary law in Uganda is patent in the context of land ownership. The tendency to handle land relationally, and thus informally, is strong. Moore rightly notes '[p]roperty in land is surely one of the most socially embedded of the elements of a legal order' and is 'not about things but about relationships between and among persons with regard to things'.[348]

Customary land tenure is the dominant form of land holding in Uganda.[349] According to estimates approximately 75 per cent of the total land holdings are customary[350] and untitled customary ownership is the dominant form of land ownership.[351] This is a remarkably high percentage given the dominance of formally titled Mailo land tenure in central Uganda[352] as well as the formal and political disfavouring of customary

---

[345] Ibid at 68.

[346] Ibid at 68.

[347] Ibid at 68.

[348] SF Moore 'Changing African land tenure: reflections on the incapacities of the state' (1998) 10(2) European Journal of Development Research 33, at 34.

[349] Ministry of Lands, Housing and Urban Development, Uganda Land Policy (2013) policy statement 38.

[350] DR Olanya 'Colonial legacy, access political economy of land, and legal pluralism in Uganda: 1900-2010' Gulu University (2011) at 8.

[351] JMB Tukahirwa 'Policies, people and land use change in Uganda: case study in Ntungamo, Lake Mburo and Sango Bay sites, LUCID working Paper Series No. 17 (2002) at 19.

[352] Mukono District is located in the region designated as Central Uganda.

land holding.[353] The way the land is held and titled indicates that a large percentage of Ugandans are not applying the formal laws of inheritance that would inevitably lead to formalisation of land titles and reduce the predominance of customary tenure.

Legal behaviour in Mukono District reflects the tendency of Ugandans to transfer land outside of formal legal frameworks. For example, IJM observes the ongoing preference of patrilineal kinship and the control of estates by male customary heirs in Mukono District despite the gender neutrality formally required by the Ugandan Constitution and the Succession Act.[354]

Emerging Appreciations of Customary Law

Contemporary scholars and judges challenge the premise that customary law is immutable. South Africa is home to several noteworthy decisions grounded in an appreciation of the dynamic and communal nature of customary law.[355] Although the influence of South African jurisprudence has yet to substantially impact formal law in Uganda, these cases speak to the potential for fresh judicial engagement with customary law.

Although Ugandan formal law has largely adhered to the 'time immemorial' requirement, there are indications of progressive incursions.

---

[353] Tukahirwa (note 73) policy statement 47 (Noting that Ugandan formal law allows for the transition of land from customary tenure to freehold tenure but it does not permit the reverse); V Bennett, G Falk, A Kovina et al 'Inheritance law in Uganda: the plight of widows and children' (2006) 7 *Georgetown Journal of Gender & the Law* 451-530, at 459; Ministry of Lands, Housing and Urban Development (note 71) policy statement 38(i) (stating that customary land tenure is 'regarded and treated as inferior' to other forms of land tenure).

[354] IJM (note 64) at 16-17.

[355] Bhe v Magistrate Khayelitsha 2005 (1) SA 580 (CC); Shilubana and Others v Nwamitwa and Other 2009 (2) SA 66 (CC); S v Shiluban 2008 1 SACR 295 (T); Mabena v Letsoala 1998 (2) SA 1068; Alexkor Ltd. and Another v Richtersveld Community and Others 2004 (5) SA 460.

Notably the Uganda Land Policy proclaims that all land tenure regimes (including customary) must have the opportunity to 'evolve and develop'[356] in response to changing social and economic circumstances and that customary tenure should have the opportunity to 'progressively evolve'.[357] In addition, Justice Mpagi–Bahigeine's opinion in the case of *Mifumi (U) Ltd and 12 Others v Attorney General* reflects a growing appreciation among the Ugandan judiciary that customary practices change over time.[358] In *Mifumi* the Lady Justice opined that the specifics of the alleged practice of bride price needed to be proven by the petitioners because those customary practices 'keep on changing with the times'.[359]

Today customary law is increasingly appreciated as flexible and situational. Human Rights Watch offers instructive and pragmatic advice regarding custom in Northern Uganda:

Customary rules, like the common law in general, evolve naturally are not static. Therefore the question is not whether or not to apply customary rules, but rather how to ensure that these rules are allowed to evolve organically in order to take into account changing circumstances.[360]

This thesis' field research confirms that customary legal content and scenarios are evolving and open to integrating change. Customary law's flexibility persists in part because it is generally unwritten. Unwritten

---

[356] Ministry of Lands, Housing and Urban Development (note 71) policy statement 33(i).

[357] Ibid 38(v) (noting that despite constitutional protections customary tenure continues to be '[d]isparaged and sabotaged in preference for other forms of registered tenures, denying it the opportunity to progressively evolve').

[358] Mifumi (U) Ltd and 12 Others v Attorney General UGCC 2 Const Petition No. 12/07 [2010].

[359] Ibid.

[360] Human Rights Watch 'As If We Weren'*t Human*': Discrimination and Violence Against Women with Disabilities in Northern Uganda (2010).

law is more easily adjusted and applied situationally.[361] The flexibility of customary law can make it more attractive to legal forum-shoppers. A recent study from South Sudan noted that '[w]here government courts impose more rigid statutory penalties, litigants seek alternative forums in which to negotiate positive outcomes of compensation and, if appropriate, marriage.'[362]

Despite the emerging acknowledgment of the flexibility and mutability of customary law, it is important not to uncritically assign these characteristics. The dividing line between customary law and formal law can be difficult to draw.[363] History and culture give the Baganda people a uniquely formal customary heritage which includes the top-down law making power of the Kabaka (king) and prior colonial era codifications of customary law.[364] This unique legal heritage is given consideration in research findings and analysis set forth in Chapter 8, Section II(3).

Practical and Strategic Challenges Posed by Customary Law

The prevalent qualities and tendencies of customary law can pose socio-legal challenges. While customary law remains flexible and unwritten, it also remains ripe for manipulation. Customary legal practices can be used to maintain structural authority and inequality at the family and community level.[365] In addition, the fact that customary law is un-

---

[361] R Odgaard & AW Benton 'The interplay between collective rights and obligations and individual rights" (1998) 10(2) European Journal of Development Research 105-16 (Describing the ability of people in Tanzania to choose between formal or customary law within semi-autonomous social fields).

[362] United States Institute of Peace & the Rift Valley Institute (note 15) at 5.

[363] Woodman (note 23) at 11.

[364] These aspects of Baganda customary law are discussed in ch 4, s IV of this thesis.

[365] United States Institute of Peace & the Rift Valley Institute (note 15) at 28.

written can make it more difficult for judges and others to discern with specificity.

Some view the formal transcription of customary law as a means for increasing legal awareness and certainty as well as limiting abuse. They believe that recording customary law can bolster its legitimacy and help to provide judges with better access to customary law.[366] Others voice concern over the tendency of written customary law to become rigid and stagnant.[367] For its part, unlike neighboring Kenya, Uganda never developed written restatements of customary law.[368]

Customary law has been criticised for its susceptibility to discrimination and abuse of power. Some observe a tendency to 'designate older male members as authority figures, particularly in matters relating to law.'[369] Thus the recording of customary law as discerned and pronounced by elder males can result in the propagation of distorted power relations. Leonardi and others posit:

If male elders and chiefs dominate the process of recording it—which seems highly probable—the resulting recorded law is likely to represent a conservative version of contested, changing norms, and its application could have an unwelcome or retrogressive effect.[370]

In Uganda, customary law has been linked to practices that are discriminatory and harmful to women.[371] Similarly customary legal sys-

---

[366] Ibid at 73.

[367] A Armstrong, C Beyani, C Himonga et al 'Uncovering reality: excavating women's rights in African family law' (1993) 7 *International Journal of Law and the Family* 314-369, at 326-27.

[368] Kakooza (note 65).

[369] P Kameri-Mbote, C Odote, C Nyamu-Musembi et al Ours by Right: Law, Politics and Realities of Community Property in Kenya (2013) at 50.

[370] Leonardi (note 17) at 121.

[371] Ministry of Lands, Housing and Urban Development (note 71) policy statement 38.

tems are accused of failing to support the rights of persons with disabilities in Uganda.[372]

Despite aspects of patrimony, discrimination and potential for abuse, some scholars and human rights actors contend that customary land tenure in Uganda has the capacity to defend the rights of the vulnerable.[373] In the context of women, Gä'ber contends that '[c]ustomary land tenure explicitly recognizes women's vulnerabilities arising from their dependence upon men and for a long time proactively provided for the protection of their land rights in both, their maiden and matrimonial homes.'[374]

The fieldwork explored the possibility that customary legal content includes aspects that are helpful to persons with disabilities. Instead it largely found discriminatory practices gilded with protective intentions. For example, the research identified a practice where land that should be inherited by a person with a disability is given to another family member with the expectation that the family member will care for the person with a disability.

That said, it is important not to hastily dismiss customary law on the grounds of perceived discriminatory and anachronistic tendencies. As Kane *et al* write

---

[372] Human Rights Watch (note 82) (noting the rules of traditional clan structures along with the weakness and corruption of local councils as reasons why women with disabilities are being denied their rights to land in Northern Uganda).

[373] J Adoku & J Akin Understanding and Strengthening Women's Land Rights under Customary Tenure in Uganda Land Equity Uganda Working Paper (April 2011) available at <http://landportal.info/sites/landportal.info/files/2._understanding_and_strengthening_womens_land_rights_under_customary_tenure_in_uganda_lemu_ug.pdf> last accessed 1 December 2016.

[374] B Gärber 'Women's land rights and tenure security in Uganda: experiences from Mbale, Apac and Ntungamo' (2013) 13(24) *Stichproben, Wiener Zeitschrift für kritische Afrikastudien* 1-32.

'[i]f indeed Customary Law has remained such a potent and powerful force it must be on account of some degree of resonance that it enjoys within the existing social fabric, rather than on account of some vague linkage to an atavistic practice from the past.'

Thus '[a] serious and meaningful reform of the institution can thus only result from an internal critique, debate and engagement that respects the essential attributes of the institution'.[375] This thesis starts its assessment with engagement and investigation as opposed to preconceived notions about the discriminatory character of customary law. It does not seek to debunk or chastise customary law; it seeks to present it accurately and instructively.

When customary law is demonised and marginalised the legal systems that shape the lives of people can be unsettled and weakened. Yet, customary laws and practices endure in the lived environment regardless of the posture of custom before formal bodies and courts. The legal fact of customary law's persistence regardless of formal institutions and proclamations is at the core of an appreciation for deep legal pluralism.

Conclusion

This chapter sets forth crucial grounding for the thesis in the related areas of legal pluralism and legal anthropology. It discusses the need to approach the field research with an appreciation of the reality and dynamics of deep legal pluralism.

The chapter presents the colonial heritage and formal legal treatment that influence the substance and operation of customary law in Mukono District. Although customary law is durable and persistent, it does not exist in a vacuum. Understanding the historic forces that shape customary legal practices offers richer understanding. Similarly awareness of

---

[375] Kane, Oloka-Onyango & Tejan-Cole (note 34) at 22.

the official place of customary law within the formal law enables one to appreciate where, when and how customary law can be marginalised and where, when and how it can retain significance and influence.

This chapter endorses a pragmatic, informed and inclusive framework for the consideration and study of customary law— a framework that entails both deep legal pluralism and an appreciation of legal formalism in the descriptive and functional assessment of customary law. Customary law is a nuanced, idiosyncratic and place-specific. Thus strategies for customary engagement should be informed by the specific cultural setting where they will be employed.

The next chapter presents and explores various approaches to change and strategic legal engagement in contexts where formal law does not play the dominant role in lived legal experiences. The theoretical groundwork from this chapter and the next inform and direct the thesis' fieldwork approach and the analytical treatment of the fieldwork findings found in Chapters 8 and 9.

4

A CRITICAL SURVEY OF CHANGE STRATEGIES FOR IMPROVING THE STATUS, RIGHTS AND TREATMENT OF PERSONS WITH DISABILITIES IN THE MAJORITY WORLD CONTEXTS

Introduction

This thesis concerns the status, rights and treatment of persons with disabilities within customary legal frameworks. Meaningful appreciation of this topic requires more than a descriptive snapshot. To understand the situation facing persons with disabilities, it is important to be aware of possibilities and means for bringing about positive change.

Persons with disabilities in developing societies face formidable obstacles. Examples include unfavorable social attitudes, inaccessible physical environments, governments with severe budget limitations and limited medical and rehabilitative services. These challenges call out for strategies that can improve the lives of persons with disabilities in the Majority World.

This chapter presents descriptions and critical assessments of change strategies. For the purpose of this chapter the change strategies are categorised as top-down or bottom-up. Yet they typically encompass both top-down and bottom-up elements. Moreover, these strategies are rarely applied in isolation. Results driven change actors often employ a combination of strategies and approaches.[376]

This chapter's survey of change strategies speaks to the value of this thesis' fieldwork. Particular knowledge about the rights, status and treatment of persons with disabilities in lived environments is an essential component to bottom-up change strategies and a key barometer for gauging the effectiveness of top-down strategies.

Top-Down Change Strategies

Top-down strategies seek to precipitate, and in some cases force, change through formal institutions. Human rights reform has an inherently top-down character. Universal proclamations of human rights necessarily entail the abeyance of all humankind.[377] Disability advocates commonly employ top-down strategies to improve the status and treatment of persons with disabilities and to establish and enforce domestically and supra-nationally proclaimed rights.

Top-down strategies are not autonomous and free-standing. To be effective these strategies should be informed by specific cultural understanding. As Wilson observes, '[h]uman rights doctrine does get reworked and transformed in different contexts.'[378]

Predominant top-down strategies include the creation, promulgation and implementation of international human rights instruments, domestic legislative reform, government policy, litigation and institutional en-

---

[376] Y Sezgin 'How to integrate universal human rights into customary and religious legal systems' (2010) 60 Journal of Legal Pluralism and Unofficial Law 5-40, at 31 (writing that a 'multipronged strategy' is necessary for inducing internal reform in customary legal systems).

[377] E Grant 'Human rights, cultural diversity and customary law in South Africa' (2006) 50(1) Journal of African Law 2-23.

[378] RA Wilson (Ed) Human Rights, Culture and Context: Anthropological Perspectives (1997) at 12, 23.

gagement. This section addresses predominate top-down change strategies and demonstrates the significance of customary and cultural contexts to these strategies.

Categories of Top-Down Change Strategies

The creation, promulgation and implementation of human rights instruments

One dominant top-down strategy is the creation, promulgation and implementation of international human rights instruments. This strategy follows a standard progression. First, human rights treaties are formulated at the international level. Once the treaties are introduced, the nations of the world are encouraged to formally adopt the treaty. The United Nations Convention on the Rights of Persons with Disabilities (CRPD) progressed through this second stage briskly with the rapid adoption by an overwhelming majority of nations.[379]

The next phase in treaty-based change is implementation. This often entails other top-down reform mechanisms. Examples include domestic law reform, compliance reporting, strategic litigation and organisational advocacy.[380]

Cultural relativism has political resonance in post-colonial settings where indigenous values have been historically marginalised.[381] Cultural relativists regard norms and morals as situational and legitimately varied

---

[379] 'United Nations enable Convention and Optional Protocol signatures and ratifications' available at <http://www.un.org/disabilities/countries.asp?id=166> last accessed 19 December 2015.

[380] P Harpur 'Time to be heard: how advocates can use the Convention on the Rights of Persons with Disabilities to drive change (2011) 45(3) *Valparaiso Univ LR* 1271-1296, at 1292.

[381] O Roy & P Annichino 'Human rights between religions, cultures and universality' in AF Vrdoljak (ed) Cultural Dimension of Human Rights (2013) 14-25.

and situational.[382] As such, cultural relativism poses a threat to normative conceptions of human rights.[383]

Certain cultural beliefs in sub-Saharan Africa present stern challenges to the realisation of universal human rights.[384] For example, social norms about the roles of women in family and society often collide with the right to gender equality.[385] Olako-Onyango notes that a key impediment to achieving gender equality in Uganda 'is the resilience of the structures of patriarchy, tradition and established practices of discrimination'.[386] Cultural intransigency can stymy human rights reform.

Deep implementation through community-level acceptance and integration poses challenges to top-down strategies.[387] Rights are 'continually contested and negotiated at different levels of society'.[388] As Moore notes, '[l]ocal persons with personal and local concerns can undo grand plans of reform.'[389] This local undoing need not be the result of an or-

---

[382] R Benedict Patterns of Culture (1934).

[383] J Donnelly 'Cultural relativism and universal human rights' (1984) 6(4) Human Rights Quarterly 400.

[384] S Ntagali & EE Hodgetts More Than One Wife: Polygamy and Grace (2011).

[385] United States Institute of Peace & the Rift Valley Institute Local justice in Southern Sudan (2010) at 6.

[386] J Oloka-Onyango 'The problematique of economic, social and cultural rights in globalized Uganda: a conceptual review' HURIPEC Working Paper No 3 (March 2007) at 38.

[387] P Armstrong 'Beyond (human) rights?' (2009) 29(4) Disabilities Studies Quarterly.

[388] C Himonga 'Exploring the concept of ubuntu in the South African legal system" (2011) 15(17) *Ideologie und Weltanschauung im Recht* 1-22, at 7 referencing SE Merry 'Changing rights, changing culture' in JK Cowan, MB Dembour & RA Wilson (eds) Culture and Rights, Anthropological Perspectives (2001) 31-55.

[389] SF Moore 'Changing African land tenure: reflections on the incapacities of the state' (1998) 10(2) The European Journal of Development Research 33-49, at 34.

ganised collective movement. 'Seemingly trivial actions of individuals can demolish state policy just as effectively.'[390]

Thus top-down reform often requires some level of community integration to enable it to become operative and effective. Writing in the context of women's rights, Himonga notes the importance of community-based processing and ownership of human rights:

Recognizing that a community can align its customary law with constitutional rights encourages the protection of women's rights from a bottom-up rather than a top-down approach. The former is more likely to have the support of the community, with no cost to women. Otherwise the community's opposition makes it harder, if not impossible, to implement women's rights by any mechanism.[391]

Himonga further observes that customary law is not static and self-contained. It is subject to incremental changes which can be caused in part by formal law and outside influences. This phenomenon is referred to as the 'passive development' of customary law.[392] In this thesis' field research, interview participants credited outside groups and foreign nations with improving local attitudes and beliefs about persons with disabilities. This affirms the capacity of outsider engagement to effect socio-legal change.

The modern human rights movement can encounter challenges exporting tenets and principles in Sub-Saharan communities. Universal rights-based ideology may run counter to the flexibility needed to foster reform from within local systems and structures. This can lead to 'rup-

---

[390] Ibid.

[391] C Himonga 'Constitutional rights of women under customary law in Southern Africa' in B Baines, D Barak-Erez and T Kahana (eds) Feminist Constitutionalism: Global Perspectives (2012) 317-335, at 319, 324.

[392] C Himonga 'The future of living customary law in African legal systems in the twenty-first century and beyond, with special reference to South Africa' in J Fenrich, P Galizzi and T Higgins (eds) The Future of African Customary Law (2011) 31-53, at 48.

tures' with established ways of life.[393] For example, efforts to stop practices such as male inheritance and clan land ownership can hurt marginalised and vulnerable people.[394] Nyamu-Musembi cautions that 'abolitionist approaches are not likely to bring about the desired results, not the least because they might be perceived as cultural imperialism'.[395] Corradi advises rights-based change operatives to 'focus on discussing the concrete negative consequences of certain local practices in order to forge a common ground with local actors to pursue solutions to problems that are locally identified as such'.[396] These cautionary points speak to the relevance of this thesis' field research.

The field research noted minimal pushback against international human rights standards. Instead the interviewees without disabilities demonstrated a general openness to the rights of those with disabilities. However, the impact of human rights dissipates due to a lack of appreciation and understanding. The international human rights agenda can seem alien and irrelevant to people's lives unless it comes bearing resources. Thus Corradi's challenge of making rights tangible is highly applicable to Mukono District—especially in the complex context of disability rights.

---

[393] G Corradi *Advancing Human Rights in Legally Plural Africa: The Role of Development Actors in the Justice Sector* (2013) PhD thesis Ghent University at 107 citing AA An Na'im (ed) Human Rights Under African Constitutions, Realizing the Promise for Ourselves (2003) and A Swidler 'Culture in action: symbols and strategies' (1986) 51(2) American Sociological Review 273-286.

[394] Ibid (Corradi) at 120.

[395] Ibid at 107 paraphrasing C Nyamu-Musembi 'Are local norms and practices fences or pathways? The example of women's property rights' in AA An-Na'im (ed) Cultural Transformation and Human Rights in Africa (2002) 126-150.

[396] Ibid at 107.

Change through Domestic Law Reform

Domestic legal reform is a ubiquitous top-down strategy. Legal reformers use law to effect change. Existing laws are critiqued and changes proposed especially in light of the requirements and specifications of international rights instruments.[397]

The implementation of change through legislation can be cumbersome. Benda-Beckmann observes that '[v]illagers are . . . confronted with local versions of State law, which often have nothing to do with the original version.'[398] Poor communication of laws to citizens makes the process of genuine reform through legislation more challenging at the community level.[399]

Griffiths questions the effectiveness of legislation in achieving change.[400] He finds top-down instrumental approaches to legislative reform to be 'unsociological' and 'untenable'.[401] Griffiths remarks that '[t]hose who have seriously considered the matter concluded long ago that instrumentalism is a sterile approach to legislation, one that cannot lead to the development of significant theory.'[402] Instead he contends

---

[397] S Philpott 'Too little, too late? The CRPD as a standard to evaluate South African legislation and policies for early childhood development' (2014) 2 ADRY 51-74.

[398] F Von Benda-Beckmann 'Scape-goat and magic charm: Law in development theory and practice' (1989) 28 Journal of Legal Pluralism and Unofficial Law 129-148, at 135.

[399] Ibid.

[400] J Griffiths 'Is law important?' (1979) 54 New York University Law Review 339-374.

[401] J Griffiths 'The social working of legal rules' (2003) 48 Journal of Legal Pluralism and Unofficial Law 1-84.

[402] Ibid at 13 citing A Allot The Limits of Law (1980); GR Woodman 'The limits of law' (1983) 21 Journal of Legal Pluralism and Unofficial Law 129; Von Benda-Beckmann (note 23).

that legislation should be considered as a factor within a wider sociological framework that has the potential of impacting behavioral choices.[403]

This thesis' fieldwork offers little justification for the present emphasis on revising domestic legislation. There was no indication of any knowledge of domestic laws concerning the rights of persons with disabilities other than the Ugandan Constitution and the provisions that establish special political representation for persons with disabilities. There is no indication that any of the interviewees were aware of the actual language or content of Ugandan statures addressing disability.

Change through Litigation

Another prominent top-down change strategy is litigation. Change seekers bring legal actions in the hopes of righting wrongs, bringing written laws to life and effecting systemic, cultural and political change. Chapter 5 includes a discussion of specific Ugandan case law addressing disability rights and social and economic rights resulting from strategic litigation initiatives.[404]

Kalaluka extolls the merits of disability rights litigation in Zambia.[405] She writes that litigation has 'the potential to bring to the open the many challenges persons with disabilities face'.[406] She asserts that denouncing discrimination through legal advocacy and resulting judicial action 'encourages society to embrace persons with disabilities as persons with

---

[403] Griffiths (note 26) at 19.

[404] This discussion appears at ch 5, s III(1)(c).

[405] L Kalaluka 'Towards an effective litigation strategy of disability rights: The Zambia experience' (2013) 1 ADRY 165-189, at 167 (Kalaluka defines 'disability rights litigation' as 'the entire process of prosecuting the rights of persons with disabilities before national or international courts or tribunals. This includes obtaining instructions to litigate, preparing briefs for trials, conducting trials and enforcing court decisions.').

[406] Ibid at 169.

rights equal to others'.[407] She sees litigation as offering the potential for displacing harmful societal norms that value diversity and human dignity.[408]

Conversely, Jjuuko and Kibalama take a measured stance on litigation as a change strategy. They contend that litigation should only be used as a matter of last resort due to its hostile and confrontational tendencies.[409] They also view cultural values as more positive and durable and voice concern over the negative impacts of disrupting and displacing traditional norms and practices.[410] The potential of litigation to impact change in customary contexts can be especially challenging.[411]

Efforts to bring about change through litigation can be viewed as disempowering when formal courts are largely inaccessible to the people strategic litigation seeks to assist. The United Nations estimates that at least four billion people are financially disenfranchised from the benefits of formal rule of law.[412] In Uganda the formal legal process is complex, lengthy and takes place in English. The net result is drastically low participation in the formal legal system.[413] Thus most Ugandans are effectively alienated from the benefits of court-based change efforts.

---

[407] Ibid at 169.

[408] Ibid at 169.

[409] FW Jjuuko & E Kibalama Culture and Women: The Position of Women in Buganda (2011) at 96.

[410] Ibid at 5, 9-10, 22-24.

[411] D Brinks & V Gauri 'A new policy landscape: legalizing social and economic rights in the developing world' in G Varun & D Brinks (eds) Courting Social Justice: Judicial Enforcement of Social and Economic Rights in the Developing World (2008) 303 at 317.

[412] The United Nations Commission on the Empowerment of the Poor Making the Law Work for Everyone (2008) at 3.

[413] International Justice Mission (IJM) Property Grabbing from Ugandan Widows and the Justice System: A Mixed-Methods Assessment in Mukono County, Uganda (2015) at 65 (finding that only 1.3 per cent of widows participated in the formal probate of their husbands' estates).

Thus, Tushnet cautions against overestimating the impact of law suits to bring about 'progressive' change. A legal victory does not necessarily result in a political or material victory.[414] He observes that legal actors tend to overestimate the impact of their legal activities and underestimate their ability to damage long term prospects for change in the hope of gaining short term legal advances.[415] Tushnet also cautions against the potential for cultural dissonance between communal based cultural outlooks andWestern rights-based litigation.[416] Each of his concerns are relevant to the Ugandan context.

Uganda has formal laws that are facially capable of fueling litigation-based disability reform.[417] However, the impact of such litigation has been mixed. The Uganda Persons with Disabilities Act (PDA) 2006 is representative of the challenges to effecting change through litigation. Notably the Ministry of Justice takes the position that the PDA is not enforceable through the courts. Instead it considers the language of the PDA to be aspirational without the collaboration of other branches of government judicial action to 'legalize' existing laws can be pyrrhic victories with limited political and material impact in nations struggling with widespread poverty and limited state resources.[418]

---

[414]M Tushnet 'The critique of rights' (1994) 47 SMU L Rev 23 at 24; See also S Gloppen 'Social movement activism and the courts' in Mobilizing Ideas (February 2013) available at https://mobilizingideas.wordpress.com/2013/02/04/social-movement-activism-and-the-courts/ accessed 7 October 2017. Noting various challenges facing strategies to effect social change though litigation including political backlash, the tendency states to use courts as weapons to weaken social movements and the ineffectiveness of litigation based change strategies in states with weak judiciaries.

[415] Ibid at 26 and 34.

[416] Ibid at 27.

[417] C Mbazira 'Enforcing rights of persons with disabilities to have access to barrier-free physical environment in Uganda: is litigation an option' (2009) A position paper written for Legal Action for Persons with Disabilities.

[418] D Brinks & V Gauri (note 36) at 345.

Change through Government Policy

Government policy is a significant top-down mechanism for bringing about desired change. Policy initiatives seek to improve the lives of vulnerable and marginalised people in society through programs, beneficial treatment and strategic expenditures.[419] Uganda's disability policy is discussed in Chapter 5, Section III.

Policy based initiatives face challenges in terms of implementation and capacity in nations with limited resources. Special interest groups in low resource environments need strong and persistent lobbies to ensure equitable resource allocation. Njoroge and others believe 'the disability movement in Uganda lacks the technical capacity to effectively lobby the government to include persons with disabilities within the [National Development Plan]'.[420] They call for a strategy of increasing the awareness of policy makers about disability issues, educating the members of the disability movement on the government's development policy processes, increasing the lobbying capacity of disability organisations and improving societal attitudes about persons with disabilities.[421] Others stress inclusion of those with disabilities in the policy development process.[422]

I encountered very little in terms of policy-based impact in the lives of the interviewees with disabilities. Many interviewees expressed the belief that there are government programs in existence that are intended to benefit persons with disabilities. However, the interviewees have not seen such programs operating in Mukono District.

---

[419] Ministry of Gender, Labour and Social Development, National Policy on Disability in Uganda (2006).

[420] TN Mwendwa, A Murangira & R Lang 'Mainstreaming the rights of persons with disabilities in national development frameworks' (2009) 21 J Int'l Dev 662-672, 669.

[421] Ibid at 669.

[422] Ibid at 666.

Change through Institutional and Organisational Engagement

International entities dedicated to the interests of persons with disabilities are another potential source of legal and social change. For example, Van Reenen and Combrinck describe the ongoing efforts of the World Bank and the International Monetary Fund through targeted development and incentive based programs.[423] Others look to initiatives such as the Millennium Development Goals to direct or encourage positive changes.[424]

Many non-governmental organisations specifically promote the rights and interests of persons with disabilities. Uganda is home to a growing number of such organisations as reported in Chapter 2, Section II(3).

This thesis' field research speaks to the benefits of institutional and organisational change initiatives. Several interviewees praised the work of foreign non-governmental organizations in promoting the cause of disabilities in Uganda. They expressed beliefs that foreign advocacy groups are key actors in helping to change local perceptions about persons with disabilities. Others specifically noted that North Americans and Europeans seem to have a keen interest in helping and promoting persons with disabilities and have been effective in their work.

---

[423] T Van Reenen & H Combrinck 'International financial institutions and the attainment of the UN Millennium Development Goals in Africa – with specific reference to persons with disabilities' in I Grobbelaar-du Plessis & T van Reenen (eds) (2011) Introduction to Aspects of Disability Law in Africa 197-230.

[424] United Nations Disability and the Millennium Development Goals (2011) available at <http://www.un.org/disabilities/documents/review_of_disability_and_the_mdgs.pdf> last accessed 17 December 2016; NE Groce & JF Trani 'Millennium development goals and persons with disabilities' (2009) 374(9704) The Lancet 1800-1801 (Noting that persons with disabilities are not specifically mentioned in any of the Millennium Development Goals, but arguing that persons with disabilities are implicitly included in each of the eight goals and the accompanying targets and indicators).

Certainly this positive feedback speaks well of the work of foreign-based initiatives in Uganda. However, the fact that several interviewees view foreign actors as the key agents of change for persons with disabilities in their communities is also troubling. There is a danger that disability rights and empowerment will be considered to be the responsibility of outside actors as opposed to matters that need to be addressed by the indigenous population.[425]

The flow of top-down human rights agendas from the 'developed' West to the majority world can engender resistance and resentment.[426] Compliance with international human rights instruments can be seen as the new external standard of review, replacing the colonial-era standard of 'repugnancy'.[427] Bennett observes that when international rights run counter to cultural practices, the global human rights movement can

---

[425] For literature that discusses the negative impacts of foreign aid see e.g. D Moyo Dead Aid: Why Aid is not Working and How There is a Better Way for Africa (2009); W Easterly White Man's Burden; Why the West's Efforts to Aid the Rest Have Done so Much Ill and so Little Good (2006).

[426] F Banda, 'Global standards: local values' (2003) 17 International Journal of Law, Policy and the Family 1-27; B Ibhawoh 'Cultural relativism and human rights: reconsidering the Africanist discourse' (2001) 1 Netherlands Quarterly of Human Rights 43-62; T Nhlapo 'Cultural diversity, human rights and the family in contemporary Africa: lessons from the South African constitutional debate' (1995) 9 International Journal of Law and the Family 208-225, at 215; ME Adjami 'African courts, international law, and comparative case law: chimera or emerging human rights jurisprudence?' (2002) 24 Michigan Journal of International Law 103-167, at 118; M Mutua Human Rights: A Political and Cultural Critique (2002) at 1-9.

[427] C Leonardi, D Isser, L Moro et al 'The politics of customary law ascertainment in South Sudan' (2011) 63 Journal of Legal Pluralism and Unofficial Law 111-142, at 114 (offering descriptions of the process of writing 'harmful customary practices' out of customary legal frameworks in South Sudan).

mirror the hegemony practiced by Western powers in the 19th Century.[428]

I did not detect this brand of backlash in the fieldwork. However, I am an American national and this might have had an impact on the responses that interviews provided about Western involvement in the furtherance of disability rights.[429] Thus any backlash may have been hidden from my observation.

An Instructive Lesson in Top-Down Change Initiatives from Mukono District

Recent fieldwork by International Justice Mission (IJM) in Mukono District offers a telling case study about the importance of understanding local practices and beliefs when championing human rights and justice sector reform. As a matter of change philosophy, IJM sees knowledge of and access to the formal legal system as integral to improving justice delivery at the community level.[430] IJM's targeted justice issue in Uganda is the problem of 'property grabbing' where women and children are stripped of their land rights after the death of male heads of households.

---

[428] TW Bennett 'Human rights and the African cultural tradition' (1993) 22 Transformation: 30-40 citing JW Nickel 'Cultural diversity in human rights' in JL Nelson & VM Green (eds) International Human Rights Contemporary Issues (1980) 43-56; and BA Rwezaura Traditionalism and Law Reform in Africa (5 July 1983) Lecture before the European Institute of the University of Saarland, Saarbrücken.

[429] Ugandans are notoriously welcoming people and it is my experience that many Ugandans tend to avoid confrontation and choose not to say negative things. Thus it is possible that the way the interviewees characterised those from the West could have been impacted by the fact that they were being interviewed by an American.

[430] G Haugen & V Boutros The Locust Effect (2014).

In an extensive field study concerning the problem of land grabbing in Mukono District[431], IJM identifies three variables that decrease unlawful property grabbing: 1) marriage formalisation, 2) the existence of a will written by the male head of household prior to his death, and 3) documentation of land ownership.[432] Conversely, factors that increase the likelihood of property grabbing include kibanja[433] land ownership, customary marriage, the presence of co-wives and the deceased husband having children with women other than a lawful wife.[434]

Based on its research findings, IJM calls for greater integration and implementation of legal formalism. It proposes strategies to increase the reach of legal formalism including increased access to the courts system; easier processes for formalising legal rights and status, heightened community level knowledge of the state justice system, the promotion of will write and the expansion of marriage formalisation.[435]

Yet even as IJM champions access to legal formalism, it recognises that Uganda's formal justice system is deeply flawed.[436] It refers to the state system of estate administration as a 'failed endeavor' in terms of clarity for users and functionality.[437] The probate process involves numerous steps and must be conducted in English instead of Luganda.[438] It also describes the estate administration process as 'maze-like', 'confusing, disorganized, hard to access and inconsistent'.[439] This assess-

---

[431] IJM (note 36) at 11 (This field study consisted of interviews of 1,806 widows in Mukono County, 187 case studies and 13 focus groups).

[432] Ibid at 11.

[433] Kibanja land ownership is discussed in detail at ch 5, s IV(5).

[434] IJM (note 38) at 11.

[435] *Ibid* at 12, 95-97.

[436] Ibid at 12.

[437] Ibid at 12.

[438] Ibid at 70 (according to IJM 66 per cent of the widows in Mukono County cannot speak English).

[439] Ibid at 65.

ment regarding the dis-functionality of formal Uganda law speaks against the workability of IJM's proposed way forward.

The limitations of pure legal formalism necessitate multi-faceted approaches to human rights and rule of law based reforms. Formal legal content and institutions should be supplemented with other strategies that can address gaps resulting from cultural dissonance as well as the barriers and costs of bureaucracy. Such eclectic and inclusive strategies should not ignore the relevance, durability and functionality of customary law and process.

Transformational strategies seeking to leverage state laws and institutions should be locally grounded and informed. Legal reformers need to understand the varying needs and aspirations of specific cultures.[440] They should account for the effectual legal phenomena in the semi-autonomous fields where change is sought. This includes knowledge of current customary law and cultural practices.

Ultimately top-down legal change strategies need to be grassroots aware. Top-down strategies should be informed by what takes place in the lived environment and how people navigate legal occurrences outside and parallel to the formal legal system. Top-down actors need to appreciate how formal laws are referenced, received, and applied in informal legal occurrences such as customary succession and customary guardianship. The next section addresses change strategies designed to bring about socio-legal changes from the bottom-up.

Bottom-Up Approaches to Change

Today a growing number of theorists and change actors embrace 'bottom-up' approaches to promote international human rights-based

---

[440] S Wiessner 'Culture and the rights of indigenous peoples' in AF Vrdoljak (ed) Cultural Dimension of Human Rights (2013) 117-156, at 119.

development.[441] Weak central governments, cultural resistance and limited justice sector resources push change advocates and operatives to consider grassroots engagement. Thus organizations set out to disseminate knowledge and empower people to uphold and enforce human rights norms in their own social contexts.

Yet, there are reasons for skepticism about the promise of bottom-up strategies. Indigenous cultural views and practices pertaining to persons with disabilities often lag behind current human rights standards and formal laws. This can result in greater discrimination and unchecked abuses of power in customary contexts.[442] However, these problems do not necessitate the jettisoning of bottom-up change strategies. On the contrary, the prominence and proclivity of such problems heighten the importance of bottom-up approaches.

Categories of Bottom-up Legal Change Strategies

The labeling and categorizing of bottom-up strategies is ongoing and fluid. In addition, many bottom-up strategies are blended. Nonetheless, this section is organised by selected designations of bottom-up strategic approaches. These designations and the strategies they encompass are not exhaustive nor are they exclusive to one another. The designations discussed below include facilitative change strategies, acculturation, strategies of directed engagement and participatory change strategies

---

[441] JE Lord & MA Stein 'The domestic incorporation of human rights law and the United Nations Convention on the Rights of Persons with Disabilities' (2008) 83 Washington U LR 449-479, at 475 citing M Keck & K Sikkink Activists Beyond Borders: Advocacy Networks in International Politics (1998).

[442] AF Vrdoljak 'Liberty, equality, diversity: states, cultures, and international law' in Ana Filipa Vrdoljak ed Cultural Dimension of Human Rights (2013) 26-70, at 67 citing art 4 of the UNESCO Cultural Diversity Declaration and the Preamble of the African Charter of Human and Peoples' Rights; M Kane, J Oloka-Onyango & A Tejan-Cole 'Reassessing customary law systems as a vehicle for providing equitable access to justice for the poor' a paper presented at New Frontiers of Social Policy, Arusha (2005).

Facilitative Change Strategies: Framing, the Receptor Approach and the Soft Approach

Facilitative change strategies entail the purposeful integration and leverage of indigenous beliefs, norms and practices for achieving desired changes. This section presents three types of facilitative change: framing, the receptor approach and the soft approach.

An-Na-im endorses a facilitative strategy he calls 'framing' whereby 'international standards are framed in terms of local symbols and terminology, and on the other hand, local struggles and grievances start to be understood and fought in the language of human rights'.[443] Rights 'framers' face the challenge of presenting ideas at the local level in a way that 'generates shared beliefs, motivates collective action and defines appropriate strategies for action'.[444] One framing strategy involves collaboration with local actors with the power to 'translate' or 'broker' change. Local actors include religious leaders, customary leaders, traditional healers, local NGOs, community mediators and legal professionals.[445]

Other terminology is used to describe similar approaches. Examples include 'negotiating'[446] social norms, the 'vernacularlization'[447]

---

[443] Corradi (note 18) at 106 citing SE Merry *Human Rights* and *Gender Violence:* Translating *International Law* into Local *Justice'* (2006a) and SE Merry 'Transnational human rights and local activism: mapping the middle' (2006b) 108 American Anthropologist 38-51.

[444] Ibid at 106 citing Merry (2006b).

[445] Ibid at 106 citing Merry (2006b) at 41.

[446] *Ibid* at 103.

[447] Ibid at 143 citing Merry (2006a) at 219.

of human rights language and concepts, imagining 'legal sensibilities'[448] and the 'societal internalizaton' of human rights.[449]

A similar facilitative change is the 'receptor approach.'[450] According to Corradi '[t]his approach seeks to identify local values which can act as "receptors" for human rights principles.'[451] This can entail 'detecting and making visible social arrangements that protect human rights'.[452] When these efforts fail to effectively promote human rights the receptor approach calls for adding mechanisms to make local and traditional institutions protect human rights without eliminating them.[453]

Like the framing approach, the receptor approach targets traditional leaders. Corradi notes '[i]n view of the prominent role traditional authorities play in their chiefdoms and their influence over their communities, development actors cannot afford to ignore them in their programmes'.[454] This is all the more important in light of customary leaders' capacity to be both change agents and inhibitors of change.[455] In the context of this research, the Kabaka's reputed power to establish and change Baganda law and practices offers a highly leveraged opportunity for the receptor approach.

Another facilitative strategy is the 'soft approach'. This approach 'grounds human rights on indigenous foundations while emphasizing the

---

[448] Ibid at 144 citing C Geertz Local Knowledge: Further Essays in Interpretive Anthropology (1983) 175.

[449] Ibid at 144 citing AD Kent 'Custody, maintenance, and succession: the internalization of women's and children's rights under customary law in Africa' (2007) 28 Michigan Journal of International Law 507-538. at 511.

[450] T Zwart 'Using local culture to further the implementation of international human rights: the receptor approach' (2012) 34(2) Human Rights Quarterly 546-569.

[451] Ibid; Corradi (note 18) at 107.

[452] Ibid.

[453] Ibid.

[454] Ibid at 139.

[455] Ibid.

latter's flexibility to respond to new needs and demands.'[456] According to Corradi both the 'receptor approach' and the 'soft approach' require 'detailed analysis of how social institutions work and how their internal logic relates to human rights'.[457] A robust appreciation of existing social and cultural contexts can inform the development of workable 'home-grown solutions'.[458]

Acculturation

Acculturation is 'the general process by which actors adopt the beliefs and behavioural patterns of the surrounding culture'.[459] The goal is the diffusion and adoption of human rights norms at the micro level.[460] Education is a component that works along with other factors such as social and economic changes, population migration, and media content to bring about local changes in community principles and social practices.[461]

Sensitisation is a key means of acculturation. Sensitisation efforts can be conducted in a myriad of ways including community based trainings, radio broadcasts, engagement through religious institutions and print media. Uganda's Ministry of Gender, Labour and Social Development includes media and theatre among its acculturation strategies for disability rights reform.[462] This thesis' field research indicates that radio

---

[456] Ibid at 107 citing MO Hinz 'Justice for justice and justice for peace: legal anthropological observations on traditional and informal justice systems' in MO Hinz & C Mapaure (eds) (2010) In Search of Justice and Peace, Traditional and Informal Justice Systems in Africa 3-23.

[457] Ibid at 107; Zwart (note 75).

[458] Ibid at 107.

[459] R Goodman & D Jinks 'How to influence states: socialization and international human rights law' (2004) 54 Duke Law Journal 621-703, 625.

[460] R Goodman & D Jinks 'Toward an institutional theory of sovereignty' (2003) 55 Stanford Law Review 1749-1788.

[461] United States Institute of Peace & the Rift Valley Institute (note 10) at 84.

[462] Ministry of Gender, Labour and Social Development (note 39) at 19.

is an influential medium for increasing formal legal knowledge and impacting beliefs in Mukono District.

Disability is an area where effective sensitisation is particularly critical. Writing in the Ghanaian context, Baffoe sees 'education campaigns aimed at eliminating the myths, negative perceptions, stereotyping, superstitions and their resultant discrimination and marginalization of persons with disabilities' as crucial to making a 'positive difference in the lives of persons with disabilities'.[463] Baffoe believes that such campaigns should be structured as a two-step process. The first step involves getting the wider public to appreciate the personhood of persons with disabilities.[464] The second step entails generating support within the community for services that will benefit persons with disabilities.[465]

The field research indicates that people in Mukono District are open to modifying their beliefs about persons with disabilities through sensitisation activities. Community leaders without disabilities indicated that they were not opposed to the reception of so-called 'enlightened' views about the rights of person with disabilities.

This thesis' field research confirms the importance of people's views about persons with disabilities in the context of customary status, rights and treatment. This is especially true when it comes to views about the capabilities and usefulness of persons with disabilities.

Sensitisation efforts can have limited impact when desired changes conflict with local norms.[466] Although there are local norms in Mukono District that hamper the rights of persons with disabilities, the norms identified in the field research do not appear to be especially intransigent. For example, a traditional belief that persons with disabilities con-

---

[463] M Baffoe 'Stigma, discrimination & marginalization: gateways to oppression of persons with disabilities in Ghana, West Africa' (2103) 3(1) Journal of Educational and Social Research 187-198, at 195.

[464] Ibid.

[465] Ibid.

[466] United States Institute of Peace & the Rift Valley Institute (note 10) at 84.

taminate crops and food appears to be waning. In addition, beliefs about the cause and impact of disability appear to be in flux with some people attributing physical conditions to genetics and others attributing them to witchcraft. Thus norms and beliefs concerning disability appear to be open to change through education.

Acculturation initiatives should be culturally informed. To impact local knowledge and beliefs it is important to understand local knowledge and beliefs. Moreover, in the context of disability rights, it is important to appreciate how and why local knowledge and beliefs impact the status, rights and treatment of persons with disabilities. This thesis' field research confirms both the necessity and usefulness of specific local knowledge.

Strategies for Directed Engagement with Customary Laws and Practices

A growing number of development actors adopt directed engagement with customary law as a means for improving the rule of law.[467] This rise in customary engagement reflects a growing theoretical rejection of legal centralism[468] and a rising acceptance of the brand of deep legal pluralism championed by Griffiths, Merry and Moore.

An-Na-im stresses the importance of contextualising human rights reforms in strongly pluralistic contexts.[469] He posits that the combination of 'internal reinterpretation' and 'cross cultural dialogues' offers a

---

[467] HM Kyed 'Introduction to the special issue: legal pluralism and international development interventions' (2011) 63 Journal of Legal Pluralism and Unofficial Law 1-23, at 2.

[468] HM Kyed 'The politics of legal pluralism: state policies on legal pluralism and their local dynamics in Mozambique' (2009) 59 Journal of *Legal* Pluralism and Unofficial Law 87-120.

[469] AA An-Na'im 'Toward a cross-cultural approach to defining international standards of human rights: the meaning of cruel, inhuman, or degrading treatment or punishment' in AA An Na'im (ed) Human Rights in Cross-Cultural Perspectives: A Quest for Consensus (1995) 19-43.

means of accomplishing grass roots human rights reform.[470] He appreciates the necessity of instilling and creating local ownership over conceptions of human rights. For him, simply inserting new law from alien sources is inherently dysfunctional.

This thesis' field research identified an outward willingness to accept international human rights standards as legitimate. The global movement for disabilities rights is not seen as a threat in Mukono District and the interviewees without disabilities largely held themselves out as open to revising their attitudes and beliefs about disability. However, there appears to be little substantive awareness as to what rights should be afforded to persons with disabilities. For many interview participants disability rights are synonymous with access to resources. Thus rights are seen by many as support the government should provide. Similarly international human rights are associated with the provision of resources and benefits from international bodies as opposed to international standards requiring societal compliance.

Moreover, the language of human rights can be considered mere words of little tangible impact. Remarkably, even efforts to use African terminology such as ubuntu can be perceived as words and messages from elsewhere. Thus the field research speaks to An-Na-im's concern about meaningfully integrating rights standards into the culture as opposed to simply delivering them through laws or information.

Customary engagement strategies are especially prevalent in developing countries where the formal justice sector is inaccessible, unfamiliar and illegitimate for much of the population.[471] The rapid growth of a

---

[470] Ibid at 21.

[471] Leonardi, Isser & Moro (note 52) at 109; D Isser (ed) Customary Justice and the Rule of Law in War Torn Societies (2011).

'rule of law' industry[472] over recent decades has generated customary law engagement strategies and guidance materials.[473]

Allot was a key figure in directed engagement with customary law.[474] He championed the written memorialisation of indigenous customary law to make it official, stable and consistently applied.[475] His ideas were influential in the creation of written restatements of customary law in various nations including Kenya.[476] Over the past several decades Allot's approach has fallen largely out of favour. Today's prevailing scholarly position critiques customary codification as contrary to the oral, flexible and mutable qualities of customary law.[477]

The mutability that makes customary law ill-suited for codification makes it a viable target for other reform efforts.[478] Claasens and Mnisi advocate changing the substantive customary law rather than overcoming it.[479] They point to the flexibility of customary law and the rising capacity of previously marginalised actors such as women to renegotiate the content of customary law as reason for optimism.[480]

---

[472] Ibid at 133.

[473] Ibid at 109 fn 2 (reporting that 'guidance notes on how to engage customary justice systems have been issued and commissioned by the United Kingdom Department for International Development, the United Nations Development Program, the Organization for Economic Cooperation and Development and the International Development Law Organization.').

[474] A Allot 'Introduction' in E Cotran (1987) Case Book on Kenya Customary Law, i, xi-xv.

[475] Ibid at xi-xv.

[476] A Harrington 'Key issues in customary justice: a comparative study' USIP Research *Report* (2010).

[477] T Ranger 'The invention of tradition in colonial Africa' in E Hobsbawm & T Ranger, The Invention of Tradition (1983) 211-263.

[478] Himonga (note 17) at 37-38.

[479] A Claasens & S Mnisi 'Rural women redefining land rights in the context of living customary law' (2009) 25 SAJHR 491-516, at 493.

[480] Ibid at 493.

Some customary engagement strategies seek to capitalise on '"positive" aspects of customary justice, while endeavouring to minimise the "negative" aspects'.[481] A rich appreciation of the local context is necessary to devise rights-based reform strategies that are culturally palatable and workable at the grassroots level.[482] Land Equity Movement Uganda (LEMU) distributes people group specific collections of principles, practices, rights and responsibilities of customary law aligned with this approach.[483] LEMU has not compiled a collection for the Baganda.

Despite its potential for broad-based empowerment, customary law can be manipulated for discriminatory purposes.[484] The 'fluidity of customary law' can be a point of weakness in its capacity to protect the socially and economically marginalised.[485] The pretext of maintaining social order can result in interpretations and applications of customary law that benefit the powerful.[486] Nyamu-Musembi observes that 'belatedly, law reformers recognised the centrality of customary tenure but

---

[481] Leonardi, Isser & Moro (note 52) at 109.

[482] Merry (2006a) (note 68).

[483] Kuman Elder's Forum & Land Equity Movement in Uganda *Kumam Principles, Practices, Rights and Responsibilities (PPRR) for Customary Land Tenure Management* (2011); Lango Cultural Foundation & Land Equity Movement in Uganda *Principles, Practices, Rights and Responsibilities (PPRR) of Customary Land Tenure in Lango Region - No. 1* (2009); Ker Kwaro Acholi & Land Equity Movement in Uganda *Principles and Practices of Customary Tenure in Acholiland* (2008); Einos Iteso Kopiteny and Land Equity Movement in Uganda *Principles, Practices, Rights and Responsibilities (PPRR) of Customary Land Management in Teso Region* (2009).

[484] J Oloka-Onyango (note 11) at 38.

[485] L Khadiagala 'Negotiating law and custom: judicial doctrine and women's property rights in Uganda' (2002) 46 Journal of African Law 1-13.

[486] Ibid.

celebrated its benefits (e.g. flexibility) without critical analysis of the power relations that shape it'.[487]

As reported in Chapter 7, this thesis' field research confirms the unpredictability of customary legal scenarios. This is particularly the case when it comes to land inheritance. Moreover, customary scenarios present opportunities for individuals to manipulate the process through discriminatory biases and abuses of power. Thus the fact that customary legal scenarios are accessible does not mean that they are pro poor. To the contrary, as discussed in Section III(4) of Chapter 3, they can be the preferred forums where the rich and powerful can carry out abuses that the formal law does not allow.

Customary change initiatives face resistance. Those who work to champion international human rights can find themselves ostracised by the targeted society.[488] However, the field research did not detect significant pushback over the promotion of disability rights. Unlike matters of gender which challenge patrilineal land succession, treating persons with disabilities in a non-discriminatory manner does not threaten to cause structural disruption to existing customary frameworks. An instance where there would be resistance in the context of disability rights is a scenario where complying with or fulfilling the right would not make practical sense such as allowing someone with an 'unsound mind' to be a clan leader.

Despite the challenges, proponents of customary engagement see customary law as a pragmatic opportunity to advance human rights rather than a regressive problem to be fixed.[489] Customary engagement entails leveraging the positive aspects of custom, tradition and culture

---

[487] C Nyamu-Musembi 'Ruling out gender equality? The post-cold war rule of law agenda in Sub-Saharan Africa' 27(7) Third World Quarterly 1193-1207, at 1201.

[488] Leonardi, Isser & Moro (note 52) at 119.

[489] Himonga (note 16) at 328.

towards the desired targets.[490] Such engagement requires a deep knowledge of the relevant customary and cultural context.

Actor-oriented and participatory change strategies

Many endorse actor-oriented approaches for effecting change.[491] Class struggle is often at the theoretical core of actor-oriented approaches.[492] Self struggle ensures local grounding, and human rights need to be grounded within local communities to reach their full potential.[493] Actor-oriented approaches recognise the need for rights-bearing individuals to work out the law in the grey zones where cultural norms and formal rights intersect.[494]

The importance of direct engagement in the struggle for positive change is well known in disability circles. The viewpoint is reflected in disability rights refrain 'nothing about us without us'.[495]

The field research demonstrates that rights realisation often hinges on persons with disabilities. Obtaining land through customary succession may require a person with disabilities to engage formal legal actors. Overcoming discrimination in clan meetings often requires a willingness to stand up to discrimination. Appointment as a customary guardian can turn on whether a person with disabilities demonstrates the capacity to earn money. The mantra 'disability is not inability' is not taken at face value; it is proven through the lives of persons with disabilities. Thus

---

[490] Ibid at 330.

[491] G Corradi 'Access to justice in Pemba City: How exploring women's lived realities with plural law uncovers programmatic gaps' (2011) 64 Journal of Legal Pluralism and Unofficial Law 1-31, at 3.

[492] Wilson (note 3) at 23; C Nyamu-Musembi 'Towards an actor-oriented perspective on human rights' in N Kabeer (cd) Inclusive citizenship: Meanings and expressions (2005) 31-49.

[493] Corradi (note 18).

[494] C Nyamu-Musembi 'An actor oriented approach to rights development' (2009) 36(1) IDS Bulletin 36 (2009) 41-51.

[495] J Charlton Nothing About Us Without Us (1998).

customary status and rights are often earned and defended by persons with disabilities.

The actual voices and input of persons with disabilities are at the centre of actor-based initiatives. Muller describes his rights-based approach to disability as 'premised on the ability and inclusion of persons with disabilities'.[496] This approach seeks to bring down barriers to fuller participation in society and allows persons with disabilities to contribute their own voices to technocratic assessments of their rights and needs.

Disabled persons organisations (DPOs) are cooperative variants of the actor-oriented approach. DPOs are collectives of persons with disabilities that seek to increase their influence and impact through solidarity and collective action. Harpur sees disabled persons organisations (DPOs) as key actors in disability rights reform.[497] Given the importance of persons with disabilities in working out their rights and status in customary contexts, DPOs can be instrumental in sharing knowledge and connecting persons with disabilities to social support systems.

Actor-based change models often include a hermeneutic component. Inkstater endorses a 'transformative' approach to legal change within deeply pluralistic settings that uses 'emancipatory knowledge' to build up an intentional strategy for change grounded in a shared consciousness.[498] Similarly Sezgin sees 'hermeneutic communities' as the key to improving the status of marginalised groups within 'pluralistic personal status systems'.[499] Sezgin believes that these communities can contest 'the validity of various categories of subjectivity . . . by offering deviant

---

[496] G Muller 'On considering alternative accommodation and the rights and needs of vulnerable people' (2014) 30 SAJHR 41-62, at 54.

[497] Harpur (note 5).

[498] K Inksater 'Transformative juricultural pluralism: indigenous justice systems in Latin America and international human rights' (2010) 60 Journal of Legal Pluralism and Unofficial Law 105-142, at 107.

[499] Sezgin (note 1) at 8.

interpretations'.[500] In Mukono District key hermeneutical players include persons with disabilities and those who are seen by the community as the knowledge bearers and curators of customary law. These two groups are the two cohorts of interviewees selected for this thesis' field research.

Community Care Delivery Models

Community care delivery models leverage community and kin to efficiently provide needed care and services for persons with disabilities.[501] In wealthier nations one of the intended benefits of community based models is the removal of persons with disabilities from institutional settings.[502] On the other hand, community based models in the developing world are often employed to provide care and services to persons with disabilities that the state is unable or unwilling to provide.

Community Based Rehabilitation (CBR) is a 'capacity building approach to disability' touted as a 'cost effective mechanism by health care professionals in delivering outreach services'.[503] CBR is a relevant disability empowerment model in the developing world.[504] This model is built on the recognition that there is a lack of specialised medical rehabilitation services in low income nations.[505] At its best[506], CBR empow-

---

[500] *Ibid* at 8.

[501] D Johnstone, An Introduction to Disability Studies 2 Ed (2001) at 39-40.

[502] Ibid at 71.

[503] D Eade Capacity-Building: An Approach to People-Centred Development (1997).

[504] GO Fefoame, J Walugembe & R Mpofuat 'Building partnerships and alliances in CBR' in G Musoke & P Geiser (eds) Linking CBR, Disability and Rehabilitation (2013) 37-51, at 41 (noting that Uganda includes CBR in its programmes and efforts directed towards persons with disabilities).

[505] M Wickenden, D Mulligan et al 'Stakeholder consultations on community-based rehabilitation guidelines in Ghana and Uganda' (2012) 1 African J of Disability 1-10, at 2.

ers families and community members to improve the lives of persons with disabilities in contexts where access to services is limited due to geographic logistics, meagre finances or limited professional capacity.[507]

Uganda has been home to CBR initiatives since the 1990s.[508] These initiatives were launched with the assistance of foreign support including the Norwegian Association of the Disabled.[509] While Ugandan CBR initiatives have been successful at a certain scale, there are significant challenges including the high expectations of target groups, inadequate funds to expand the project and the persistence of negative attitudes.[510] Only a small portion of Uganda has been served through these initiatives.[511]

To assess the viability and potential of community delivery models one must understand community and family settings. In Mukono District, customary law and practices are key structural components in community and family life. Thus this thesis' field research has something to offer CBR initiatives.

---

[506] Concerns have been lodged regarding the ethics and effectiveness of CBR initiatives. For a prominent critique see M Turmusani, A Vreede A & SL Wirz 'Some ethical issues in community-based rehabilitation initiatives in developing countries' (2002) 24(10) Disability Rehabilitation 558.

[507] P Geiser & M Boersma 'The role of the community in CBR' in G Musoke & P Geiser (eds) Linking CBR, Disability and Rehabilitation (2013) 24-36, at 33.

[508] World Health Organisation (WHO) 'World Report on Disabilities' at 141, Box 5.2 available at <http://www.who.int/disabilities/world_report/2011/report.pdf> last accessed 9 October 2017.

[509] Ibid.

[510] Ibid.

[511] Norad Evaluation Department Mainstreaming Disability in the New Development *Paradigm: Uganda* Country Study Summary (2012) at 4.

Research Implications in Light of the Prevalence and Viability of Bottom-up Rights Reform

Bottom-up reform strategies place a premium on small-scale community-based field research. Specific contextual knowledge concerning lived environments and community practices can generate findings that point to potential areas and means of societal improvement.[512] Anthropologically informed legal theorists such as Griffiths, Merry and Moore advocate shifting focus from the formal law to the 'shop floor' of social life.[513] The result is an emphasis on lived experiences and bottom-up approaches to human rights reform that places the focus on the 'small places'[514] of life. Moore advises that '[m]icro level anthropological research is well placed to contribute to the practical and operational aspects of human rights questions.'[515] After all, '[h]uman rights discussions in the abstract, with an emphasis on what is morally desirable, seem quite aimless without a concomitant discussion of the physical conditions under which action could be taken.'[516]

'[T]he strength of the fieldwork perspective is that anthropology provides a specific description of what is happening on the ground at a particular time and place.'[517] This thesis' field research frames struggles faced by persons with disabilities and provide insights as to the means of change, the possibilities of reform and the hermeneutical context.

---

[512] SF Moore 'Certainties undone: fifty turbulent years of legal anthropology' (2001) 7 Journal of the Royal Anthropology Institute 95-116.

[513] Griffiths (note 26) at 19.

[514] 'Where, after all, do universal human rights begin? In small places, close to home - so close and so small that they cannot be seen on the maps of the world.' Remark made by Eleanor Roosevelt at a presentation of the Universal Declaration of Human Rights, New York, 27 March 1948.

[515] SF Moore 'Changing African land tenure: reflections on the incapacities of the state' (1998) 10(2) European Journal of Development Research 33-49, at 47.

[516] Ibid at 47.

[517] Ibid at 45.

Formalism and Change in Baganda Customary Law

Customary law is dynamic and discerning the causes of change can be challenging. It is subject to multi-agent change processes where overlapping social structures interact to create unique legal stews.[518] However, there are some distinctively formal aspects of the Baganda legal culture pertaining to change that warrant special attention.

First, the Baganda have long-standing top-down mechanisms for changing customary law. These mechanisms include the changes adopted by the Kabaka, changes presented by the Lukiiko (the parliamentary body of the Buganda kingdom) before the Kabaka, and those initiated by clan leaders or the Katikkiro (prime minister) through consultation with the Kabaka.[519] For example, Kabaka Mutesa I changed customary succession practices from male inheritance passing to paternal nephews[520] to male inheritance by children or grandchildren[521], Kabaka Ssuuna II introduced the death penalty for the offence of defilement, and Mutesa II revoked the law that prevented his mother from remarrying.[522] This thesis' field research confirms that Baganda in Mukono District continue to view the Kabaka as having customary law making authority.

Second, Baganda customary law has a written heritage. During the British colonial era laws of the Buganda Kingdom were codified and published. As a result, the ongoing conception of Baganda customary law is prone to stolidity resulting from a sense that the true customary law is what was written down in these colonial era codifications. Alt-

---

[518] SF Moore 'Law and social change: the semi-autonomous social field as an appropriate field of study' (1973) 7(4) Law & Society Review 719-746.

[519] ES Haydon Law and Justice in Buganda (1960) at 18.

[520] *Ibid* at 218 (At the time of Haydon's book female customary succession continued to run from aunts to maternal nieces instead of to the children of the aunt).

[521] Ibid at 214; Jjuuko & Kiblama (note 34) at 15.

[522] Ibid at 15-16.

hough these written codes are no longer in place or easily accessible they seem to live on in the collective memory of the substance of the Baganda customary law. For example, findings in the IJM study referenced in section II(2) of this chapter indicate that community practices concerning succession have greater alignment with the extant colonial Baganda code than the modern formal law. For some Baganda people, the customary law of 'time immemorial' might actually be a memory of the extant colonial era codes.

Understanding the possible means of change and the legal forces that resist change is important for those who seek to improve the lives of vulnerable people. For example, appreciating the Kabaka's continued role as supreme customary lawmaker within Baganda culture might lead change actors to directly engage the Kabaka. In addition, appreciating the heritage of written customary law among the Baganda can help change actors locate both beneficial and problematic provisions that might persist in the post-codified customary milieu. Moreover, although Uganda is not home to a post-colonial customary code like other nations, the staying power of colonial era codes might offer insights as to the persisting substance of Baganda customary law. Among the Baganda customary law has aspects of grassroots flexibility, institutional dominance and historic formalism.

Conclusion

This chapter presents a broad variety of change strategies that can be implemented to positively impact the rights, status and treatment of persons with disabilities. Despite the diversity and range of strategies a common thread emerges—contextual knowledge about lived environments matters. Transformative strategies do not operate in a vacuum. Change strategies should be calibrated through grassroots knowledge to effectively impact the community level.

In light of the fact of strong legal pluralism[523] it is critical to examine the living law as it is discerned and applied at the local level. This thesis investigates the lived experiences of persons with disabilities in Mukono District to assess the places where the social working of legal rules manifests.[524] This is the living law that persons with disabilities in Mukono District negotiate and apply on a daily basis. Understanding this local living law is a valuable component for strategies intended to make a positive impact on the rights, status and treatment of persons with disabilities.

An emphasis on localised rights delivery and engagement can help make distant and abstract rights tangible in lived environments. This is especially true with respect to rights that require cultural buy-in. Moreover, grassroots approaches are crucial in nations with limited resources to implement top-down change strategies.[525]

The effective leveraging of customary institutions and practices requires contextual knowledge and understanding. This thesis' fieldwork presented in Chapters 6, 7 and 8 offers insights on the state of customary law in Mukono District as it pertains to the rights, status and treatment of persons with disabilities. The information within those chapters can meaningfully inform and empower those seeking to bring about positive changes through a range of strategies and approaches. Possible applications of the fieldwork findings will be presented in Chapters 8 and 9.

Next this thesis turns to Chapter 5 which presents an overview of the law relevant to disabilities at the international, national and customary level in in Mukono District.

---

[523] J Griffiths 'What is legal pluralism?' (1986) 24 Journal of Legal Pluralism and Unofficial Law 1-55, at 5.

[524] Griffiths (note 26).

[525] M Maboreke 'Understanding law in Zimbabwe' in Ann Stewart (ed) Gender, Law & Social Justice (2000) 101-116.

5

THE DISABILITY LEGAL AND POLICY FRAMEWORK IN MUKONO DISTRICT

Introduction

This chapter presents the legal and policy framework with particular relevance to the status, rights and treatment of persons with disabilities in Mukono District. It begins with a discussion of the United Nations Convention on the Rights of Persons with Disabilities (CRPD). Next it covers Ugandan domestic law and policy with an emphasis on the relevant statutory law and case law. It concludes with a survey of Baganda customary law with particular pertinence to the status, rights and treatment of persons with disabilities.

This chapter's content serves as a foundational backdrop to the fieldwork findings presented in subsequent chapters. With respect to Chapter 7, it primes the reader with a baseline understanding of the customary law and practices of the Baganda people. As for Chapter 8, this chapter equips the reader with an appreciation of the multiple layers and sources of legal content that pertains to the status, rights and treatment of persons with disabilities in Mukono District.

The United Nations Convention on the Rights of Persons with Disabilities

Adopted in 2006, the CRPD[526] is the first international human rights treaty of the 21st Century.[527] It is a landmark treaty for persons with disabilities with wide reaching implications. Uganda signed and ratified the CRPD promptly in 2008.[528]

Although there are other international[529] and regional instruments[530] relevant to disability rights that are operative in Uganda, the CPRD's

---

[526] Convention on the Rights of Persons with Disabilities (CRPD), adopted 13 December 2006 by GA Res 61/106, Annex I, UN GAOR, 61st Sess, Supp No. 49 at 65, UN Doc A/61/49 (2006), entered into force 3 May 2008, UN Doc. A/61/61, signed by Uganda on 30 March 2007 and ratified by Uganda on 25 September 2008.

[527] JE Lord & MA Stein 'The domestic incorporation of human rights law and the United Nations Convention on the Rights of Persons with Disabilities' (2008) 83 Washington U LR 449-468, at 450.

[528] Ibid 1.

[529] International Covenant on Civil and Political Rights (ICCPR), adopted 16 December 1996, GA Res 2200A (XX1), 21 UN GAOR Supp (No 16) at 52, UN Doc A/6316 (1966), 999 UNTS 171, entered into force 23 March 1976, acceded to by Uganda 21 June 1995; International Covenant on Economic, Social and Cultural Rights, GA Res 2200A (XXI), UN Doc A/6316 (1966), entered into force 3 January 1976, acceded to by Uganda 21 January 1987; Convention on the Elimination of Discrimination Against Women (CEDAW), adopted 18 December 1979 by GA resolution 34/180, entered into force on 3 September 1981, ratified by Uganda on 22 July 1985; Convention on the Rights of the Child, GA Res 44/25, annex, 44 UN GAOR Supp (No 49) at 167, UN Doc A/44/49 (1989), entered into force 2 September 1990, ratified by Uganda on 17 August 1990.

[530] African [Banjul] Charter on Human and Peoples' Rights, adopted 27 June 1981, OAU Doc. CAB/LEG/67/3 Rev 5, 21 ILM 58 (1982), entered into force 21 October 1986, ratified by Uganda 10 May 1986; Protocol to the African Charter on Human and Peoples' Rights on the Rights of Women in Africa (the Maputo Protocol), adopted 11 July 2003, entered into force November 2005, signed by Uganda on 18 December 2003, ratified by Uganda, 22 July 2010;

extensive treatment of disability rights effectively subsumes other human rights instruments on matters specific to persons with disabilities.[531] Thus this discussion of the substance of international and regional human rights instruments is limited to the CRPD. Scholarly treatments outlining the rights and protections set forth in other international instruments and African regional instruments are available elsewhere for reference.[532]

The extensive breadth and detail of the CPRD prevents an exhaustive treatment. Instead this section focuses on the theoretical underpinnings of the CPRD, the structure and substance of the CRPD with special relevance to customary legal frameworks, and the status of compliance and implementation of the CPRD in Uganda.

The Theoretical Underpinnings of the CRPD

The CRPD eschews ideological purity. It contains elements of the social model of disability while retaining the tangible benefits of the medical model.[533] It seeks to effect change from both the top down and

---

Draft Protocol to the African Charter on Human and Peoples' Rights on the Rights of Persons with Disabilities in Africa, adopted at the 19th Extra-Ordinary Session of the African Commission on Human and Peoples' Rights, 16-25 February 2016, in the Islamic Republic of the Gambia.

[531] MA Stein & JE Lord 'Future prospects for the United Nations Convention on the Rights of Persons with Disabilities' in G Quinn & OM Arnardotti (eds) The United Nations Convention on the Rights of Persons with Disabilities: European and Scandinavian Perspectives (2009) 17-40, at 18-19 (noting the general ineffectiveness of earlier human rights instruments in addressing disability related claims and concerns despite the fact that such instruments are technically applicable to disability issues).

[532] Ibid at 18-22 (addressing international instruments and activities predating the CRPD including scholarly references included in fns 8-33); TP van Reenen & H Combrinck 'The UN Convention on the Rights of Persons with Disabilities in Africa: progress after 5 years' (2011) 8(14) SUR International Journal on Human Rights 133-165, at 134-142 (addressing the African regional context).

[533] CRPD pre (j).

the bottom-up. As a human rights treaty, it also emphasises social and economic rights, human dignity, and non-discrimination.

The Preamble of the CRPD includes pronouncements concerning the social quality of disability,[534] the importance of mainstreaming,[535] the link between non-discrimination and human dignity[536], the significance of gender in the context of disability rights[537], and the crucial role of families in the context of disabilities[538] and the classification of disability concerns as human rights concerns.[539] The CRPD also specifically includes participation and empowerment as human rights principles.[540]

As touched on in Chapter 2, Degener classifies the non-exclusivist theoretical approach of the CRPD as a human rights approach.[541] In the context of disability this approach enables the CRPD to address the civil and political rights stressed by the social moment while also accounting for the needs recognized by the medical model. In addition the CRPD goes further by placing an emphasis on personal agency, legitimizing the prevention of disability and the accounting for the impact of poverty. For Degener, the fundamental recognition of human dignity is the theoretical ground norm that undergirds and encompasses the CPRD's wide ranging content.

The CPRD's general principles proclaim its core values.[542] These principles are: 1) respect for inherent dignity, individual autonomy including the freedom to make one's own choices, and independence of persons; 2) non-discrimination; 3) full and effective participation and

---

[534] CRPD pre (e).

[535] CRPD pre (g).

[536] CRPD pre (h).

[537] CRPD pre (q) and (s).

[538] CRPD pre (x).

[539] CRPD pre (j) and (r).

[540] CRPD pre (e), (o) and (p) and arts 4(3) and 6(2).

[541] T Degener 'Disability in a Human Rights Context' (2016) 5(3) Laws 35.

[542] CRPD art 3.

inclusion in society; 4) respect for difference and acceptance of persons with disabilities as part of human diversity and humanity; 5) equality of opportunity; 6) accessibility; 7) equality between men and women; and 8) respect for the evolving capacities of children with disabilities and respect for the right of children with disabilities to preserve their identities.

The CRPD seeks to effect social change from the top down and the bottom-up. As an international treaty, it is a top-down instrument that requires member state compliance. However, it also includes bottom-up components. It is designed to address negative social constructs, recast norms from the grassroots and impact lived environments.[543] Lord and Stein observe that the CPRD moves beyond standard top-down reform strategies such as law reform and court-based advocacy to 'include strategies that support deeper domestic internalization of human rights norms'.[544] For example, it includes 'an affirmative duty to alter social norms regarding persons with disabilities, which includes the responsibility to eviscerate harmful stigmas and stereotypes and promote positive imagery'.[545] This duty combats key causal factors of discrimination in customary legal scenarios in Mukono District.

The Structure and Substance of the CRPD

The CRPD is an integrative treaty. It 'melds civil and political rights with economic, social, and cultural rights'.[546] It consists of introductory

---

[543] Lord & Stein (note 2) at 475; Stein & Lord (note 6) at 31-32.

[544] Ibid (note 2) at 449.

[545] *Ibid* at 476 (citing CRPD art 8 which requires states parties to 'to adopt immediate, effective and appropriate measures: (a) To raise awareness throughout society, including at the family level, regarding persons with disabilities, and to foster respect for the rights and dignity of persons with disabilities;').

[546] Stein & Lord (note 6) at 24.

articles of general application, enumerated substantive rights, monitoring provisions and rules for governing operations.[547]

The CRPD takes a detailed approach to substantive rights. By way of example, it does not merely state that persons with disabilities have a right to education. Instead, it offers extensive treatment on what this right entails[548] and takes similar approaches with respect to employment, awareness raising, accessibility, personal mobility, respect for the family and health.[549]

There are features of the Convention with special relevance to customary legal frameworks. Article 4 requires state parties to 'abolish or amend existing laws, regulations, customs and practices that constitute discrimination against persons with disabilities'.[550] The CRPD calls for proactive engagement with customary and informal legal procedures.[551] Article 12 requires the reform of laws that deprive persons with disabilities of their right to exercise legal capacity. This requirement specifically includes customary law.

The CRPD also promotes the communal rights of persons with disabilities.[552] It calls for States Parties to take effective and appropriate measures for achieving inclusion and full participation of persons with disabilities within the community[553] and asks signatories to consider what is entailed in community life.[554]

---

[547] Ibid at 24.

[548] CPRD art 24.

[549] CRPD arts 9-30.

[550] CRPD art 4(1)(b).

[551] J Borg, AK Bergman & PO Ostergen 'Is "legal empowerment of the poor" relevant to people with disabilities in developing countries? An empirical and normative review' (2013) 6:22854 Global Health Action.

[552] CRPD art 19.

[553] Ibid; E Kamundia 'Choice, support and inclusion: implementing Article 19 of the Convention on the Rights of Persons with Disabilities in Kenya' (2013) 1 ADRY 49-72, at 69.

[554] Ibid (Kamundia) at 67.

The Convention addresses the need for states to address cultural attitudes that impact the rights, status and treatment of persons with disabilities. It calls on member states to promote awareness at all levels of society about the rights and human dignity of persons with disabilities.[555] In addition states parties are required to 'combat stereotypes, prejudices and harmful practices relating to persons with disabilities' and 'promote awareness of the capabilities and contributions of persons with disabilities'.[556] This thesis' field research confirms the particular importance of the attitudes of family and community members to the rights, status and treatment of persons with disabilities in contexts of pervasive customary practices.

State Implementation of the CRPD

The CRPD charges state parties with the task of implementation. Article 4 sets out the 'general obligations' of states parties which range from enacting appropriate laws to training of disability service professionals.[557] Article 31 requires states to collect appropriate information relevant to the Convention's implementation.[558]

An initial state report of Uganda to the Committee on the Rights of Persons with Disabilities was distributed in 2015.[559] This report catalogues a number of state initiatives to implement the mandates of the CRPD and discusses the challenges of limited resources and impact. The fidelity of Uganda's compliance with CRPD mandates is also addressed

---

[555] P Harpur 'Time to be heard: how advocates can use the Convention on the Rights of Persons with Disabilities to drive change (2011) 45(3) *Valparaiso Univ. LR* 1271-1296, at 1280 quoting art 8(1) of the CRPD.

[556] Ibid.

[557] CPRD art 4.

[558] Ibid art 31.

[559] Committee on the Rights of Persons with Disabilities 'Consideration of reports submitted by States parties under article 35 of the Convention: Initial Report of Uganda' (received 22 January 2013; distributed 10 March 2015).

in a report issued to the United Nations Committee on the Rights of Persons with Disabilities by the National Union of Disabled Persons of Uganda (NUDIPU).[560] This report critiques the absence of concrete steps taken by the Ugandan government in twenty-two areas. Examples include health, education, liberty of movement and participation in cultural life, recreation, leisure and sport. The report points to a lack of concrete government action to strengthen and protect various rights provided for under the Convention.

In terms of legislation, the report critiques the harmonisation of disability laws and the definitions of disability under the current laws.[561] The report joins others in lamenting the fact that Ugandan law reflects more of a medical model than a social model of disability.[562] NUDIPU also criticises the lack of robust anti-discrimination laws to protect persons with disabilities, the presence of outdated and discriminatory language referring to persons with disabilities in existing statutes and the ongoing potential for abusing legal rights of persons with mental health impairments.[563] Yet to a large extent the report acknowledges that written legislative framework is adequate under the CPRD's standards and requirements. The next section addresses the formal disability laws and policies in place in Uganda.

---

[560] National Union of Disabled Persons of Uganda Implementation of the UN Convention on the Rights of Persons with Disabilities in Uganda: Submission of National Union of Disabled Persons of Uganda (NUDIPU) in response to the List of issues of the Committee on the Rights of Persons with Disabilities for the initial review of the Republic of Uganda on the implementation of the Convention on the Rights of Persons with Disabilities (January 2016).

[561] Ibid 7-8.

[562] Ibid 7.

[563] Ibid 10.

Disability Law and Policy in Uganda

Uganda is an intriguing setting for the study of disability policy and practice. It is a developing sub-Saharan nation that has willingly enacted a considerable body of law and policies intended to promote the status, rights and treatment of persons with disabilities. This section outlines Ugandan formal law and policy.

Ugandan Laws Concerning Disability

Uganda is home to a growing body of laws addressing the status, rights and treatment of persons with disabilities.[564] Observers credit Uganda for its legislative efforts made on behalf of persons with disabilities.[565] Although there are ongoing calls for legislative reforms[566], one is hard-pressed to attribute the substance of the current written domestic laws to the primary challenges persons with disabilities experience in Uganda.

The Constitution of Uganda

The Constitution is the supreme law of Uganda.[567] Article 2(2) provides that 'if any other law or any custom is inconsistent with any of the provisions of this Constitution, the Constitution shall prevail, and that

---

[564] For comprehensive treatment of the laws in Uganda that have special relevance to persons with disabilities in the context of accessibility please refer to Uganda National Action on Physical Disability's 'Publication of selected legal provisions in domestic and international laws on physical accessibility' (2010) available at <http://www.medbox.org/ug-disability/publication-of-selected-legal-provisions-in-domestic-and-international-laws-on-physical-accessibility/preview?> last accessed 28 October 2015.

[565] T Degener 'International disability law - a new legal subject on the rise: the Interregional Experts' Meeting in Hong Kong December 13-17, 1999' (2000) 18 Berkeley J Int'l Law 180.

[566] See for example The Persons with Disabilities Bill, 2014, Bills Supplement No. 5 to the Uganda Gazette, 9 May 2014.

[567] Constitution of Uganda 1995 (as amended in 2005) art 2(1).

other law or custom shall, to the extent of the inconsistency, be void'.[568] Thus, from a formal standpoint all customary content that conflicts with constitutional provisions is legally invalid.

The Constitution proclaims and protects the rights of persons with disabilities. National objective XVI declares that '[s]ociety and the State shall recognise the right of persons with disabilities to respect and human dignity.'

Article 21(2) prohibits discrimination against people with disabilities. It broadly defines discrimination as giving 'different treatment to different persons attributable only or mainly to their respective descriptions' including disability.

Article 32(1) requires the state to take affirmative action to assist groups that have been marginalised on the basis of disability. Article 32(2) prohibits laws, cultures, customs and traditions which oppose or undermine the dignity, welfare or interest of marginalised groups. Article 35(1) provides that '[p]ersons with disabilities have a right to respect and human dignity, and the State and society shall take all appropriate measures to ensure they realise their full mental and physical potential'. Article 35(2) requires Parliament to 'enact all laws appropriate for the protection of persons with disabilities'. Thus, on the surface the Constitution is equipped to protect and empower persons with disabilities.

In addition to the core articles referenced above, Article 59 requires Parliament to pass laws to ensure that persons with disabilities are able to meaningfully participate in elections and Article 79 designates persons with disabilities as a group are entitled to special representation in Parliament. This constitutional allocation of political representation to persons with disabilities has been recognised as exceptional.[569] Statutes in place to implement this mandate are discussed in the next sub-section.

---

[568] Ibid art 2(2).

[569] G Dewsbury, K Clarke, D Randall et al 'The anti social model of disability' (2004) 19(2) Disability, Poverty and Development 145-158.

Statutory Laws

The centrepiece of disability specific legislation in Uganda is the Persons with Disabilities Act (hereinafter the 'PDA').[570]   The PDA seeks to foster 'equal opportunities and enhanced empowerment, participation and protection of persons with disabilities irrespective of gender, age and type of disability'.[571]

The PDA defines disability as a 'substantial functional limitation of daily life activities caused by physical, mental or sensory impairment and environmental barriers resulting in limited participation'.[572] As discussed in Chapter 2 in Section III(3), adherents to the social model of disability critique the Act for its emphasis on functional impairments as the cause of disability as opposed to attributing disability to social causes.[573] While the PDA might be dated in terms of its theoretical underpinnings, such critiques are more a matter of ideological veneer than legal substance. Its substantive provisions provide considerable legal protections.

The PDA addresses a wide range of substantive areas including education, health services, rehabilitation, vocational rehabilitation; access to employment, government based affirmative action, prohibitions regarding punishment, the protection of privacy and measures to address discrimination in the context of food, services and facilities. The ambitious scope of the Act can be a double-edged sword when it comes to the realisation of disability rights. Its expansive and generous provisions led the Ministry of Justice to deem the legislation 'aspirational' and therefore not presently enforceable.[574]

---

[570] The Persons with Disabilities Act of 2006 (Uganda).

[571] Ibid pre.

[572] Ibid s 2.

[573] van Reenen & Combrinck (note 7) at 150; NUDIPU (note 35) at 7.

[574] Human Rights Watch 'As If We Weren'*t Human*': Discrimination and Violence against Women with Disabilities in Northern Uganda (2010) 65.

One section with particular relevance to customary contexts is section 36 on the 'Rights of the family'. It addresses familial relationships including marriage and guardianship that are regularly established and maintained under customary law. This section's 'right to a home and a family' includes the rights 'to experience his or her sexuality and to have sexual and other intimate relationship', the right to 'at the age of eighteen years and above, to marry a spouse of his or her own choice and to found a family', and the right 'to guardianship, trusteeship and adoption of children under the relevant laws'.

At this time there is a pending bill that would amend certain content in the PDA. The Persons with Disabilities Bill, 2014 was added to the Uganda Gazette on 9 May 2015.[575] The purported object of the bill is to replace and reform existing law by operationalising Article 35 of the Constitution and other human rights and freedoms of persons with disabilities with special emphasis in the areas of education, health and employment.[576] In particular, the existing PDA was implemented prior to the promulgation of the CRPD and the proposed revisions seek to align the Act with the terminology and standards used in the Convention.

The National Council for Disability Act[577] establishes a council for monitoring and evaluating the rights of persons with disabilities in Uganda. The Council is mandated to 'act as a body at a national level through which the needs, problems, concerns, potentials and abilities of persons with disabilities can be communicated to Government and its agencies for action'.[578] However, the National Disability Council has demonstrated some unwillingness to act on complaints and to monitor the implementation of the CRPD.[579] In fairness to the Council, the

---

[575] The Persons with Disabilities Bill, 2014, Bills Supplement No. 5 to the Uganda Gazette, 9 May 2014.

[576] Ibid para 1.

[577] The National Council for Disability Act of 2003, amended in 2010 (Uganda).

[578] Ibid s 5.

[579] Human Rights Watch (note 49) at 66-67.

CRPD is so extensive and integrative that monitoring for compliance would be a massive undertaking in a nation with limited bureaucratic capacity.

Government resistance to oversight and accountability can be troubling, but it is not surprising given the weighty challenge of human rights standards for developing nations with limited capacity to implement resource dependent mandates. If nations such as Uganda considered themselves truly accountable for fully implementing the requirements included in instruments such as the CRPD they would be unlikely to ratify them. The willingness of a nation like Uganda to adopt the Convention often comes with a presumption of an unofficial moratorium, for the foreseeable future at least, from legal accountability. This aspirational approach to human rights runs the risk of delegitimising human rights and weakening the rule of law.[580]

Uganda has domestic laws that ensure political representation by persons with disabilities. The Parliamentary Elections Act provides that five seats in Parliament are specifically allocated to persons with disabilities.[581] The Local Governments Act[582] and the Movement Act of 1998[583] set requirements for involving persons with disabilities in local councils. These laws ensure access to the political sphere. By 2008 government officials reported that approximately 47,000 persons with disabilities were involved within local government structures in the country.[584]

---

[580] C Stern 'Human rights or the rule of law—the choice for East Africa?' (2015) 24 Michigan State Int'l L Rev 45.

[581] The Parliamentary Elections Act of 2005 (Uganda) (cap 140) s 8(2)(d).

[582] The Local Governments Act 1997 (Uganda) (cap 243).

[583] The Movement Act 1998 (Uganda) (cap 261).

[584] H Katsui 'Ugandan disability movement: political achievements and social challenges of WWD' (2008) available at <disability-uganda.blogspot.com> last accessed on 27 October 2015.

Other Ugandan laws address disability concerns in various contexts. There is legislation that addresses disability concerns in the context of customary land tenure which is discussed later in this Chapter. In addition there are a number of acts that touch on matters of disability in contexts that are unlikely to overlap with customary legal contexts. These laws are referenced in Table A as an addendum to this chapter.

Ugandan case law

In recent years noteworthy cases concerning the rights of persons with disabilities have come before Ugandan courts. The judicial decisions offer mixed results.

In *Centre for Health, Human Rights and Development (CEHURD)*[585] *and Iga Daniel v the Attorney General*[586] the petitioners challenged discriminatory provisions in Uganda's criminal laws.[587] The Constitutional Court struck down the use of outdated and offensive language in the statutory law such as 'imbecile' and 'lunatic' and replaced that language with terms such as 'mentally handicapped' and 'mentally disabled'.[588] The Court also found that the current criminal provisions appli-

---

[585] CEHURD is a Non-Governmental Organisation that uses strategic and public interest litigation to address matters concerning health related rights. It is a lead plaintiff in two cases referenced in this section of the thesis.

[586] CEHURD and Iga Daniel v the Attorney General UGCC Const Pet No 64 of 2011 [2015].

[587] Treaties referenced in the opinion include the Universal Declaration of Human Rights, the International Convention of Civil and Political Rights, the CRPD and the African Charter of Human and Peoples Rights.

[588] Uganda's revised terminology remains dated in terms of current approved parlance in Western contexts when referring to persons with disabilities. Using the term 'disabled' as opposed to the clause 'with disabilities' is now considered objectifying and dehumanising, while the term 'handicapped' has been criticized due to its origins in the practice of begging on the streets. See, for example PJ Devlieger 'From handicap to disability: Language use and cultural meaning within the United States' (1999) 21(7) Disability and Rehabilitation 346.

cable to persons with mental illness—including indefinite detention—denied due process under the law. Notably the relief granted in *CEHURD and Iga* did not include a court directed allocation of substantial government resources.

A 2008 case brought against a private bank alleging discrimination against persons with disabilities based on inaccessibility produced another impactful result.[589] The ruling court required the bank to increase accessibility at the subject branch, pay a financial settlement to the plaintiff and adopt nation-wide steps to improve accessibility at other branches. However a similar case involving public, as opposed to private, institutions produced a different result.

In *Legal Action for People with Disabilities v. Attorney General and Another*[590] the plaintiffs asserted that buildings operated by the city of Kampala and Makerere University were not accessible by persons with disabilities and sought remedies to force these public institutions to make their facilities more accessible. The High Court chided the applicants for implying 'that their own right must be enjoyed irrespective of the negative effects that it may have on public interest, the costs to the respondents and the overall costs to other (students) or people'. The court noted that 'enjoyment of their rights is not absolute' and that the court must 'take into account the rights of others as well as public interest'. Citing limited government resources, the court held that it 'cannot order prompt enforcement of the provisions of the law because of the hardship it involves, but shall encourage whoever is responsible and the respondents in particular to ensure continued compliance with the law as

---

[589] H Lubwama 'Accessibility law bites Centenary Bank' (Sept.-Oct. 2008) 6(4) UNAPD Update available at <http://www.unapd.org/userfiles/September _october_2008.pdf> accessed 12 November 2015 reporting on Uganda High Court case Santo Dwoka & Anor v Centenary Rural Development Bank Ltd [2008].

[590] Legal Action for People with Disabilities v. Attorney General and Another [2014]. UGHC 42.

required'. This judgment speaks to the reticence of the Ugandan judiciary to order the specific governmental provisions of economic and social rights.

In *Centre for Health Human Rights and Development (CEHURD) and Three Others v. Attorney General*[591] the Constitutional Court of Uganda initially abstained from considering the merits of a right to health claim on the grounds that government health policy is a non-justiciable political question.[592] However, this decision was reversed by the Supreme Court of Uganda[593] with an instruction for the Constitutional Court to make substantive rulings as to whether the Government had met its obligations to provide citizens the right to health and not to deny citizens the right to life.[594] In a separate concurring opinion, Chief Justice Bart Katereeba indicated that the government should be held to the standard of providing 'all practical measures to ensure the provision of basic medical services'.[595] Given the resource dependent aspects of disability rights, the Supreme Court decision is a significant development. In its holding the Supreme Court recognises the existence of a social and economic right that is not specifically delineated in the Constitution (the right to health) and provides that the judiciary has the power and responsibility to provide oversight over governmental policy decisions concerning the allocation of resources to meaningfully account for that right. If applied to the rights to persons with disabilities to accessibility and accommodation, this holding could significantly increase the potential for effecting change through litigation.

---

[591] UGCC 4, Const Pet No 16 of 2011 [2012].

[592] *CEHURD & Three others v Attorney General*, Constitutional Petition No. 16 of 2011, UGCC 4 [2012].

[593] The Supreme Court of Uganda stands above the Constitutional Court in terms of appellate review. Constitution of Uganda art 132.

[594] *Centre for Health Human Rights and Development (CEHURD) & Three others v Attorney General* UGSC Constitutional Appeal No. 01 of 2013 [2015].

[595] Ibid opinion of CJ Katureeba at 17.

In sum, litigation's capacity to bring about change in Uganda is increasing, but remains limited. Isolated success appears possible, but courts tend to shy away from imposing substantial financial hardships on the government. Resource strapped governments in Sub-Saharan nations have a tendency to view 'individual rights and freedoms as a superfluous luxury that (can impede) national growth'.[596] Thus disability rights face the potential of political and judicial backlash.[597] While the Supreme Court opinion in *CEHURD and Three Others* offers fresh hope in the judicial enforcement of social and economic rights, court oversight of government spending and policy decisions remains politically and functionally problematic.

Formal Law, Customary Law and Disability

Both formal and informal considerations are relevant to customary law in Uganda. The formal law provides official recognition of customary law in areas such as land tenure and marriage as well as minimum overarching standards for customary law based on the repugnancy test and the Constitution, as discussed in Section III(1) of Chapter 3. Meanwhile the actual substance of customary law springs from the unwritten traditions and practices of diverse cultural groups inhabiting Uganda. The customary law—both substantive and procedural—of these people groups is not codified in a post-colonial extant document.

Ugandan formal laws preempt and displace customary laws and practices when those formal laws specifically apply to situations and

---

[596] TW Bennett 'Human rights and the African cultural tradition' (1993) 22 *Transformation* 30-40 citing SKB Asante 'Nation building and human rights emergent African nations' 2 Cornell Int Law Jnl 72-107; TR Nhlapo 'The African family and women's rights: friends or foes?' (1991) Acta Juridica 135-146.

[597] J Srem-Sai 'The hugger-mugger of enforcing socio-economic rights in Ghana: A threat to the rights of persons with disabilities' (2015)135 ADRY 135-159.

scenarios.[598] A noteworthy example of formal preemption and displacement is the Succession Act.[599] This Act governs the distribution of all property in the case of both testate and intestate succession. Thus, it subsumes all matters of succession and leaves customary succession law with no formal legitimacy. Similarly, formal laws that address the award of guardianship of children technically displace ongoing customary practices.[600] However, as acknowledged by IJM[601] and as further confirmed in this thesis' field research, customary succession and guardianship practices persist despite formal displacement.

When customary law is not preempted by formal legislation, Ugandan law provides for some protections for persons with disabilities in the context of customary land tenure. The procedure established for the issuance of certificates of ownership in customary land provides that such certificates shall give effect to customary entitlements that inure to the benefit of persons under a disability.[602] In addition, Section 27 of the Land Act of 1998 provides that any decision taken concerning land held under customary tenure is null and void if it denies a person with a disability access to ownership, occupation or use of land on the basis of disability.[603] Yet these provisions are of little legal relevance in Mukono District given the absence of unregistered customary tenure in the area.

---

[598] Mustafa Kadala Nsubuga v. Mawandu Balumu and Others, High Court of Uganda at Kampala, Civil Suit No. 1086 of 2000.

[599] Succession Act of 1906 (Uganda) (cap 162).

[600] The Children Act of 2003 (Uganda) (cap 59), the Judicature Act of 1996 (Uganda) (cap 13) and the Civil Procedure Act 2002 (Uganda) (cap 71).

[601] International Justice Mission (IJM) Property Grabbing from Ugandan Widows and the Justice System: A Mixed-Methods Assessment in Mukono County, Uganda (2015) at 65.

[602] S Coldham 'Land reform and customary rights: the case of Uganda reviewed' (2000) 44(1) Journal of African Law 65-77, at 66-67.

[603] The Land Act of 1998 (Uganda).

Policies

In addition to the laws discussed above, there are government policies that specifically concern the status, rights and treatment of persons with disabilities.

The National Policy on Disabilities (NPD) 2006 provides for 'a human-rights based framework for responding to the needs of persons with disabilities'.[604] It acknowledges existing problems with access and structural exclusion and calls for resource allocation and service provision to persons with disabilities from all levels of government.

The National Health Policy (NHP) addresses disability concerns. It adopts a 'minimum health care package' approach due to limited financial resources and low health care capacity in Uganda.[605] This package seeks to deliver the most urgent and necessary health care due to the fact that limited resources restrain the level of medical services the government can provide. Thus, the NHP's minimum package approach is not aligned with the right to the highest attainable standard of health without discrimination pronounced in the CPRD.[606]

Other policies make some effort to promote the status, rights and treatment of persons with disabilities. The Land Sector Strategic Plan and Uganda's Land Policy both call for measures to protect vulnerable groups including persons with disabilities.[607] Uganda's Land Policy states that '[l]egislation and management practices shall accord all vulnerable groups equal rights in acquisition, transmission and use of

---

[604] C Nyombi & MW Mulimira Mental Health Laws in Uganda: A Critical Review (Part 1) (2012) at 5, available at <http://www.researchgate.net/publication/228124324_Mental_Health_Laws_in_Uganda_A_Critical_Review_(Part_1)> accessed on 15 June 2015.

[605] Ibid at 3.

[606] CRPD art 25.

[607] MA Rugadya Women's Land Rights in Uganda: Status of Implementation of Policy and Law on Women's Land Rights for ECA a paper offered at ACGS Addis Adaba (June 2010) at 13-14.

land'[608] and commits the Government *inter alia* to guarantee access to land by persons with disabilities and 'mainstream disability interventions in strategic land sector activities'.[609]

Uganda Vision 2040 mentions disability concerns although there is little in terms of specific substance addressing disability issues in the document.[610] The Vision recognises the need to 'provide assistance' to people who are vulnerable because of age, social class, location, gender, disaster or lack of income.[611] It mentions the need for a universal pension and social protection systems to respond to the specific needs of these vulnerable groups. Thus, the Vision is consistent with the perception of many of the interviewees in the field research that the government should provide for persons with disabilities.

Regardless of the plans and proclamations asserted in Ugandan policies, the field research indicates that there is a high level of suspicion and skepticism about the legitimacy and effectiveness of government initiatives. Community members believe that those persons with disabilities should receive governmental assistance, but they indicate that such assistance rarely benefits such persons. There is a collective sense among the interview participants that policies pertaining to persons with disabilities are 'just words'

Survey of Key Areas of Baganda Law

This next section surveys substantive areas of Baganda customary and traditional law that are highly consequential to the lives of persons with disabilities. These areas include marital relations, clan leadership,

---

[608] Ministry of Lands Housing and Urban Development, Uganda Land Policy (2013) s 73(a).

[609] *Ibid* s 74(i) and (v).

[610] Ministry of Finance, Planning and Economic Development (Uganda) Uganda Vision 2045 (2013).

[611] Ibid s 5.4.

succession, guardianship and land rights. These areas were selected based on the literature review, as well as my knowledge and experience.[612] These are observed areas where customary law has a major impact on people's lives in Mukono District.

Marriage, Divorce and Bride Wealth

Achieving official status as a married person is important to protecting one's legal rights in Mukono District.[613] Thus, a person's ability to marry is a significant matter in terms of status, rights and treatment.

Baganda culture places heavy emphasis on the importance of marriage. Traditionally 'an unmarried man could not hold office and when he dies his body would be taken out through the back door'.[614]

The key ceremonial event in Baganda customary marriage is the okwanjula.[615] This is an introduction ceremony where the man seeking marriage visits the family of the bride.[616] It has become a highly public and social ceremony.[617]

The okwanjula presents the potential for public shaming or embarrassment to persons with disabilities. Field interviewees indicated that the crowds that participate in the okwanjula can be rude and disrespectful. The fear of exposing oneself to public ridicule can prevent persons with disabilities from pursuing formal customary marriage.

There are also concerns that the customary betrothal process has become increasingly materialistic and economically exploitive.[618] Justice

---

[612] I served on the Faculty of Law at Uganda Christian University. During that time her coordinated a clinical legal education program that engaged law students in various projects to address local justice and rule of law concerns.

[613] IJM (note 76) at 60.

[614] FW Jjuuko & E Kibalama Culture and Women: The Position of Women in Buganda (2011) at 64.

[615] Also referred to as 'kwanjula'.

[616] ES Haydon Law and Justice in Buganda (1960) at 87-89.

[617] Jjuuko & Kibalama (note 84) at 10.

[618] Ibid at 10.

Mpagi–Bahigeine articulated this concern in the *Mifumi* case when she observed that 'these days when prospective grooms out of sheer egotism are obliged to take lorryfuls of goods to their future in-laws' it amounts to 'an adulteration of the time honored "kwanjula"'.[619] Furthermore, the financial burden posed by bride wealth (omutwalo) demanded by the families of brides presents an obstacle to male suitors with limited means. Given the reciprocal relationship between disability and poverty[620] the practice of bride wealth presents opportunities for the disparate treatment of male suitors with disabilities.

Ethnographic literature does not point to traditional systemic discrimination against persons with disabilities within Baganda customary marriage law. According to Haydon, physical and mental illness were not considered grounds for divorce among the Baganda.[621]

A predominate health-related ground for divorce is male impotency. Male sexual potency is required to consummate a marriage.[622] In fact, an impotent bridegroom was not even permitted to recover his marriage consideration.[623] This thesis' field research confirms that impotency still disqualifies a man for marriage and is grounds for terminating a marriage. Conversely, the sterility of a wife is not a basis for terminating a marriage.[624] Thus Haydon's assertion that the Baganda do not consider sterility the fault of either the husband or wife appears to ring true to-

---

[619] Mifumi (U) Ltd and 12 Others v Attorney General UGCC 2 Const Petition No. 12/07 [2010].

[620] S Mitra, A Posarac & B Vick 'Disability and poverty in developing countries: a multidimensional study' (2012) 41 World Development 1-18; United Nations Commission for Social Development (2008) Mainstreaming Disability in the Development Agenda available at <www.un.org/disabilities/default.asp?id=708> last accessed on 27 October 2015.

[621] Haydon (note 91) at 24.

[622] *Ibid* at 98, 106.

[623] Ibid at 98.

[624] Ibid at 107.

day.[625]   Divorce is a common practice among the Baganda.[626] One need not have cause for divorce. For example, a wife may obtain a divorce under Baganda customary law by leaving the husband and not returning.[627] This thesis' field research indicates that customary separation takes place primarily when husband and wife choose not to remain together. The customary status of divorce appears to be less important than actual living arrangements. Little was made of any formal distinction between separation and divorce among the interview participants. Chapter 7, Section II includes a discussion of the limited relevance of disability in the context of customary marital termination in Mukono District.

There are discrepancies concerning the practice of returning bride wealth.[628] In her opinion in the *Mifumi* case[629] Justice Mpagi–Bahigeine opined that 'there is no such concept as refund of "mutwalo" "bride price" in Buganda as it is in the Eastern region (of Uganda)'. Yet according to Haydon, traditionally, the technical legal challenges associated with the termination of a customary Baganda marriage largely concerned the potential return of bride wealth paid to the wife's family.[630]

Haydon wrote that when a wife leaves, the husband is entitled to the return of bride wealth unless there are certain grounds for not return-

---

[625] Ibid at 107.

[626] J Tumusiime & CO Bichachi (Eds), The People and Culture of Uganda 4th Ed (2011) at 17.

[627] Haydon (note 91) at 108.

[628] There is considerable controversy over the proper English term for this practice in Uganda. Concern over the implications and baggage associated with the term 'bride price' is discussed by Justice Tumwesigye in Mifumi (U) Ltd and 12 Others v Attorney General UgSC Const App No. 2/14 [2015] with Justice Tumwesigye ultimately deciding to use the term 'bride price' to describe the practice despite his dislike of the term.

[629] Mifumi (supra note 94).

[630] Haydon (note 91) at 108.

ing.[631] Long-standing grounds for retaining bride wealth include general incompatibility, sexual abomination (bestiality, sodomy, incest) by the husband, impotence, neglecting the wife, rudeness to the wife, cruelty to the wife, expelling the wife from the marital home, practicing wizardry, theft by the husband and consorting with sexually promiscuous women.[632] Conversely, the wife's family was required to return bride wealth if the wife is sexually frigid, refuses a husband's conjugal rights or in any other instance where the husband was not at fault for the breakdown of the marriage.[633] With the exception of male impotency and female frigidity, none of these traditional grounds concern disability and the field research failed to detect any additional grounds existing in practice that are directly connected to disability.

Haydon reported that the process for obtaining the return of bride wealth typically involves going to the wife's family and presenting one's case.[634] If disputes over bridal wealth cannot be resolved at the family level, the matter can be taken to a clan head or chief.[635] This thesis' field research indicates that the wife's family members continue to play the key role in the disposition of bride wealth after marital termination.

In August of 2015 the Supreme Court of Uganda held that making divorce contingent on the return of the bride wealth is unconstitutional.[636] This court ruling formally outlaws a traditional element within Baganda customary law that disincentivises undesirable conduct within a marriage. Going forward it will be interesting to see what impact, if any, the formal disallowance of the return of bride wealth has in the

---

[631] *Ibid* at 108.

[632] Ibid at 109.

[633] Ibid at 109.

[634] Ibid at 109.

[635] Ibid at 109.

[636] Mifumi (supra note 103).

lived environment. The timing of the fieldwork precedes the August 2015 decision.

Clan Leadership

Another relevant aspect of Baganda customary law is clan leadership. The Baganda have a clan system and the clan leader administers significant cultural and legal roles in that system. Traditionally these clans served as cohesive social units that practiced the reciprocity that one might expect to find in nuclear families.[637] Clans continue to play an important role and designation as clan leader is a significant honour and responsibility.

Clan leadership among the Baganda is hereditary with leadership passing to a male heir in the line of past clan leaders.[638] Traditionally clan elders choose a successor in the male line of the prior leader.[639] Although the oldest male son stands in a favoured position, the selection process involves more than primogeniture. This thesis' fieldwork indicates that because qualities other than birth order are considered, this is a zone within Baganda customary law where discrimination against persons with disabilities can occur.

There is no indication in existing literature concerning the impact of disability on one's eligibility or qualifications to serve as a clan leader. This thesis' fieldwork indicates that disability can be a negative factor. This is especially true for individuals with mental illness and those unable to hear and speak. The research indicates that physical disabilities and blindness can also present hurdles to clan leader appointment.

Guardianship

In guardianship relationships one individual with full legal autonomy assumes the role of providing care for and acting on the behalf of anoth-

---

[637] Jjuuko & Kibalama (note 89) at 4.
[638] Haydon (note 91) at 195.
[639] Ibid at 195.

er person. Legal guardianships typically entail a child, known as the ward, who is placed in the care of a guardian. In customary guardianships, wards are placed in the care of guardians outside of the formal legal system.

This thesis investigated both guardianships with child wards and guardianships where adults are placed in the care of other adults. However, there was nothing in the existing literature about a Baganda practice of adult custodianship. Therefore this sub-section is limited to prior reports on the customary guardianship of children among the Baganda.

Traditionally a Baganda child is considered to belong to the clan as opposed to the parents.[640] Thus, when a minor's parent died there was no need for a formal adoption process under customary law. Matters of guardianship were handled at the clan and family level.

Under Baganda customary law a surviving male family member would take on the role of successor of the deceased man's estate. Traditionally the successor would follow "'in the footsteps of the deceased" (ajja mu bigere by'omufu) from the moment he dons the barkcloth (okusumuka) of succession, taking over the duties and responsibilities of the deceased as well as his rights'.[641] This includes assuming responsibility for the care of the deceased's children[642] and holding the property of the deceased's children in trust.[643]

Today the customary successor's role has been bifurcated and modified by the formal law. The role of administrating estate property is assigned by statute to executors and administrators.[644] In guardianship,

---

[640] Ibid at 81.

[641] Ibid at 221.

[642] Ibid at 225.

[643] Ibid at 226.

[644] The formal law also provides for estates to have a customary heir, but the role of the heir is essentially ceremonial. The formal customary heir is stripped of any functional or fiduciary responsibilities. The Succession Act (cap 162) (Uganda) ss 2(e), 27(1)(a)(i) and 31.

statutory law provides for the legal role of a guardian that accepts the responsibility of caring for the minor children of the deceased.[645] Thus the right to administer the property of the deceased ansd the responsibility to care for the deceased's children are not necessarily linked.

Ugandan statutory law entails formal processes and procedures for establishing the custody and care of children through guardianships.[646] However, customary guardianship arrangements continue to arise with great regularity in Central Uganda outside the formal law.[647]

This thesis' field research presented in Chapter 7, Section IV confirms the ongoing prevalence of customary guardianship and the relevance of disability to the customary guardianship process. In particular the research indicates that someone's status as a person with a disability often has a negative impact on the likelihood that a person will be named a customary guardian.

Succession

From a purely formal standpoint there is no customary law of succession in Uganda. Uganda's Succession Act completely subsumes succession law. Yet customary law and process maintain dominant roles in people's lives. As noted in Chapter 2, a recent field study conducted by IJM in Mukono District found that only 1.3 per cent of widows use the formal probate procedures.[648] Similarly this thesis' fieldwork is bereft of stories where people probated an estate through formal channels. Instead succession matters are worked out at family and clan levels.

In Mukono District the key actor in the customary succession process is commonly referred to as the customary heir. This person assumes the administrative role over estate property in the customary context.

---

[645] The Children Act (cap 59) (Uganda) ss 1(k), 4, 5, 65, 51, 71.

[646] Ibid.

[647] Jjuuko & Kibalama (note 89) at 21.

[648] IJM (note 76) at 65, 91.

Under the formal law the customary heir is a token role. The Succession Act provides that the customary heir receives one per cent of the estate in intestate succession and plays no role in administering the estate.[649]

Yet the consequential role of customary successor persists among the Baganda.[650] Customary heirs continue to manage and administer estates outside of any formal legal process. Traditionally the heir is a brother of the deceased or a son of a brother of the deceased male head of household.[651] Interviewees described a tendency to name the oldest son of the deceased as the customary heir. Perhaps this shift is aligned with a shift in inheritance rights to the male children of fathers in Baganda customary law[652] and a shift to the inheritance of children in the formal law.[653] Despite the minimal rights and powers granted to customary heirs by the Succession Act, uncles and nephews continue to serve as heirs and often use their traditionally dominant role in the succession process to 'grab' property they do not rightfully own.[654]

The broad power held by the customary heir to manage the estate is susceptible to abuse.[655] Customary heirs often distribute the estate in accordance with customary traditions and their own discretion instead of adhering to the schedules provided by the Succession Act.[656] Discriminatory customary practices such as larger distributions to males continue despite prohibitions in the formal law.[657]

There are many actions taken within the process of customary succession that can work to the disadvantage of persons with disabilities.

---

[649] Succession Act ss 27, 31, 180-207.

[650] IJM (note 76) at 21 fn 29, 87, fn 95.

[651] Haydon (note 91) at 222.

[652] Ibid at 214; Jjuuko & Kiblama (note 89) at 15.

[653] Succession Act s 27.

[654] IJM (note 76) at 45, 60, 68, 74, 77, 83 and 86.

[655] Ibid; Haydon (note 91) at 17-18, 48-49, 67.

[656] Ibid at 68.

[657] Ibid at 65.

This thesis' field research indicates that persons with disabilities face discrimination with respect to inheritance of real property. In addition, persons with disabilities face difficulties in the customary heir appointment process. Thus although customary law does not appear to require discrimination in the context of succession or the appointment of heirs, the customary process and the absence of clear bars to such discrimination enables discrimination to occur.

Baganda culture has long recognised the operative legitimacy of oral wills and oral designations of customary heirs and clan leaders.[658] The arrival of the British introduced written wills which became popular with the Baganda.[659] Buganda's Succession Order of 1926 adopted formal requirements for written wills that are similar to the requirements found in the Succession Act.[660] The fieldwork indicates that family, clan and customary heirs tend to honour the asserted terms of wills regardless of technicalities despite their general disregard of formal probate. Informal wills, including oral wills, which are not subjected to formal probate, create legal occurrences with opportunities for discriminatory conduct which is largely free from formal restraints.

Land Rights

The Baganda have a unique land holding system that is a mixed product of indigenous practices and colonial policy. While this system is not purely customary, it has customary elements and land rights are the penultimate concern in customary succession. This section presents aspects of real property law that are instructive in understanding the rights, status and treatment of persons with disabilities in Mukono District within customary legal frameworks.

---

[658] Haydon (note 91) at 222.

[659] Ibid at 223.

[660] The Succession Order of 1926, found in Haydon (note 91) app 4 at 320.

Land is at the centre of African society. Land offers sustenance, economic opportunities and social status.[661] There are certain features that are prevalent in traditional Sub-Saharan land tenure systems. These include: 1) the imbedding of land rights within households, kinship networks and community relationships; 2) an inclusive character that treats land as a resource to be shared; 3) the attribution of land rights to a wide range of occurrences such as birth, group allegiance, political authority and transactions; 4) a distinction between access to land and ownership of land; 5) the exercise of authority and control over land to regulate the use of common resources, guarantee and enforce rights, resolve disputes, and equitably distribute resources; and 6) flexibility in terms of boundaries and legal application.[662] These factors are present in Mukono District.

The economic pressures and uncertainties connected with cultural, social and economic transitions spawn 'land fever'.[663] Rapid population growth, government and administrative management deficiencies pertaining to land, rapid urbanisation, and unchecked development add to this socio-economic malady.[664] The importance of land increases in settings where it seems to offer the only basis for economic security.[665] Present demographic data presents an ominous picture of increasing land

---

[661] P Kameri-Mbote, C Odote, C Nyamu-Musembi et al Ours by Right: Law, Politics and Realities of Community Property in Kenya (2013) at 17 (addressing the Kenyan context).

[662] Ibid at 38 citing B Cousins 'Potentials and pitfalls of communal land reform: experience in Africa and implications for South Africa' Paper presented at the World Bank Conference on Land Governance in Support of the MGDs: Responding to New Challenges (2009).

[663] Ibid at 34.

[664] Ibid at 42.

[665] Kameri-Mbote, Odote & Nyamu-Musembi (note 136) at 34.

related strife in Uganda.[666] Rugadya cites the deterioration of traditional land tenure systems and customary norms as contributive factors in the prevalence of land disputes.[667]

The heightened state of land fever places vulnerable groups in precarious situations.[668] For persons with disabilities land ownership, land access, and agricultural land use are crucial matters.

The dominant form of land tenure in Central Uganda is Mailo tenure.[669] Mailo is a unique tenure system that results from a colonial modification of the traditional Buganda tenure system.[670] Unlike customary tenure where land titles are rarely written or registered, Mailo titles are formally registered.[671] Yet, Mailo tenure retains customary vestiges. Mailo's customary heritage and the importance of land interests in customary legal scenarios calls for a brief excursus on this tenure system.

Prior to colonial rule, all land in the Kingdom of Baganda belonged to the Kabaka and was held for use in trust by the clans.[672] Prescriptive title was held by clan chiefs on behalf of the Kabaka.[673] These chiefs allowed peasants to occupy and cultivate the land at the chiefs' pleas-

---

[666] Rugadya (note 82) at 4-5 (citing a young population, a current housing shortage, a population growth of 3.2% and an average of 6.7 live births for a Ugandan woman in her lifetime.

[667] MA Rugadya 'Escalating land conflicts in Uganda: A review of evidence from recent studies and surveys' A paper commissioned by the International Republican Institute (2009) available at <http://mokoro.co.uk/wp-content/uploads/escalating_Uganda_landconflicts.pdf> last accessed on 15 June 2015.

[668] Ibid.

[669] International Justice Mission Property Grabbing Prevention Handbook (Mukono, Uganda) (2009).

[670] Haydon (note 91) at 132-135.

[671] Registration of Titles Act of 1924 (cap 230) (Uganda) ss 27, 37.

[672] Haydon (note 91) at 127; E Obaikol 'Women's land rights and the law' (2009) Uganda Land Alliance policy paper at 2.

[673] Ibid (Haydon) at 128.

ure.[674] The peasants' interests in these feudal plots were known as kibanja. Peasants paid the Kabaka's tribute through their chiefs from the produce of kibanja land.

British colonialism disrupted this customary form of land tenure.[675] In 1900 the British converted all Buganda Kingdom land into crown land held in the name of Queen Victoria. That land was granted back in freehold to chiefs and members of the Kabaka's family to hold out for feudal use.[676] This took the tribute and title away from the Kabaka and transferred formal land ownership rights to the local chiefs.[677]

This tenure system became known as Mailo. The word Mailo derives from 'mile', the unit of measurement the British used to inventory and divide the land. Unlike customary land, all Mailo land is formally titled with the Uganda Lands Registry.[678] Mailo interests are transferable and inheritable.[679]

The tenants of Mailo land are called kibanja holders. Kibanja holders pay an annual tribute to maintain their legal right to the land. This tribute is called busuulu. Kibanja holders have the right to occupy and use kibanja land without interference from the land owner as long as they pay busuulu.[680] Busuulu is not rent. Rent is typically set by property owners at market rates. Instead, busuulu is a token amount that officially recognises the owner of the land.[681]

---

[674] Ibid 131.

[675] Kameri-Mbote, Odote & Nyamu-Musembi (note 136) at 17.

[676] Coldham (note 77) at 65.

[677] Haydon (note 91) at 133.

[678] Registration of Titles Act (cap 230) (Uganda) s 55.

[679] HW West Land Policy in Buganda (1972).

[680] The Land (Amendment) Act 2010 (Uganda) codified the practice of ground rent for kibanja holders by protecting bonafide and lawful occupant and his or her successors against any arbitrary eviction as long as the ground rent is paid.

[681] IJM (note 76) at 172; F Bwengye 'Land as a sensitive matter in Uganda in the eyes of the law' (2007) 5(1) Uganda Living Law Journal 1 at 15.

Ownership disputes are frequent in the context of Mailo tenure.[682] '[T]he nominal ground rent (busuulu) provided for is largely ignored' and this creates 'a land use deadlock between the tenants and the registered land owner' and results in 'conflicts and in many instances evictions'.[683] Thus 'the landlord-tenant relationship as legally regulated is not amicable or harmonious'.[684] Mailo title owners often manipulate the legal system to force rightful kibanja holders off their plots.[685]

Legitimate kibanja claims can be difficult to protect at law.[686] Power is abused and the formal law fails to offer certainty and protection, especially with respect to vulnerable people.[687] This thesis' research confirms that the kibanja holdings of persons with disabilities are considered vulnerable to abuses of power by Mailo title owners.

Conclusion

This chapter offers a wide-ranging treatment of laws that impact and concern the status, rights and treatment of persons with disabilities in customary legal scenarios in Mukono District. It canvasses international law, domestic law and customary law.

---

[682] CK Petracco & J Pender, 'Evaluating the impact of land tenure and titling on access to credit in Uganda' (2009), IFPRI Discussion Paper 00853 at 6.

[683] Land Policy of Uganda (note 83) policy statement 44.

[684] Ibid policy statement 44.

[685] Rugadya (note 142) at 7.

[686] Bwengye (note 156) at 16.

[687] J Oloka-Onyango 'The problematique of economic, social and cultural right in globalized Uganda: a conceptual review' at 38 available at <http://makir.mak.ac.ug/handle/10570/656> last accessed on 22 March 2017 ('However, to the extent that the local context may remain insensitive to the concrete situation of significant sectors of the population such as women and other marginalised groups, then there are serious issues of access that arise simply from the content of the substantive (statute or customary) law sought to be applied.')

The first half of the chapter presents international and domestic formal law that seeks to foster and protect persons with disabilities. Most significantly the CRPD and the Constitution of Uganda make strong assertions about the legal status and rights of persons with disabilities that can serve to challenge all laws and legal practices that discriminate against or mistreat persons with disabilities.

Yet despite the extensive legal content that touches on matters of disability, the chapter leaves us doubting the efficacy of formal law. Despite the expansive body of written law and policy addressing disability issues in Uganda[688], the lives of most persons with disabilities are largely unaffected by the formal law.[689] In addition, there are discrepancies between what is written and what is implemented.[690] Policies reflect encouraging government stances, but little in terms of action and resource allocation.

On the other hand, customary legal frameworks are highly relevant. While the formal law remains inaccessible, people continue to work out the legal relationships of their lives through customary legal scenarios. Therefore the social and legal dynamics at play in these customary scenarios must be understood in order to appreciate the status, rights and treatment of persons with disabilities.

This chapter provides necessary context for the fieldwork findings presented in subsequent chapters. Its content offers foundational guid-

---

[688] S Cooper, J Ssebunnya, F Kigozi et al 'Viewing Uganda's mental health system through a human rights lens' (2010) 22(6) International Review of Psychiatry 578-588.

[689] Uganda National Action on Physical Disability 'Publication of selected legal provisions in domestic and international laws on physical accessibility' (2010) at 4.

[690] Norwegian Agency for Development Cooperation (Nored) Mainstreaming Disability in the New Development Paradigm, Evaluation of Norwegian Support to Promote the Rights of Persons with Disabilities: Uganda Country Study (2012) at 6.

ance for findings concerning specific categories of customary scenarios such as marriage, guardianship and succession. In addition, the chapter's inclusive coverage of potential legal sources enables the reader to appreciate the fieldwork findings through an inclusive analytical lens.

Table A

Other Uganda Domestic Legislation Concerning Matters of Disability

Name of Act and Citation	Description of Disability Rights Related Mandate or Provision
Children Act of 2006 (Uganda) (cap 59) s 8	Requiring the assessment and identification of children with disabilities as well as their treatment, rehabilitation and education
The Universities and Tertiary Institutions Act of 2001, amended 2006 (Uganda) (cap 59)	Requiring public universities to disseminate knowledge and give the opportunity of acquiring higher education to all persons including persons with disabilities wishing to do so and including representation by persons with disabilities on the university councils of public universities.
The Employment Act of 2006 (Uganda) (cap 219) ss 2, 6, 34	Prohibiting discrimination based on disability in the context of employment
The Equal Opportunities Commission Act of 2007 (Uganda)	Establishing a committee charged with eliminating discrimination and inequality in the employment sector

The Workers Compensation Act of 2000 (Uganda) (cap 225)	Providing compensation to workers who become disabled as a result of industrial accidents
Business, Technical, Vocational Education and Training Act of 2008 (Uganda) (cap 130) s 4(h)	Pronouncing an intention to increase equitable technical training and employment access to disadvantaged groups including persons with disabilities
The Traffic and Road Safety Act of 1998 (Uganda) (cap 361) s 41(c)	Generally prohibiting the denial of a driving permit on the basis of disability
The Uganda Communications Act of 1998 (Uganda) (cap 106)	Promoting research for the development and use of new communications techniques and technologies that promote accessibility to new forms of communication to persons with hearing impairments.

6

DISABILITY IN CONTEXT: THE SOCIAL PLACE OF HUMAN IMPAIRMENT IN MUKONO DISTRICT AND APPLIED ANALYSIS OF THEORETICAL APPROACHES

Introduction

In Mukono District the rights, status and treatment of persons with disabilities within customary frameworks are significantly impacted by perceptions, attitudes and beliefs about human impairments. This is especially true in the context of customary legal scenarios where family members and clan mates take consequential actions. This chapter presents the fieldwork findings concerning attitudes and beliefs about persons with disabilities. The chapter also offers a contextual analysis of various theoretical approaches to disability in light of the fieldwork.

Disability in Context in Mukono District

What is Disability?

Interviewees with disabilities were asked '[w]hat is disability?' Approximately two thirds of them offered descriptions of disability that placed a major emphasis on functionality. Representative examples include 'disability means that you cannot do something' and 'disability means one can't do what other people can do'. Certain names used for persons with disabilities reflect the importance of functionality in the conception of disability. Other names reflect a perceived link between disability and uselessness. Examples include 'kateyamba' (someone who cannot help themselves) and 'omubogo' (a helpless child).

Another predominate feature in these descriptions[691] was the presence of a physical impairment. In Luganda the broader categorial words for persons with disabilities are built on the lexical root 'lema' (e.g. 'mulema', 'omulema', 'balema') which means someone who is lame or has a limb-based impairment. Thus, general terms for persons with a disability are associated with physical disability. Eleven interviewees with disabilities described disability as an injury or impairment without reference to any other qualification. Another 27 included the element of an impairment or injury in their descriptions.

20 of the interviewees with disabilities referred to disability as not 'normal' or to people with disabilities as an out-group from 'normal' people. One described persons with disabilities as 'inhuman'.

Few of the interviewees tended to attribute disability to social causes. One example was a man with a disability who said that the community tells you that you are disabled, then you believe yourself to be disabled, and the environment can also make you disabled. Tellingly, of the four interviewees who attributed disablement to social causes, three were involved with either disability movement organisations or the political representation of persons with disabilities. Thus consciousness of the social model of disability in Mukono District appears to be the relatively exclusive purview of disability rights insiders.

The interviews also explored people's awareness concerning the varieties of disability. Physical disabilities, blindness and deafness were

---

[691] In this section many of the findings are expressed in generalities because the interview outline that sought responses about disability was open ended and did not elicit categorical responses that lend well to clear statistical tabulation. The matrix attached in Appendix IV provides the reader the opportunity to inspect specific interview responses that are generalised in this chapter.

the most commonly named disabilities. Less than half of the interviewees mentioned mental conditions as a type of disability. The limited listing of psychosocial and cognitive forms of disability could be attributable to people's categorising mental disabilities as illness, unsound mind or madness (mulalu in Luganda) as opposed to bodily impairments.

Some interviewees referred to persons with unsound minds as a distinct category of disability which requires different social and legal treatment. One woman amputee indicated that 'people with mental disabilities are treated worst of all'. A man with a physical disability said that 'if someone has a mental disability and cannot be contained families will just let them go'. Some interviewees with disabilities as well as customary knowledge bearers were at a loss as to how persons with mental disabilities can be treated in a way that is not discriminatory. As a polio survivor said, 'no one knows what to do with them'.

Society and Persons with Disabilities

The interviewees with disabilities overwhelmingly characterized the treatment of persons with disabilities as negative. 47 of the depictions were highly negative. One woman stated that persons with disabilities are treated very badly, undermined, abused, called names, stigmatized, not invited to functions, and not given jobs. A man reported that '[w]hen a person with a disability dies they dig a pit, put their body in there, then they urinate on him.' Another man said that '[t]he majority of people do not know that persons with disabilities are human beings' and they 'presume you cannot do'. One man reported that persons with disabilities are 'treated like animals' and 'left to sleep on the street'. Others said that persons with disabilities are treated as if they are not human.

One young woman with polio related how she was thrown into a rubbish pit by her mother when she was a small child. The child's aunt came and took custody of her after the police found her. This event took place in Eastern Uganda.

Eleven of the depictions offered mixed reports. For example one woman noted that although persons with disabilities are presumed to be 'incapable' and are 'not trusted' in terms of work, there are people who show concern for persons with disabilities. Another woman noted that although many people are indifferent to persons with disabilities, her neighbour torments her with witchcraft because of her disability. A man with physical disabilities reported that while persons with disabilities are often treated badly and ignored, there are people who push him on his tricycle and who let him know when meetings are taking place.

Five of the depictions could be characterised as largely positive. One man stated that although 'in the past there was discrimination', 'now persons with disabilities are treated like normal people'. Another man connected with the disabilities movement stated that 'things are improving these days'. He credited the current government for working to improve social conditions. He reported that '[a]t functions the President gives respect and recognition to persons with disabilities' and that '[c]hurches are supportive of marriages involving persons with disabilities.' Notably most of the positive reports were provided by people who are connected with disability rights organizations and local government.

Most customary knowledge bearers affirmed the largely negative impressions of the interviewees with disabilities. They acknowledged that persons with disabilities are disregarded, isolated and segregated. Negative portrayals such as 'they are not treated as human' and 'they are laughed at and ridiculed' outnumbered positive depictions. However, these interviewees reflected a general sense that society's treatment of persons with disabilities is improving and many attributed this improvement to the national government. For example, one customary knowledge bearer indicated that '[a]ttitudes about PWDs have changed . . . because of the current government.' Another stated that now persons with disabilities have a voice and 'it is getting better for them'.

This sense of improvement was shared to some extent by the interviewees with disabilities. Persons with disabilities who reported improving social conditions were more likely to credit NGOs, foreign actors and the national government as opposed to local community members. Interviewees with disabilities residing in semi-urban areas indicated that conditions for persons with disabilities had undergone greater improvement in more urbanised settings. One repeated refrain was that people in rural areas were more likely to tie up persons with disabilities behind their homes like goats.

A large number of interviewees with disabilities indicated that persons with disabilities are despised, undermined and seen as useless. One woman with a disability reported that she was chosen as a treasurer for a women's saving circle but when a healthy woman came along they replaced her saying 'what can you do?' People often presume that persons with disabilities are only fit for certain stereotypically assigned work such as mending shoes.

Interviewees with and without disabilities indicated that there is a traditional belief that persons with disabilities are unfit to farm vegetables or cook food, although that belief appears to be waning. Nonetheless, one woman with a disability stated that people still refuse to eat the food she prepares because of stigma.

One interviewee noted incredulously that

'[w]hatever you do or whatever you own, people say "how did he manage to get that or do that?"' Another interview with a disability stated '[y]ou are treated like a tomato in the market stall— (they act) as if you cannot make it on your own. People see you as useless.'

A woman with albinism said that she overhead someone refer to her and say '[i]f it was me who gave birth to such a kid I would kill it or I would throw it away.' Another interviewee said that society views persons with disabilities 'as people who have been killed by God and just dumped here'.

Beliefs about the inability of persons with disabilities to perform tasks are problematic in the job market. While some persons with disabilities said that they receive better treatment from society when they prove that they can perform tasks, many interviewees complain that they are never given the opportunity to prove themselves in the workplace.

The customary knowledge bearers affirm society's tendency to simply ignore persons with disabilities. Some said that persons with disabilities are simply 'never helped' and are 'treated the same'. Others said that the society 'lets them relax' and people with disabilities are 'just left there'. There was a tendency among knowledge bearers to put the onus on the government to provide care and support rather than members of society.

One recurring concern is the poor treatment of pregnant women with disabilities in hospitals and health clinics. According to several interviewees many hospital staff members do not think that women with disabilities should be getting pregnant and they are often treated with general disdain. Remarkably one of the interviewees with a disability who works in a clinic indicated that he believes women with disabilities should not get pregnant. He unapologetically agreed that such women are treated poorly at the health facility where he works.

Many interviewees with disabilities also mentioned challenges in the context of dating and marriage. Some described society members' views towards persons with disabilities as indifferent or hateful. One woman with a disability reported that 'men think it is a curse and will not want to marry a woman with a disability.' One man with a disability reported that he has a friend who uses a wheelchair who struggled to get married in a customary wedding so he and his wife opted for a church wedding. A woman reported that young women with disabilities are often sexually exploited.

I uncovered little in terms of customs, cultural beliefs and practices that benefit persons with disabilities. 40 of the 63 interviewees with disabilities stated that there is no custom of special care for persons with disabilities in their community. One interviewee said that all persons with disabilities get from society are 'pity'.

Interviewees in both cohorts tended to list individual acts of kindness and decency as opposed to actions deriving from cultural traditions. One woman told the story of how her sewing machine was repaired promptly at a fair price. Others mentioned courteous acts such as assistance getting on taxis. As one interviewee representatively stated, 'some people help (persons with disabilities) but it is not about culture'. Another said '[t]he way people treat persons with disabilities is about the heart and not custom'.

Some interviewees told of supportive acts by past Kabakas. Several related the story of a Kabaka giving land for the benefit of blind people in Mukono District. One man with a disability spoke of Kabaka Daudi Chwa II (1897-1939) who treated persons with disabilities particularly well. Yet there was no indication that Baganda customary law has any aspect or feature that improves the lives of persons with disabilities or accommodates their differences.

Although many interviewees indicated that life in Mukono District is improving for persons with disabilities, when interviewees spoke about initiatives and efforts to bring them special care there was little that could be fairly characterized as indigenous or cultural. Instead interviewees mentioned government initiatives and the work of Non-Governmental Organisations (NGOs) and outside advocacy groups. One interviewee observed that the things were better for persons with disabilities in Arua, a town in Northwest Uganda, because of the higher level of NGO activity.

The major source of care in Mukono District is family. As a customary knowledge bearer stated: 'It is for the family to take care of their own. If you do not take care of your own people then nobody will take care of them.'

Family is pivotal. Parents have the power to devastate the lives of persons with disabilities through discriminatory action and denial of educational opportunities. Interviewees criticised parents in rural areas who tie children with disabilities up and hide them from public view. Another interviewee said that parents do not count their children with a disability as their children. For example, if they have four children and one of them has a disability the parent will say that they only have three children. Nonetheless, interviewees with and without disabilities indicated that treatment at the family level is improving.

Disability and Supernatural Beliefs

Local notions about disability include supernatural beliefs. Several customary knowledge bearers indicated that local gods cause disabilities if people believe in them. Others stated that disabilities can be caused by abusing a disabled person or by failing to fulfill cultural obligations. Another knowledge bearer indicated that eating your totem (e.g. a member of the Buganda sheep clan eating sheep) can cause disability. A princess in the Buganda Kingdom told the story of an evil spirit who caused a local woman who traveled to Great Britain to crawl like an animal upon her return.

There is a widely held Baganda belief in a 'small god' called Wanema that causes physical disability. Wanema is a petty deity who causes people to have disabilities in order to insure that he gets respect. When a family member is affected by disability Wanema becomes a patron spirit of the family. He is appeased by keeping a special enchanted walking stick in the home, by making small sacrifices (e.g. a libation of beer) to him, and by building him a small shrine.

Many of the names given to persons with disabilities in Mukono District demonstrate the centrality of Wanema to conceptions about disability. Commonly used names include 'wanema', 'kawanema' (meaning little Wanema), 'kaddu wanema' (meaning the slave of Wanema), and 'wanema yakwatamwana' (the spirit of Wanema has captured the child). These names reinforce the idea of disability as bondage to or possession by Wanema.

Buganda's Mamba (lungfish) clan is associated with a high prevalence of disabilities. One customary knowledge bearer claimed that this is because Wanema is more active in certain clans. Another knowledge bearer credited the heightened level of impairments in Mamba clam to genetics.

Harmful practices arise out of local supernatural beliefs. An interviewee with albinism recounted how an aunt ripped out her hair because the aunt could sell it to others who believed that the hair had the power to bring wealth. This same interviewee stated that women with albinism face a threat of rape due to a belief that sex with them can cure HIV/AIDS. Customary knowledge bearers reported that people have begun using persons with disabilities in human sacrifices to obtain financial prosperity.

None of the interviewees self-reported as followers of a traditional indigenous religion. All of those interviewed identified themselves as adherents of non-indigenous monotheistic faiths. Many Christian and Muslim interviewees asserted that 'disability comes from God', and multiple Christian interviewees indicated that God has the power to heal physical impairments. One interviewee with a disability said '[m]any people will say that God made you disabled because you are very dangerous.' However, few people asserted that God punishes people by giving them physical impairments or those impairments can be cured or warded off by appeasing God.

There was little to indicate that interviewees that self-identified as Christian or Muslim have rejected the attribution of impairments to Wanema as false or contrary to their faith. Despite one customary knowledge bearer's contention that 'people are not believing in curses as much', traditional beliefs linking disabilities to supernatural causes persist.

Diversity within Disability in Terms of Status, Rights and Treatment

The status, rights and treatment of persons with disabilities is not monolithic. Within Mukono District there are discrepancies and differences based on the type and extent of impairment. As one interviewee with disabilities remarked, '[t]here are many categories of persons with disabilities and their experiences are very different.' For example, the interviewees with hearing-based impairments expressed a deep sense of separation from culture and society.

Both customary knowledge bearers and interviewees with disabilities confirmed the presence of significant challenges for those with severe hearing impairments in Mukono District. As an initial matter, being unable to hear makes it difficult to know the customary law. A deaf interviewee complained that '[d]eaf people are left out from learning the customary laws of the Baganda.' He lamented that '[n]o one shares knowledge with you.' A broad section of the interviewees from all stages in the interview process noted that those who are deaf and unable to speak are often given less rights and social status than other persons with disabilities. Many indicated that those with difficulty hearing and speaking would not be eligible to serve as an heir or a clan leader because of the importance of communication in those roles. The Luganda word most commonly used for someone who is unable to speak is 'kasiru' which roughly translates 'a host of stupid ideas'. The highly negative connotation of this word was pointed out by several interviewees.

Another impairment that results in negative social treatment is epilepsy. Many people in Mukono District see epilepsy as a contagious disorder. There is a traditional local belief that everything touched by a person with epilepsy must be burned to prevent spreading the disease. This can cause considerable hesitation prior to one dating or marrying someone with epilepsy. This also makes transfers of land to persons with epilepsy less likely for fear of contaminating the land.

As noted in Chapter 7, Section II's discussion of marriage and disability, male impotence is a prohibitive impairment when it comes to customary marriage. From a cultural standpoint a relationship between a man and a woman cannot amount to marriage unless a man is able to perform sexually. The inability to produce children can also impact a man's ability to inherit property as families and clans seek to provide land to people who can produce the legacy of children.

Another group of people who are broadly despised are people who move around by sliding and writhing on the ground. A name given for such people is 'magobwe' which means people that belong to a snake god. Several interviewees indicated that what might hold true for most persons with disabilities in terms of fair and equitable treatment would never apply to this category of people.

Persons with mental impairments are also set apart from other persons with disabilities. Interviewees in all three stages of the field research indicated that mental disabilities can be the basis for the denial of various rights under customary law including the right to marry, the right to serve as an heir, the right to inherit property, and the right to be a clan leader.

Disability Theory: Contextual Assessment

Chapter 2 included a treatment of the ongoing theoretical debates in disabilities studies and advocacy.[692] This section offers an applied assessment on the appropriateness and usefulness of various approaches to disability introduced in Chapter 2.

---

[692] This treatment can be found at ch 2, s III.

To a certain extent, the debate over disability theories that originated from the West[693] is alien from the lived environment studied in the fieldwork. In particular, the disparagement of medical and welfare models of disability is difficult to appreciate in a context where programmatic assistance for persons with disabilities is largely nonexistent and access to basic medical services and assistive devices is limited. Yet, despite the contextual divide, the theoretical content from the various approaches to disability finds ample points of relevance and application in the fieldwork.

The Medical and Welfare Model

Basic needs for persons with disabilities go unmet in Mukono District. People need functioning wheelchairs and they are happy to receive them. Medical care and assistive services are not taken for granted. Fortunately, the human rights model embodied by the CRPD includes rights that cover these vital social and economic needs.[694]

While an over emphasis on individual pathology may cut against the development of nuanced and holistic appreciation of disability-based discrimination[695], any present discounting of unmet medical needs and the physical challenges flowing from impairments is problematic. Tellingly at no point during the research did any person with disabilities complain about being treated as someone who needs medical care or government assistance. On the contrary, interviewees with disabilities commonly spoke with frustration about a broken government system that prevents them from receiving the provision of health care or assistive devices.

---

[693] Ibid.

[694] CPRD arts 25 and 26.

[695] C Nwenga 'Deconstructing the definition of "disability" under the Employment Equity Act; Part II (legal deconstruction)' (2007) 23 South African J on Human Rights 116.

The Social Model of Disability

The fieldwork speaks to the insight and value of the social model of disability. The fieldwork demonstrates the importance of the 'lived community' which is at the centre of the social model. People and their attitudes, beliefs and actions are highly consequential to the lives of persons with disabilities. The fieldwork demonstrates how beliefs about the functionality of persons with disabilities impact the outcome of customary legal scenarios.

There is a tendency to view persons with disabilities as targets of exploitation. Family members and others are known to grab the land of persons with disabilities based on the belief that such persons are vulnerable targets that cannot stand up for their rights. Similar beliefs underlie risks to sexual exploitation faced by women with disabilities. The absence of effective and accessible legal redress within formal law and the longstanding disempowerment of formal customary legal systems leave individuals to fend for themselves. Thus it is not the existence of a system or superstructure that results in the oppression and exploitation of persons with disabilities. Instead the opportunities for impunity provided by weak state and weakened formal institutions appear to be the pressing challenge facing persons with disabilities.

In addition, while some view persons with disabilities as vulnerable people to exploit, others view them as burdens. Thus there is a prevalent social dynamic to just leave persons with disabilities as they are and force them to fend for themselves. They are not seen as people worth investing resources in and thus they are prevented from accessing land and wealth through customary channels.

The field work brings out the legitimacy of two of Priestly's three variants of the social model referenced in Section III(2) of Chapter 2.[696] It reflects the 'individualist model' of disability because the field re-

---

[696] For a concise overview of Priestly's typologies see M du Plessis *Access to work for disabled persons in South Africa: A rights critique* (2017) Ch 2.6.

search demonstrates the way particular personal experiences and negotiated social roles can produce disability. Moreover, the findings stress the importance of cultural perceptions and interpretations. In Mukono District the shared social value in human usefulness and perceptions about the limited usefulness of persons with disabilities impact the rights, status and treatment of people with impairments. Thus Priestly's communal belief typology of social disability has credence in this context. In this sense, Priestly's 'idealist' typology of the social model shares ground with the 'ableist' model that is plainly validated by the research.[697]

The research also affirms the current view of Oliver, Priestly and others that the social model should not be applied exclusively.[698]. The clear need for medical services and interventions for persons with disabilities in Mukono District warns against viewing the medical model as a irreconcilable enemy of the social model..

Yet the expectation and hope of government assistance presents certain challenges for persons with disabilities. The fieldwork identified a belief that it was the government's responsibility to assist persons with disabilities. Dependence on the government support is contrary to goals of autonomy, independence and community integration espoused by the CRPD.[699] Moreover, this belief has the potential of diminishing collective and individual responsibility for the positive and negative impacts community members are causing, enabling or allowing in the lives of persons with disabilities. The potentially debilitative social impact on expectations of government welfare is well considered phenomena.[700]

---

[697] The 'ableist' model is discussed at ch 2, s III(6).

[698] See for example M Oliver 'Defining impairment and disability: issues at stake' in C Barnes & G Mercer (Eds) Exploring the Divide (1996) 29-54.

[699] CRPD arts 3(1) and 19.

[700]L Mead Beyond Entitlement: The Social Obligations of Citizenship (1986); J Habermas The Structural Transformation of the Public Sphere: An inquiry into the Category of Bourgeois Society (1991)

Any reduction in communal responsibility for the care and assistance of persons with disabilities is troublesome in a context where the government has limited resources and where society members wield considerable power and influence.

Ableist Models of Disability

The above discussion of Priestly's 'idealist' typology leads us to the merits of ableist models of disability. These models stress the need to enhance and emphasise the capabilities of persons with disabilities. Society's beliefs about the abilities and capacities of persons with disabilities are at the center of the status, rights and treatment of persons with disabilities. Thus the wisdom of disabilities theories that stress awareness of the ability and potential of persons with disabilities are affirmed.

As discussed in Chapter 2, Uganda's Persons with Disabilities Act (PDA) adopts the Americans with Disabilities Act (ADA) approach to disability.[701] This approach considers people to have a disability when they are not able to perform essential life tasks despite the use of assistive devices. Officially correlating disability with inability is problematic in light of the research findings because the cultural and familiar rights and responsibilities allocated to persons with disabilities are highly dependent on people's perceptions about their abilities. Although there is little indication that people in Mukono District are attuned to the nuance entailed in the definition of disability under the PDA, the fieldwork findings validate those who seek to ensure that the abilities of persons with disabilities are emphasised at all levels.

Although the fieldwork points to the importance of seeing people with disabilities as capable, there is little indication that possibility or provision of medical treatment is causing an objectification of persons with disabilities. Instead the potential of care and assistive devices to

---

[701] This discussion appears at ch 2, s III(2).

increase the functioning of persons with disabilities presents a means for better social treatment. Interviewees noted the potential of medical advancements and technology to enable persons with disabilities to perform tasks and contribute to their communities. Thus the functional repercussions of the medical model are arguably aligned with the ablest models as well as Priestly's 'idealist' typology.

The Minority Group Model of Disability

The fieldwork paints a challenging picture for those who endorse and promote the minority group model of disability empowerment. Persons with disabilities are aware of their diversity of impairments and concerns. Disability is a difficult aspect of human identity and experience to unite under for the purposes of identity politics.

The needs of persons with disabilities vary based on their disabilities. For example, access ramps are important for persons with physical disabilities and braille signage is important to those with vision impairments. Notably most of the references that customary knowledge bearers made about government assistance concerned the provision of wheelchairs and access and egress to buildings.

There are also challenges of communication amongst persons with disabilities. Those who are unable to hear or speak are hard pressed to communicate with persons who are unable to see without translators or technology. Thus groups of people that could be connected in community are socially separated by the impact of their impairments.

Persons with limb-based physical disabilities are the politically dominant cohort in Mukono District. Most political offices allocated to persons with disabilities are held by persons with such disabilities. This is a source of discontent for persons with other impairments.

However, the findings also point to benefits in disability solidarity. Persons with disabilities are key actors in combatting discrimination in customary contexts. The actor-oriented and participatory changes strategies outlined in Chapter 3 are dependent on joint effort and collaboration for general effectiveness and broader and social impact.[702] Yet often times they are unaware of their rights or unwilling to stand up for their rights. Thus a strong and supportive community of persons with disabilities could help to equip and encourage them to champion their own customary causes. Applied implications of the research on this point are discussed in Chapter 8.[703]

The Human Rights Approach to Disability

The human rights approach to disability has latent potential in Mukono District. The customary knowledge bearers did not present as opposed to the concept of human rights. Moreover the idea that persons with disabilities are entitled to human rights appears to have moral currency.

The key challenges for the human rights approach are increasing awareness and accountability. The layers and complexity of disability rights can make them difficult to share and infuse within a culture. The research indicates that aphorisms which package the essence of human rights concepts (e.g. 'disability is not inability') might offer an effective means for integrating of disability rights principles at the grassroots. Thus as discussed in Section IV of Chapter 8, the emphasis of raising awareness in the CRPD in apropos in this context.

In terms of accountability, the fieldwork points to the importance of the self-championing of rights. As seen in Section III(1) of Chapter 4, Ugandan formal law has the substantive content to override discriminatory acts in customary settings if the victims of discrimination are empowered to challenge such acts with formal correction. Thus it is critical that persons with disabilities are aware of their human rights and are

---

[702] The actor oriented and participatory change strategies are introduced at ch 4, s III(1)(d).

[703] See ch 8, s III(2)(d) for this analysis.

knowledgeable about formal means of challenging illegal discrimination.

The Folly of Ideological Purity

The fieldwork speaks to the folly of ideological purity and rivalry in the context of disability theory. Theoretically generous and non-exclusive approaches to disability are required to address the challenges facing persons with disabilities. Various theoretical approaches to disability offer valuable perspectives. A forced choice of one theoretical approach at the expense of others is unwarranted and unnecessary. As discussed in Chapter 8, the wisdom of the inclusive theoretical approach of the CRPD is borne out in the research.

Conclusion

The fieldwork offers a telling window into the social lives of persons with disabilities in Mukono District. Aspects of the findings can be discouraging. The social attitudes about persons with disabilities in Mukono District are prevailingly negative. Moreover, the fieldwork uncovered little in terms of positive cultural practices or actions that benefit persons with disabilities. Instead there is a growing sense that help should come from the government.

For those hoping gender grassroots change, the research points to the need for people to appreciate the abilities and capacities of persons with disabilities. This appears to be the social fulcrum on which the rights, status and treatment of persons with disabilities hinge. Uganda is a not a surplus culture. Life is challenging and poverty is rampant. Many people are not in the position to bear the loads of others. However, people will treat persons with disabilities more equitably in terms of customary matters, social relations and employment if people consider persons with disabilities to be capable of functioning well in society.

The next chapter presents findings concerning the rights, status and treatment of persons with disabilities in particular categories of customary law. It demonstrates how beliefs and attitudes about persons with disabilities impact customary legal scenarios in the context of marriage, guardianship, customary leadership and succession.

7

FIELDWORK FINDINGS CONCERNING SELECTED SUBSTANTIVE AREAS OF CUSTOMARY LAW AND PRACTICE RELEVANT TO THE RIGHTS, STATUS AND TREATMENT OF PERSONS WITH DISABILITIES IN MUKONO DISTRICT

Introduction

This chapter presents findings concerning the rights, status and treatment of persons with disabilities in various zones of customary law and practice. Topical areas addressed in this chapter include marriage and divorce, clan leadership, customary guardianship, succession and land rights.

The research findings demonstrate the significance of customary legal frameworks to persons with disabilities. Customary legal scenarios generate effectual outcomes in matters of marriage, inheritance, land ownership and caregiving. People's beliefs about disability are influential in these scenarios.

The findings in this chapter inform the integrative legal descriptions and applied analysis in Chapter 8 as well as the suggestions and conclusions in Chapter 9.

Marriage and Divorce

Customary law remains highly relevant to the institution of marriage in Mukono District. The fieldwork covered various aspects of domestic customary practices including eligibility to marry, the requirement of bride wealth, ceremonial rites, grounds for terminating a marriage and the process of separation. Over all, the fieldwork offers an encouraging account of the status, rights and treatment of persons with disabilities within these customary practices.

There was little indication of any widely applied customary bars to marriage for persons with disabilities. All of the research participants agreed that most persons with disabilities have the right to marry under customary law. A female customary knowledge bearer recounted how she recently saw a man with no limbs get married. She saw the marriage party 'carry him off on their shoulders'. A male customary knowledge bearer noted that some men with disabilities 'can even get more than one wife'.

The right of most persons with a disability to marry under customary law appears to be longstanding. Only one of the 63 interviewees with disabilities, a Batoro woman, stated that the right of a person with a disability to marry is a new development in customary law. Similarly only one of the 23 customary knowledge bearers indicated this 'has changed just now'. The balance indicated that this right has existed since time immemorial.

Although most impairments are not a bar to customary marriage, there is one physical impairment that clearly prevents marriage — male impotence.[704] Sexual intercourse is an essential component of customary marriage and a male's inability to perform sexually means that there is no marriage.[705] Interviewees spoke about this issue as a well known and accepted fact. There were male and female interviewees from the first

---

[704] ES Haydon Law and Justice in Buganda (1960) at 98. (Making a note of this fact in an earlier ethnographic study).

[705] The female parallel to impotency is what Haydon refers to as 'being like a stone' or sexual frigidity. Ibid at 109. According to Haydon this character trait was grounds for return of marriage consideration. The issue of female sexual frigidity never came up in the interviews.

and second stages of the field interviews who expressed amusement and laughter at the idea of marriage with an impotent husband.

On the other hand, infertility is not a disqualifying state and is not grounds for divorce. Interviewees described infertility as a joint problem of both the husband and wife. In addition, the ability to marry multiple wives under customary law provides husbands with other options for procreation in case one wife is infertile. The fact that up until now people have been largely unable to access scientific test results concerning the attribution of infertility may help to maintain a role in the cultural view of infertility as a joint problem.

Both interviewees with disabilities and customary knowledge bearers indicated that a certain threshold level of mental soundness is required in order to marry. One customary knowledge bearer said that the 'retarded can marry' but those with 'unsound mind' cannot. One interviewee with disabilities submitted that people who do not know what they are doing are prevented from entering into marriage or participating in sexual relations. It is difficult to know if this understanding reflects customary knowledge or if it springs from the memory of prior statutory prohibitions against sexual relations with people with mental and cognitive disabilities. The pervasive use of the British legal term 'unsound mind' by interviewees' points to a possible legal sourcing from Uganda's colonial past.

Certain impairments and conditions may prevent marriage based on scandal or taboo. Interviewees from both cohorts indicated that people who move about by sliding on the ground cannot get married. A customary knowledge bearer stated that some 'with grievous disabilities cannot marry' because 'God stops them' and because 'a woman cannot respect such a man'. Thus the limitation here appears to be more about the choice of marital partners than any legal prohibition under customary law. Other interviewees mentioned taboos against sexual relations and marriage with persons with leprosy and epilepsy.

These taboos appear to spring from the notion or understanding that epilepsy and leprosy are highly contagious. There is a local belief that everything touched by a person who has epilepsy should be burned in order to prevent the spread of the disease. Meanwhile one interviewee said that epilepsy has a special stigma because those with epilepsy are likely to fall into the fire and thus bring shame on the family or clan. Of course leprosy is infamously, even Biblically[706], contagious.

Some interviewees emphatically asserted that there are not any cultural taboos against sexual relations with and among persons with disabilities. They indicated that the customary limitations worth noting in this context are bars to sexual relations between people of the same clan or family. The primary impediments to marriage facing persons with disabilities and marriage are social and not legal. One man with a disability related that 'women do not want to date you', and one woman with a disability observed '[m]en think it is a curse and will not want to marry a woman with a disability.'

A customary knowledge bearer stated that '[p]eople tell persons with disabilities not to marry each other so they do not produce children with disabilities.' This particular social prohibition appears rooted in concerns over inherited genetic traits as opposed to cultural beliefs.

Interviewees in both cohorts and of both sexes noted that it is more difficult for women with disabilities to get married than men. There is a cultural belief that women must be physically able to perform household chores while men must merely be able to provide financially. Therefore men with disabilities who have financial means are seen as legitimate marriage partners. Meanwhile women who are not able to prove their physical capacity for housework can be viewed as unsuitable for marriage.

One aspect of Baganda custom that can present challenges to persons with disabilities is the okwanjula. This marriage introduction ceremony

---

[706] Leviticus 13:44-46.

places those seeking marriage in the middle of a public and potentially embarrassing cultural spectacle. A customary knowledge bearer stated '[t]hey don't usually do kwanjulas. They usually just cohabit because of their own shame.' An interviewee with a disability related how he had a wheelchair-using friend who 'struggled to get married in a customary wedding—so they opted for a church wedding instead'.

The customary practice of bride wealth also presents potential for discriminatory treatment. I sought to determine whether the requirement of bride wealth is used to make it more difficult for men with disabilities to marry. The results were mixed.

More interviewees with disabilities asserted that men with disabilities are likely to be charged a higher bride price than those who said that it would be the same or less. In stark contrast only 1 of the 23 customary knowledge bearers indicated that a male suitor with a disability would be charged a higher bride price.

Two Baganda men with disabilities claimed that they were charged a higher bride price because of their disability. One said that he was asked for two cows and two goats as opposed to the normal asking price of one cow and one goat. Another man with a disability told the story of a young man with a limb-based impairment who was required to provide a much higher bride price because of his disability. Due to the high cost of the bride price, it took the young man a long time to pay so the intended bride was given to another man. The father of the bride ultimately kept the money that the young man had paid.

Six other customary knowledge bearers indicated that suitors with disabilities would only be required to bring what they can or what they may desire to bring. Representative comments include '[t]hese days it depends on what someone has to offer—you bring what you can' and '[t]oday people just decide in their heart based on what they can afford.' Arguably this situational approach could actually help a male with a disability with limited financial prospects. One man with a disability related that his father-in-law simply asked him to 'bring what he could'. Regardless of whether higher bride prices are more or less common, the practice of bride wealth results in a customary scenario where both discrimination and accommodation can occur.

The interviews failed to offer clarity with respect to any specific procedure for officially terminating a customary marriage. A few participants asserted the need for formal action. One high-ranking cultural leader in the Buganda Kingdom indicated that a divorce can only be obtained through the courts and two other customary knowledge bearers noted the need to go to a local government official. However, most of the interviewees described less formal mechanisms for divorce. As one customary knowledge bearer said '[t]hey just agree; they do not decree.' Many interviewees in both cohorts described forms of family mediation where the spouses would present their situation to in-laws to see if divorce is necessary. As one knowledge bearer related, divorce proceedings are 'more about families coming together'. Others said that divorce is accomplished by merely leaving. One knowledge bearer said, '[t]hey just go; they just pack their things and go—either man or woman.' Another reported '[t]he man or the woman will just say "I am fed up with you" and they will separate'.

Some customary knowledge bearers claim that divorces can be imposed by the clan leaders. Grounds for imposed divorces include 'night-dancing' (a form of witchcraft where someone dances in the nude outside people's homes), theft, and incest (which include the prohibition of sexual relations between Baganda clan members). Disability was never identified as a basis for forced divorce.

The core reasons mentioned by the interviewees for terminating a marriage are the absence of love, dislike and conflict. Although one of the interviewees with a disability reported that he was left by his wife when he became disabled, the disability of a spouse is not considered a legitimate reason for terminating a marriage. The notable exception is male impotence which some customary knowledge bearers said was a ground for divorce even if the onset of impotence takes place after consummation of marriage. As one stated '[i]f a man becomes weak and cannot sexually satisfy, a woman can easily walk away.'

I also explored the issue of husbands leaving wives who give birth to a child with a disability. It is not uncommon for men to presume that their own bloodlines cannot produce a child with a disability. Thus some men leave their wives that give birth to a child with a disability because they believe it is not their child. Apparently it is also possible for a husband to be left by a wife based on the birth of a disabled child. One of the men with disabilities reported that his wife left him when they had a child with a disability.

Traditionally, according to Haydon, the major customary legal concern in divorce among the Baganda is whether the husband is able to recoup the bride wealth.[707] The circumstance where bride wealth is returned was not covered with particularity in the interviews. However, at no point did any interviewee indicate that a wife's disability warranted the return of bride wealth to the divorcing husband.

When a marriage ends there is a traditional belief among the Baganda that the children belong to the man or the man's family. This applies in the context of divorce and the death of a spouse. The fieldwork did not generate insights this practice of gender-based discrimination in Mukono District.

In sum, substantive customary law pertaining to marriage and divorce are not overly problematic for persons with disabilities in Mukono District. Challenges in the context of marriage and dating are primarily social. Moreover, with the exception of impotence, traditional grounds for the termination of marital relations are not connected to disability status of a spouse or to the birth of a disabled child. What is most problematic is the opportunity for social pressure associated with the

---

[707] Haydon (note 1) at 108-109.

okwanjula ceremony and the potential for fathers to use bride wealth to discriminate against male suitors with disabilities. Yet both of these customary practices also present opportunities for community members to demonstrate acceptance, affirmation and accommodation of persons with disabilities.

Clan Leadership

The clan leader appointment process is an instructive example of how disability factors into customary practices. There is diversity when it comes to the ways impairments factor into leader selection. Also, discriminatory decisions are often attributable to beliefs about the capability and usefulness of persons with disabilities. There is discrimination, but the extent and application of discrimination varies based on the customary decision makers.

Clan leaders are normally appointed at a clan meeting based on majority vote or the consensus of clan elders. The appointment process often takes place at an event connected with the burial rights of the previous clan leader.

A key factor in the appointment of a Baganda clan leader is lineage. In most cases the appointed clan leader is the first born son of the outgoing clan leader. In addition, clan leaders can be designated in advance by the outgoing clan leader. Express wishes for one's replacement are typically followed whether they are spoken or set forth in a written will. Clan leaders also must be men.

There are other factors at work when it comes to the appointment of a clan leader besides lineage, designation and sex. These factors can cause the clan elders to select someone other than the deceased clan leader's designee or his first born son. Clan elders consider various pertinent qualities of candidates for clan leadership. Key qualities include knowledge of cultural practices, past involvement in clan matters, good behaviour, personal integrity, responsibility and economic success.

It is also important that the clan leader be mature in years although one male knowledge bearer indicated that the clan leader can be as young as eighteen years of age.

Most of field interviewees indicated that disability is not a strict bar to appointment as clan leader. However, there was a discrepancy between the perspectives offered by interviewees with disabilities and the customary knowledge bearers.

The customary knowledge bearers did not view disability as a major impediment to designation as a clan leader. Only two of these interviewees said that it would be impossible for persons with a disability to be a clan leader. Another conceded that clans 'will probably select someone who is fine'—meaning not impaired.

Meanwhile, the interviewees with disabilities were less sanguine about the possibility of a person with disabilities being designated as a clan leader. 12 of the interviewees indicated that it was possible. Two of those qualified their response by noting that it would only be possible if the prior clan leader designated a person with a disability as his replacement in his will. Five of these interviewees said that it was not possible and four others indicated that they had never seen it done. Notably, all nine individuals with disabilities who provided highly negative perspectives self-identify as Baganda.

Certain impairments are deemed to be major impediments to the possibility of designation as clan leader. Intelligence and mental capacity is a key quality for clan leadership. Disabilities that negatively impact this quality can disqualify someone from clan leadership. Interviewees in both cohorts indicated that a clan leader cannot be someone with a mental disability or 'unsound mind'.

The ability to communicate and interact with others is considered a key ability for clan leaders. Thus the inability to hear or speak is widely considered a disqualifying impairment.

Five interviewees stated that someone who is blind cannot be a clan leader. Some of the interviewees were worried that a blind man would have difficulty monitoring clan matters, and could be taken advantage of by dishonest people. Others asserted that a blind person can be a clan leader and one interviewee with blindness presently serves as a clan leader. This leader and his clan mates are members of the Japadohla people group from Eastern Uganda and not Baganda.

Others named epilepsy and the tendency to writhe on the ground as forms of impairment that could disqualify someone from being a clan leader. As noted earlier in Chapter 6, there are stigmas associated with those conditions that make them culturally disfavoured.[708]

Thus the clan leadership selection process is a customary scenario where discrimination against persons with disabilities can occur. This discrimination often springs from pragmatic concerns and varies based on the appointing leaders and the impairments at issue.

Customary Guardianship

Customary guardianship is common in Mukono District and one's status as a person with a disability can negatively impact one's chances to become a guardian.

Customary guardianship entails the allocation of child rearing responsibilities to non-parents outside of the provisions and procedures set forth in the formal law. As noted in Chapter 5, customary guardianship is widely practiced in Mukono District. The fieldwork demonstrates that disability status can play a major role in guardianship decisions and eligibility.

Customary guardians are primarily designated through a will or some other pre-death instruction. Final instructions will typically be

---

[708] Ch 6, Secs II and III.

honoured although some interviewees indicated that such an appointment can be overridden by a clan leader.

When there has been no such designation, the clan leaders will typically give the children of the deceased the opportunity to decide who their guardian will be. According to Baganda tradition this decision is typically delegated to the female children of the deceased who are considered to be attuned to matters of caregiving.

Interviewees with disabilities who said that a person with disabilities can be a guardian outnumbered naysayers by a ratio of roughly five to one. These interviewees indicated that the potential for designation as a guardian would depend largely on the family or the clan. Financial capacity and past life performances are important considerations in such decisions. A guardian should be responsible, financially stable and sociable. Thus someone's impairment can cause them to be perceived as unable or unfit to serve as a customary guardian. Due to the requirement of sociability, some interviewees indicated that persons who are unable to hear or speak cannot be guardians.

The balance of interviewees indicated that the motivations behind decisions to assume customary guardianships are largely commendable. Most customary guardians faithfully serve in the interest of the wards placed in their care. Interviewees emphasised that guardians should not receive a financial benefit for their service. Instead guardians should provide their care and services out of an obligation flowing from their friendship with the deceased caregiver.

That is not to say that no benefits flow from service as a customary guardian. Interviewees from both cohorts indicated that guardianship increases social status. One customary knowledge bearer acknowledged that there are other potential benefits. She noted that '[u]sually the children will study and then become prosperous and benefit the guardian, and the children can also provide labor.' However, few interviewees joined in reporting similar sentiments. Although it is possible that the children a guardian raises will benefit guardian at a later time out of appreciation, the consensus position is that serving as a guardian is not a path to wealth.

This research confirms that there are customary guardians with disabilities in Mukono District. Six of the interviewees with disabilities indicated that they are or have been customary guardians. Of the six, three self-identify as Baganda.

Customary guardianship practices can be used to discriminate against parents with disabilities. A Baganda female polio survivor reported that when her husband died the husband's relatives took her marital land and she had to struggle to keep her children from her brother-in-law. To retain custody of her children she had to prove that she was able to function and provide for her children economically. One customary knowledge bearer contended that it is 'impossible' for persons with disabilities to be a guardian because 'they cannot dig'.

I also explored the issue of guardianship for adult wards under customary law and practices. It investigated whether or not adults with disabilities are placed in customary guardianships. It sought to determine how autonomy and legal personality are addressed in such contexts.

Many interviewees had difficulty understanding questions about adult guardianships. Roughly half of the interviewees with disabilities failed to offer any meaningful response to such questions.

28 of the 31 interviewees with disabilities who were able to appreciate the concept of adult guardianships indicated that such an arrangement is possible. Some interviewees qualified their answer by indicating that such guardianships only take place where people are 'very kind' or in close families. Others indicated that these arrangements only occur with elderly family members or with people who cannot help themselves such as 'those who cannot speak' or 'those in wheelchairs'. Only three interviewees with disabilities flatly asserted that customary guardian-

ships for adults do not exist. On the whole it appears that these arrangements are possible, but that they are very situational and are not thought of as established customary legal occurrences like guardianships for children.

The interviewees with disabilities told two stories of adult guardianships. In one story an adult female polio survivor was placed under the guardianship of a cousin without court action. In the other story a family placed a deceased father's adult son with cerebral palsy under the care of an uncle.

Family is viewed as the primary care giver and support system for persons with disabilities. Several comparisons were made with the practice of caring for an adult with a disability and the care typically provided to an older parent or grandparent. Some interviewees indicated that such care arrangements are becoming less common as family structures and support systems weaken.

When family members are unable to meet the needs of a disabled adult some clans take the initiative to place persons with disabilities into caregiving relationships that resemble guardianships. As one interviewee said of clans, 'they can sort out any problem'.

Concerning the issue of legal personality and autonomy, most interviewees addressing this issue indicated that a person with a disability who is placed in a guardianship will be consulted or in some cases will be left to make decisions. However, the responses addressing legal personality and autonomy were too scant and hypothetical to warrant a research finding.

Finally, the forced taking of children from disabled widows into customary guardianships is a troubling legacy of local custom. As mentioned in the section on Marriage and Divorce, children among the Baganda are seen as belonging to the male line. Thus when fathers die it is not uncommon for brothers of the deceased man to come seeking to take custody of the children. This practice presents problems regardless of the disability status of women. It could be useful to undertake research to determine if widows with disabilities are more susceptible of being stripped of the custody of their children. This research made no findings regarding that issue.

Succession

As discussed in Chapter 5 at Section III, succession remains a highly consequential customary practice in Uganda despite its formal displacement by statutory law. The fieldwork demonstrates that customary succession poses considerable challenges to persons with disabilities because it is a legal occurrence where significant disability based discrimination takes place.

Land Inheritance

Although any property can be inherited, chattels are of marginal consequence in Mukono District. When people speak about inheritance and succession they inevitably speak about land. Thus, this section on succession largely concerns the inheritance of land.

The treatment of persons with disabilities in customary land inheritance is not uniform. It varies based on the families and clans involved in a particular scenario. 23 of the 63 persons with disabilities interviewed stated unequivocally that a person with disabilities can inherit land. 12 of the 63 stated that persons with disabilities could not inherit land and three indicated that they had never seen a person with a disability inherit land. Another 12 reported that land inheritance depends on the families or clans involved. Five of the interviewees indicated that it was possible to inherit land but that persons with disabilities will receive less. Six indicated that it was possible for a person with disabilities to inherit land but that it was very rare or difficult to do so. Another interviewee indicated that it was only possible to inherit land if the person with a disability is an only child. The balance of interviewees with disabilities either indicated that they did not know or offered no definitive response.

Personal stories of land inheritance based on actual experiences were diverse. Five persons with disabilities indicated that they were able to inherit land without any discrimination while five others indicated that they not permitted to inherit land. Three of these five report that their disability was the reason they were not permitted to inherit, while the other two described instances of property grabbing by those in the deceased male's line that were not expressly linked to their disability status. Three others stated that they were permitted to inherit some land, but they were given smaller plots because of their disability or were given land to share with others.

One Baganda man told how he was only given a small plot from his father's estate because he was unable to walk and was not considered able to develop the land. His other brothers who did not have disabilities were given larger plots. The man sold his small plot and bought land somewhere else. He thought about challenging the distribution through the formal courts, but he ultimately decided to let the matter go and live elsewhere because his siblings were treating him badly. Another man told a similar story of how he sold his small family plot he inherited due mostly to the social pressure of family members.

A Baganda female polio survivor stated that when her father died all of her brothers and sisters received a portion of her father's unregistered kibanja holding but she received nothing. When she tried to speak for herself she was treated as if she was not a person.

Decisions not to allow a person with disabilities to inherit land can spring from concerns about maintaining the long term ownership of family land. One Baganda man with a physical disability related the story of how he was denied inheritance of his father's land in Masaka.[709]

---

[709] Masaka is a town located on the west side of Kampala in an area of Uganda that is historically a part of the Buganda Kingdom.

At the family meeting to determine the allocation of his father's property a cousin asserted that this man should not inherit arguing '[w]hat could he do with the land?' and saying '[h]e will just sell it and eat the money.' The man said that this argument was instrumental in his family's decision to give the land to an uncle. In this instance, beliefs about the inability of a person with disabilities precipitated customary discrimination.

One unique story demonstrates how established customary practice can help to rebuff pragmatic discrimination against a person with a disability. A Baganda man with a physical disability was his father's only son. His father left a will that gave his son with disability his land as long as that son had not produced a son of his own. If the disabled man had produced a son the will directed that the land would go to the disabled man's son, the testator's grandson. When the testator died in 1974 the clan met to determine who would inherit the land. Those who were knowledgeable about cultural matters claimed that the land should go to the man with a disability because he was the male heir. Others felt that the land should go to his aunt because it would be useless to let a man inherit property if that man cannot produce a child. This position was not based on the customary law, instead it was based on 'what makes sense'. Ultimately the clan chiefs were consulted and they decided that the land should go to the disabled man. Thus the established customary law prevailed over a pragmatic application of the customary principle that inheritance should go to those capable of producing children.

These inheritance stories are representative of the place of disability within Baganda customary law. The legal implications of disability within custom are not categorical. Instead disability is considered situationally in relation with other customary principles, such as the importance of keeping land within a male family line. The legal results often hinge on submissions made at family meetings appealing to pragmatic concerns and customary knowledge.

Most of the customary knowledge bearers indicated that persons with disabilities are able to inherit land under the traditional laws of the Baganda. Approximately half of these knowledge bearers gave no caveats to their affirmative responses. The other half said it could depend on whether their parents choose to give them the land or if the potential beneficiary has an impairment that would make the person unable to receive the land such as epilepsy and mental illness. Only four of the customary knowledge bearers indicated that persons with disabilities cannot inherit land and three of these respondents said this prohibition can be overcome if the land is expressly bequeathed to them in a will.

The diversity of statements provided by customary knowledge bearers concerning land inheritance speaks to unsettled and inconsistent practices and outcomes. One man flatly contends '[i]f there is no will a person with a disability cannot inherit land' while another contends '[p]eople give the property to the children regardless of disability and if they do not the child has the right to report to higher authorities.' One knowledge bearer asserts that 'there was more diversity in times past' but 'now [discrimination against persons with disabilities in the context of land succession] does not usually happen', while another contends that if a person with a disability has not been named as a beneficiary in a will 'they will not let him be a successor of land because they treat him as senseless'.

Interviewees with disabilities indicated that there are community members who consider giving land to persons with disabilities poor stewardship. One interviewee with a disability said '[g]enerally people think you cannot make use of the land so that giving it to your disabled family member would be a waste of resources'. Another stated '[p]eople will say "how can this person manage land?"' Interviewees in both cohorts repeatedly described a customary practice in Mukono District whereby persons with disabilities are only given enough land for a small residence because of a traditional belief they cannot cultivate land or that the food that they grow would be contaminated. Interviewees with disabilities indicated that traditional beliefs about the tendency of farmers with disabilities to contaminate their produce were once quite pervasive but are beginning to wane.

Along with the utilitarian concerns discussed above, there is also a cultural ethos of paternalism that impacts the substance and application of customary approaches to land inheritance. A customary knowledge bearer observed that '[u]sually when someone dies they divide the land among all the children and the other children are supposed to look after the one with disabilities.' Another knowledge bearer stated '[i]n some cases enlightened families can hold and manage land on their behalf, meanwhile families that are not enlightened can try to take away their land.' A man with a disability claimed that wherever he has lived people have always refused to allow persons with disabilities to inherit and will leave it to the other siblings to 'take care of' the sibling with a disability. A female polio survivor told how she was not given land though inheritance and was told to go and live with her sister.

A customary knowledge bearer noted that 'all [types of disabilities] can keep you from getting land. It depends on the degree of disability and the type.' One customary knowledge bearer observed that '[p]eople with mental disabilities and the deaf and dumb cannot inherit', while another said that '[s]ome people who are just sliding on the ground would not be allowed to inherit the property of the deceased.' Another customary knowledge bearer indicated that people with epilepsy are not permitted to inherit land because they would contaminate it.

Several customary knowledge bearers identified those unable to hear or speak as ineligible to inherit land. A few said that blind people cannot inherit land as well. According to comments made during the interviews, this limitation on land inheritance to the blind is linked to a concern that blind people cannot manage land and are unable to prevent others from taking advantage of the land they are given. There is a similar sense that persons with hearing impairments might require the assistance of a family member to ensure their impairments are not exploited. In such cases a family member might be assigned to manage their land. This is indicative of the heightened paternalism and reduced autonomy resulting from beliefs about vulnerability.

Indigenous culture and custom are not viewed as progressive forces in the context of succession. Although one interviewee with disabilities indicated that the culture actually gives persons with disabilities the right to inherit, this statement was an outlier. Other interviewees indicated that the traditional culture has generally opposed the inheritance of land by persons with disabilities. A customary knowledge bearer referring to the possibility of such land inheritance stated '[i]t has started just now'. This cultural opposition appears to spring from as sense that persons with disabilities are sources of shame and incapable of performing tasks. Interviewees in both cohorts related that the formal law recognises the right of persons with disabilities to inherit and those persons with disabilities who are aware of their formal legal rights and willing to enforce those rights are most likely to inherit land. Thus the formal law can serve as a check against the discriminatory tendencies in customary succession.

Persons with disabilities told of instances where non-customary influences enabled them to inherit equal shares of land. A man belonging to the Samia people group indigenous to Southeastern Uganda stated that although Samia men traditionally give most of their land to a single grandson, his father's estate was distributed according to the formal law of succession. He credited knowledge of the formal law as instrumental in this result. Similarly, a Baganda polio survivor from a Muslim family credited the involvement of Islamic clerics subject to local council oversight for his inheritance of an equal share of his father's land.

Wills

There was general uniformity amongst both cohorts concerning the capacity of persons with disabilities to make wills. One knowledge bearer asserted that '[i]f there is a will they will always follow it.' Many qualified this contention by noting that only persons with disabilities who are of 'sound mind' can make wills. For example, 14 of the 23 customary knowledge bearers indicated that a person with an 'unsound mind' or 'mental problems' cannot make a will. There is general consensus that the right of a person with a disability to make a will is a longstanding right. This is consistent with the mid 20th Century findings of Haydon who indicated that written wills have been a part of Buganda law since the early days of the British Protectorate[710] and that the practice of written wills is predated by oral wills.[711]

Some interviewees with disabilities indicated that people who cannot hear or speak are not permitted to make written wills. This belief appears rooted in the presumption that such people are illiterate and that wills must be in writing. One interviewee with a disability indicated that those who are deaf can make a will as long as they can sign their name to prove they are literate. There were customary knowledge bearers who submitted that those unable to hear and speak can make wills as long as they are able to communicate. One said 'maybe one who is mute can make a will by making signs' and another said 'if they can use sign language they can—it is all about communication'. Another customary knowledge bearer said that 'the deaf and dumb can make a will because they are intelligent'.

Customary Heirship

The customary heir is the key cultural officer in the context of succession. Among the Baganda, the heir is a male in the family of the

---

[710] Haydon (note 1) at 223.

[711] Ibid at 222-23.

deceased who is given the authority and control over estate property and its distribution. Although the formal law assigns the heir a token role[712], heirs continue to play a dominant role within succession matters in Mukono District. Due to the centrality of the heir in customary succession, the issue of eligibility of heirship is a major item of concern when assessing the rights, status and treatment of persons with disabilities.

If a customary heir is named in a will or in some other pre-death directive, that individual will generally be named the customary heir. In cases where the customary heir has not been designated by the deceased there are diverse opinions as to how the customary heir is appointed. Some customary knowledge bearers indicated that the customary heir is chosen by clan elders. Others claimed that fellow siblings will sit down and agree on someone based on factors such as responsibility and behaviour. Some said that only the female siblings carry out this task. While still others said that the family and clan leaders will vote together. Regardless of the procedure for selection, the qualities considered when selecting a customary heir include sociability, the ability to read, a certain maturity of age, good behaviour and a sound mind.

One interviewee with a disability said that 'they will even consider a younger child' before allowing a person with a disability to be a customary heir. Another interviewee with a disability said she was unsure if it was possible for a person with a disability to be a customary heir because she had never seen it happen. All but three of the customary knowledge bearers indicated that most persons with disabilities can be named customary heir and this is especially the case where the deceased has designated them as their heir. Yet several knowledge bearers qualified their response by stating that persons of unsound mind and those who have hearing impairments and are unable to speak would not be allowed to serve as heir.

---

[712] Succession Act (Uganda) (cap 162) (1906) s 27.

There can be exceptions to the general rule of customary eligibility based on the specific disability at issue. Nine customary knowledge bearers indicated that persons with mental disabilities are not considered suitable for heirship. Another seven also stated that those with hearing impairments that are unable to speak would not be allowed to serve as an heir. In addition, one knowledge bearer indicated that persons who are unable to move were also identified as being incapable of serving as a customary heir.

There was a lack of unanimity on whether persons with disabilities have always been permitted to serve as customary heirs. Nine customary knowledge bearers indicated that persons with disabilities have always been permitted while two said that eligibility for this customary office is the result of a recent change. One customary knowledge bearer offered a nuanced response when he stated 'this is the way it always has been, but now it has become better thanks to education'. Of the six persons with disabilities who were asked about this issue in the third stage of the fieldwork, four indicated that the allowance of persons with disabilities to serve as heirs is the product of a recent change and another indicated that it is still not permitted.

One man with a physical disability told the remarkable story of how he was made heir of his father's estate after his father died without a will. The clan selected him as heir out of 47 brothers, 20 of whom were older than him. He claims to have been selected based on his integrity and social relationships.

Another man with a physical disability reported that he was named the heir of his father's estate. However, despite his position of leadership he was pressured by family members to take a smaller piece of land. He claims that his brothers and sisters plotted against him and that his own mother attempted to poison him because of his disability. Yet he knew his rights and he used his position as heir to stand up for his claim to an equal portion of land.

A man with a physical disability reported that his clan made him heir when his father died. However, the day after the decision disgruntled family members deposed him and replaced him with his older brother and he ended up inheriting nothing. Instead the older brother sold three plots of land and kept one for him.

One interviewee with a physical disability who had previously served as an heir was a woman. She was made an heir of her father's estate in Western Uganda in accordance with the Batoro custom that allows for female heirship. She contended that the Batoro were not likely to discriminate against a person with disabilities in the context of succession if that person proves themselves to be capable in business as she had done.

Gender and Land Inheritance

Any discussion of customary succession in Mukono District would be incomplete without addressing gender. There is a cultural presumption in Mukono District that men are the owners of land and a sense that men's estates are more consequential than women's estates. Moreover, the persistence of the customary practice of male heirship places power and control of estate property under the control and discretion of men. A female customary knowledge bearer submitted that these discrepancies are based on the sex of the potential beneficiary with a disability. She stated that 'if they are men they get' and if they are women 'they get through marriage'.

For example, a woman with partial paralyzation indicated that when her father died the daughters were given smaller shares of land than the sons. The land that she received was equal to each of the plots the other daughters received. Thus it was her gender and not her disability that caused her to receive disparate treatment.

The prominence of gender-based discrimination can make disability-based inequities less apparent. Yet, the importance of disability in customary inheritance should not be lost in the shadow of gender-based inequity. Although the consequences of disability in succession matters are more fluid and less defined than gender, disability is an important factor in customary succession in Mukono District. Additional comparative and relational analysis addressing gender and disability appears in Chapter 8.

Land Issues Excluding the Inheritance of Land

There is near consensus that persons with disabilities can own land. Only three of the interviewees with disabilities said flatly and unconditionally that persons with disabilities cannot own land.[713] Moreover, almost all of the customary knowledge bearers indicated that persons with disabilities have always been able to own land.

Many interviewees made unsolicited comments linking the right to own land with the financial capacity. In fact, 18 of the interviewees with disabilities qualified their answer without prompting by saying that persons with disabilities can own land if they have the money to buy it.

Interviewees were largely unable to identify any customary law or legal practice that helps ensure access to land for persons with disabilities or other vulnerable people. Some mentioned the fact that the Kabaka had given land to persons with disabilities on a few occasions in the past.

The most beneficial cultural phenomenon mentioned by the interviewees is the tendency of various community leaders to stand up for vulnerable people in the context of wrongful property taking. Interviewees indicated that local community leaders could step into clan and fami-

---

[713] Interestingly each of the three interviewees with disabilities who indicated that persons with disabilities cannot own land were females. This was one of the rare instances in the data where any particular demographic characteristics was unusually linked to a response. Overall the answers from the interviews of persons with disabilities did not vary in any noteworthy way based on sex, age, religion, education or disability.

ly succession scenarios and challenge discriminatory practices. Although leader oversight in customary matters appears to be less formalised due to the disempowering of cultural institutions, cultural leaders retain some coercive social power. This soft power can be used to engage local government leaders to intervene in matters.

The understanding that land belongs to the family can limit the land rights of individuals with disabilities. The story of the man from Masaka who was not permitted to serve as customary heir reflects the cultural emphasis on keeping land in the family for future generations.

Some interviewees indicated that the responsibility for the proper use of land extends to the entire family. Interviewees with disabilities described a cultural practice whereby land that would otherwise go to a sibling with a disability is given to another sibling to manage for the benefit of the sibling with a disability. Others mentioned the practice of giving persons with disabilities a plot of land just large enough for their future burial on family land.

The fieldwork offered no indication of any historic cultural resistance to allowing persons with disabilities to possess kibanja holdings. However, this is not to say that one's status as a person with a disability is irrelevant in the context of kibanja holdings. On the contrary, of those specifically asked, approximately three quarters of the interviewees with disabilities reported that persons with disabilities with kibanja holdings face greater challenges with their landlords including wrongful eviction and constructive eviction through social pressure and intimidation. As one interviewee stated landlords 'take advantage of persons with disabilities because they are vulnerable'. Another interviewee stated that 'there is often mischief because persons with disabilities are seen as defenseless'.

Although many interviewees acknowledge the heightened vulnerability of kibanja holders with disabilities, there is a consensus that all kibinja holders have the legal right to stay on the land as long as they can prove ownership and pay busuulu. However, many people are not capable of defending and enforcing their rights in court. As one interview with a disability noted, 'usually the smaller person does not go to court so usually disputes are resolved through clan leaders or with local council members. Bigger people are the ones who go to court.'

A Rwandese man with a disability who had lived in Mukono District for several decades claimed that he was targeted as a kibanja holder on the basis of his disability. The title holder of the kibanja land sought to remove him and give the plot to the title holder's son. The man's home on the kibanja plot was knocked down, but he was able to retain his land rights based on his willingness to fight in court with the help of the Uganda Human Rights Commission. The story demonstrates how the formal law can be used to check lawless abuses for those with the requisite knowledge, resources and willingness to fight.

There is a difference between the way persons with disabilities viewed the vulnerability levels of kibanja holders with disabilities and the perspectives of the customary knowledge bearers. The customary knowledge bearers were confident in the formal law's capacity to protect kibanja holders with disabilities who pay busuulu. Several customary knowledge bearers claimed that clan leaders, community members or local government actors will come in to ensure that kibanja holders are not wrongfully chased from their land holdings. To the contrary, the perception of the interviewees with disabilities is that kibanja holders are left to fend for themselves.

The customary knowledge bearers demonstrated greater confidence in the ultimate prevailing of the formal law. Many of the customary knowledge bearers are leaders who are more connected with formal institutions and who understand how engage bureaucratic systems. On the other hand, many of the interviewees with disabilities are largely unconnected with formal mechanisms and institutions. Therefore, they have less confidence in the capacity of formal law to prevail over abusive activities on the ground.

Kibanja holdings are no longer the domain of customary law. The current formal version of kibanja is inflexible and links kibanja rights with a frozen recurring tribute that is a negligible percentage of market rental value. This unique hybrid form of land holding is under attack by title owners who cannot recognize the value of their land titles as long as kibanja holders remain. As land values increase, the incentive to take the land grows. In these scenarios people who are perceived as vulnerable are targeted, exploited and victimized. Thus kibanja holders with disabilities appear to experience disproportionate harm and displacement not because they are seen as useless, but because they are seen as weak and defenseless.

Conclusion

The research findings concerning specific areas of customary law and practice offer useful insights. Taken as a whole, the findings help us to understand how disability matters in the lives of people in Mukono District.

This chapter demonstrates how disabilities can impact a range of important legal situations. However, without understating the importance of the findings in other areas, the fieldwork especially highlights the importance of disability in the context of land inheritance. It indicates that persons with disabilities commonly experience disability based discrimination in crucial scenarios where land is divided among siblings outside of the formal probate system.

Customary legal scenarios present people with the opportunity to make decisions with legal implications in informal settings. When customary decision makers and officiants view persons with disabilities as capable and competent, persons with disabilities are more likely to be treated fairly and equally. Moreover, persons with disabilities are best able to combat discrimination in customary scenarios when they are aware of the protections afforded to them under formal law and when they are willing and able to assert their rights in customary scenarios and through formal channels.

The fieldwork findings demonstrate needs to be addressed and point to potential strategies for improving the rights, status and treatment of persons with disabilities. The implications of the thesis' research for those seeking to improve the rights, status and treatment of persons with disabilities are further discussed in Chapters 8 and 9.

8

DISABILITY AND LEGAL DEVELOPMENT IN MUKONO: A SEMI-AUTONOMOUS FIELD-BASED ANALYSIS AND APPLIED TOPICAL ASSESSMENTS

Introduction

Chapter 8 is the third and final chapter in a series of chapters presenting fieldwork findings. This chapter accomplishes two broad tasks.

First, it expands the analytical lens out from Chapter 7. It considers the place of customary law and practice with special relevance to disability from the inclusive viewpoint of Moore's semi-autonomous social field. Thus it considers how other legal sources and influences interact with customary law and practice in ways that are relevant to the rights, status and treatment of person with disabilities.

Second, it offers applied analysis on certain topics that warrant further discussion in light of the findings. These topics include an assessment of change strategies introduced in Chapter 4, a reflective discussion of substantive provisions of the Convention on the Rights of Persons with Disabilities[714] (CRPD) and a critical examination of the com-

---

[714] Convention on the Rights of Persons with Disabilities (CRPD), adopted December 13, 2006 by GA Res 61/106, Annex I, UN GAOR, 61st Sess, Supp No 49 at 65, UN Doc A/61/49 (2006), entered into force 3 May 3 2008, UN Doc A/61/61, signed by Uganda on 30 March 2007 and ratified by Uganda on 25 September 2008.

parative place and relationship of gender and disability in customary contexts.

The Legal Implications of Disability through the Lens of the Semi-Autonomous Social Field

As Moore posits, the semi-autonomous social field offers a fertile research approach for appreciating the nature, character and operation of legal activity in deeply pluralistic legal contexts.[715] Moore's semi-autonomous social field takes account of the multifarious legal sources and influences within a specific society.

There are a number of influences and sources that affect the status, rights and treatment of persons with disabilities within customary legal frameworks other than customary law and process. These include laws, government institutions and policies, customary institutions, lawyers, non-governmental organisations (NGOs), religion, societal values and widely held beliefs.

Chapter 6 presented findings about cultural beliefs concerning disability and analysis about the impact of those beliefs. Therefore this section does not include a full discussion of those beliefs.

What follows is a topical treatment of various contributing factors to the socio-legal context in Mukono's District's customary frameworks relevant to disability rights, status and treatment. Each topic is discussed in light of the fieldwork findings.

---

[715] SF Moore 'Law and social change: the semi-autonomous social field as an appropriate field of study' (1973) 7(4) *Law & Society Review* 719-746.

National and International Laws

The Uganda Constitution

The customary knowledge bearer interviews included lines of inquiry concerning the Uganda Constitution.[716] Specifically, this segment of the field interviews assessed knowledge and attitudes concerning the relationship between the Constitution and custom and culture as well as the substance of the Constitution pertaining to the status, rights and treatment of persons with disabilities.

Almost all of the customary knowledge bearers claimed to have some familiarity with the Uganda Constitution and its legal preeminence.

They generally acknowledged that customary law and practices should be consistent with any rights and protections provided for in the Constitution. One interviewee added the caveat that 'it should as long as customary laws are not completely done away with'. Another customary knowledge bearer epitomised the outward submissiveness to the formal law by stating 'I just take what they say'.

Only two of the customary knowledge bearers indicated that customary law need not be consistent with the Ugandan Constitution. One of these individuals reasoned that customary law should not have to change because it has been that way since time immemorial.

There was a sense among the customary knowledge bearers that the enforcement of the formal law, including the Constitution, must come from the outside. Several doubted the ability of the Constitution to foster positive change for persons with disabilities at the grassroots level. They cited formal agents and technocratic structures as the means for bringing life to the Constitution. A few customary knowledge bearers identified local government officials as key players in the enforcement and protection of constitutional rights of persons with disabilities. Another men-

---

[716] Constitution of Uganda 1995 (as amended in 2005).

tioned the use of lawyers to enforce the formal law when there is a conflict with applied customary law and practices. Two others posited the possibility of the Buganda Kingdom government in Mengo (Kampala) having a formal role in effecting compliance with the Constitution, but none of the interviewees identified Buganda ministries or officials as historic or current enforcers of the Constitution.

Very few of the customary knowledge bearers claimed to have read the Constitution. Instead, many indicated that their knowledge about the formal law comes from radio broadcasts and community-based sensitisation sessions.

The customary knowledge bearers' understanding of how the Constitution relates to persons with disabilities is minimal and varied. Several noted that the Constitution provides for special political representation for persons with disabilities. Others asserted that the Ugandan Constitution mandates the provision of benefits such as wheelchairs and money for persons with disabilities. Such benefits are not expressly provided for under the Constitution although they could arguably be derived from article 35 which requires 'the State and society to take all appropriate measures to ensure that (persons with disabilities) realise their full mental and physical potential'.

Customary knowledge bearers peppered their depictions of Constitutional rights with generalist rights speak and references to accessibility. One interviewee observed flatly that the Constitution calls for equality. Another said that the Constitution protects the rights of persons with disabilities and penalises rights abusers. Two interviewees indicated that the Ugandan Constitution requires buildings to be accessible to persons with physical disabilities. Others mentioned the right to access education. One interviewee said that the Constitution empowers NGOs to uplift persons with disabilities. Another interviewee indicated that the Constitution empowers persons with disabilities by giving them increased social standing in the community.

Other Ugandan Domestic Law

Several interviewees in both the first and second phase of the field research indicated that the formal law serves as a check on discriminatory practices within customary law. There is a general recognition that it is improper to discriminate against persons with disabilities. This prohibition on discrimination is perceived as something coming from the formal law generally and the Constitution of Uganda especially.

Interviewees from both cohorts largely commended domestic laws that allocate political offices to persons with disabilities. However, there are concerns over whether the persons with disabilities that hold these offices fairly represent the broad spectrum of persons with disabilities. Several interviewees with disabilities complained that such positions are typically filled by individuals with minor physical impairments such as limps.

With the exception of persons with disabilities holding designated political offices, the interviews were notably bereft of concrete instances where domestic legislation positively impacts persons with disabilities. There was no indication of any awareness of the Persons with Disabilities Act.[717] Excepting the Constitution, there was never any reference to other laws in Uganda that protects or furthers the rights and interests of persons with disabilities.

International Human Rights Instruments

The customary knowledge bearers had little or no knowledge about international human rights instruments that concern or address the rights of persons with disabilities. Some were incredulous that the interviewer asked about such instruments. As one respondent stated, '[i[f I do not know about the laws of Uganda how can I know about foreign laws?' Many customary knowledge bearers laughed at the question '[d]o you

---

[717] Persons with Disabilities Act of 2006 (Uganda).

know about any international human rights instruments that concern the rights of persons with disabilities?'

The customary knowledge bearers were unable to say anything tangible about international treaties that concern the rights of persons with disabilities. A few specifically mentioned the Universal Declaration of Human Rights but did nothing more than name the instrument.

Yet there is a sense that international human rights standards are a source of influence. Many knowledge bearers described a changing culture where persons with disabilities are given more opportunities and support. One stated that '[i]nternational laws have helped to influence the laws in Uganda so that persons with disabilities are not so marginalised.' Two interviewees attributed the freedom of speech belonging to persons with disabilities to such instruments. One indicated that the human rights instruments help persons with disabilities know about their 'right to study' and 'right to life'. Another indicated that they lead to the formation of organisations that champion disability rights. However, none of the customary knowledge bearers reported any specific knowledge of the CRPD.

Others were pessimistic about the impact of international human rights instruments in Mukono District. One customary knowledge bearer bluntly stated 'maybe that law works in other places, but not here'. Another knowledge bearer asked about whether customary law should change to account for the rights of persons with disabilities sardonically quipped 'as if it is possible'.

Despite a lack of awareness about international human rights instruments, the customary knowledge bearers indicated that they were not opposed to abiding by such instruments. Interviewees who claimed to have some knowledge of international human rights instruments indicated that customary laws should conform to such instruments. None of the customary knowledge bearers asserted a desire that customary law resist the requirements of human rights instruments concerning persons with disabilities.

Some interviewees expressed the sentiment that international human rights instruments are somehow connected with foreign aid. When addressing the line of questions about international human rights instruments, one interviewee said that international groups can come to help but the government will 'eat' the money. Another said that international human rights instruments can help provide wheelchairs and crutches.

Ultimately there is little indication from the field research that human rights instruments have a direct impact on the customary legal scenarios. Instead, the Ugandan Constitution is seen as the legal instrument that serves as the legal check on improper discrimination against persons with disabilities.

Government Institutions and Policies

The National Government

Both persons with disabilities and customary knowledge bearers attribute positive developments in disability rights, policy and social conditions to President Museveni and his long-ruling National Resistance Movement (NRM) party.

One customary knowledge bearer indicated that the right of persons with disabilities to own land has been reinforced by the government. Another noted that persons with disabilities have been permitted to be clan leaders 'since the time of Museveni'. Still another said that the current government 'has empowered' persons with disabilities. The ruling government was also credited with inviting 'people from outside countries to teach about disability' which has led to more 'enlightened' perspectives about disability.

Even those interview participants that are politically disenchanted with President Museveni and the NRM tend to acknowledge that the ruling government has been a positive force for persons with disabilities.

In terms of specifics, interviewees most often referenced laws that set aside political representative space to persons with disabilities. Also, multiple persons with disabilities appreciated Museveni's recognition of persons with disabilities at public gatherings.

There is general awareness of government institutions and initiatives that are in place to support persons with disabilities. Several customary knowledge bearers mentioned ministries that have the responsibility of furthering the interests of persons with disabilities. Both interviewees with disabilities and customary knowledge bearers indicated that persons with disabilities are supposed to be the beneficiaries of government resources. Yet there was a common sentiment that such programs, initiatives and resources rarely have an impact in Mukono District.

Interviewees with disabilities offered pessimistic perspectives on top-down disability rights initiatives. Interviewees from both cohorts voiced concerns over the fact that the benefits of the NRM's disability policies and initiatives do not seem to help persons with disabilities. As one customary knowledge bearer stated '[g]overnment programs never have an impact on persons with disabilities on the ground.' Interviewees related concerns about local government officials who 'eat' most of these intended benefits. For example, one knowledge bearer stated that '[t]he government should support persons with disabilities directly without using so many agencies because the intermediaries take the money.'

Customary knowledge bearers made statements indicative of a shift in perceived responsibility from society to the state. Instead of speaking of a communal obligation to support those with disabilities, there were some who placed the burden of care and provision on the government. One customary knowledge bearer noted that persons with disabilities 'are often neglected by the government' even though 'it should be the duty of the government to take care of them'. Another knowledge bearer related how she hears on the radio that the government is supposed to 'care for persons with disabilities by giving them wheelchairs'. While another stated that there are government ministers and local council members who are supposed 'to represent and help persons with disabilities'. It appears that government promises are used to justify a growing moral distance between community members and persons with disabilities who, in the words of one knowledge bearer, 'do not have the necessities of life, yet they can hardly do anything for themselves'.

Local Government

Reports on the role and activities of local governments in disability matters were mixed. One interviewee with disabilities said that Mukono is a 'role model' community for Uganda in the context of disability matters. He credited Mukono District with attempting to provide civil services to persons with disabilities before the government offered support. Yet, other interviewees with disabilities portrayed local government officials as corrupt stewards of monies intended for the benefit of persons with disabilities.

Two interviewees indicated that local government oversight is having a positive influence against discrimination in the context of Islamic succession. They reported that Muslim religious clerics who oversee succession rites are required to report estate distributions to local government authorities. This helps ensure that Islamic distribution of estate property is carried out in accordance with Ugandan Constitutional standards (e.g. not discriminatory against women). There was no indication that similar oversight protocols are regularly followed in non-Islamic customary succession.

Buganda Institutions

The Buganda Kingdom has structures that mirror the institutions of the national government. For example one customary knowledge bearer referred to a minister in Mengo[718] who is charged with making sure the

---

[718] Mengo is a prominent hill in Kampala which is the court home of the Kabaka and the situs of the Buganda Kingdom's central government.

rights of persons with disabilities are honoured in customary matters. Another mentioned a formal customary tribunal in Mengo that could be used to address discriminatory conduct in customary proceedings.

Yet there is no indication these institutions have any impact on the status, rights and treatment of persons with disabilities. One customary knowledge bearer noted that the Buganda Kingdom has entrusted people to take care of persons with disabilities, but often times they do nothing. He cited the deterioration of Kingdom institutions and inadequate funding as reasons for ineffectiveness.

Nonetheless, the Kabaka and other Buganda Kingdom leaders have the potential to bring about positive reforms for persons with disabilities. Interviewees in both the first and second phases confirmed that the Kabaka is the ultimate customary law maker and Kabaka still has the power to unilaterally pronounce and amend Buganda customary law. Thus the Kabaka could make potentially influential pronouncements concerning the status, rights and treatment of persons with disabilities.

A 67 year old Baganda interviewee with a disability cited the actions and leadership of Daudi Chwa II as improving the rights, status and treatment of persons with disabilities. This interviewee stated that Kabaka Daudi, who ruled from 1897 to 1939, declared that if a person dies the deceased's property should go to the children irrespective of whether or not they have a disability.

Non-governmental Actors

NGOs

Some interviewees with disabilities credit an improvement in community attitudes concerning persons with disabilities to NGOs. One said 'now society seems to care about persons with disabilities because there are organisations providing help'. Another opined that '[o]ganisations have impacted this generation to the good with respect to how they treat persons with disabilities'.

Others noted that the Western world appears keen on promoting the rights of persons with disabilities. Some credited international organisations with improving the social climate for persons with disabilities through sensitisation. An interviewee with a disability stated that 'sensitisation is helping to reduce the level of abuse and bad thinking—things are changing for the better'. Another commented that '[t]hings are not like they were—people like them—sensitisation has helped.'

Legal Advocates

One interviewee with disabilities said that 'people in the community will always try to involve lawyers to make sure the properties of persons with disabilities are protected under the law'. No other interviewees mentioned similar tendencies, but multiple stories were told of how persons with disabilities effectively engaged legal assistance to combat discrimination in the context of land rights, including the inheritance of land.

Thus the fieldwork indicates that lawyers can serve to ensure some level of interface between customary legal frameworks and the formal law. The primary challenges to litigation appear to be access to free or affordable legal services as well as the social trauma of engaging in litigation with family members and neighbours.

Non-indigenous Religions

Although it is the majority faith in Mukono District, there was little indication that Christianity has a significant impact on the status rights and treatment of persons with disabilities. When interviewees discussed Christianity the most common issue was the challenge of physical access to church buildings. A few interviewees with disabilities mentioned Christianity's hopeful prospect of miraculous healing and the view that all people are created in the image of God. Another credited Protestant churches for their involvement in an initiative to vaccinate children for polio. Yet, none of the interviewees expressly attributed a positive or negative impact to Christianity for persons with disabilities in customary legal contexts.

Similarly, the fieldwork did not indicate that Islam is a major driver in matters of disability status, rights and treatment. However, as previously mentioned, the formal oversight provided over instances of Islamic succession reportedly serves as a means of combating unconstitutional discrimination in the context of succession.

Indigenous Communitarian Ethos (Ubuntu)

I sought to assess the possible impact of an indigenous communitarian ethos on the status, rights and treatment of persons with disabilities. I explored this subject matter in two ways.

First, as discussed in Chapter 6, I examined zones of human affairs where communal beliefs can be manifested in actions, practices and customs relevant to persons with disabilities. Although the interviewees with disabilities were not pointedly asked about ubuntu, they were asked in general terms to identify and describe community practices and attitudes that were helpful or hurtful to persons with disabilities. This line of questioning failed to identify practices that reflected the manifestation of a communitarian ethos. I also sought to determine if persons with disabilities would speak about ubuntu or an ubuntu-like ethos without direct prompting. None of these interviewees with disabilities did so.

Second, I questioned the customary knowledge bearers concerning their knowledge and understanding regarding the existence, relevance and impact of a communitarian ethos in their communities and its customary practices. These interviews included direct questions about ubuntu.

The customary knowledge bearers demonstrated minimal familiarity with the word 'ubuntu'. Only one of the 23 customary knowledge bearers indicated that they had heard of ubuntu without additional prompting. In order to pursue the point, interviewees were asked whether they were familiar with the idea that 'I am because you are and you are because I am' and whether they had an understanding of common Luganda phrases that express similar sentiments. This probing line of inquiry managed to elicit some responsive answers.

Notably several customary knowledge bearers viewed the ubuntu ethos as foreign. One interviewee indicated that '[i]t is coming slowly. It did not used to be there'. Another respondent indicated that ubuntu is a good idea but that 'people do not follow it here' and that it is a foreign concept that 'comes from the people of the world'. One interviewee said 'the government talks about this sort of thing but not the Buganda'. Another said '[p]eople just speak words, but they do not practice them'.

Only three of the customary knowledge bearers reported that ubuntu, or something akin to ubuntu, has an impact on their local customs and culture. One interviewee, who described ubuntu as 'behaving humanly', said that ubuntu causes people to vote for candidates that are 'good and caring'. Another said that ubuntu can 'build confidence in people who are disabled'. Finally, one interviewee said that ubuntu has an impact on the customs and cultures in Mukono District because 'when there is donor help from abroad (the recipients in Uganda) will share what they get'. Notably, none of the customary knowledge bearers gave an example of how ubuntu inspired grassroots cooperation or assistance that benefits persons with disabilities in a tangible way.

However, some of the cultural and customary practices mentioned by the customary knowledge bearers could be fairly construed as manifestations of an ubuntu-like ethos. One knowledge bearer who was asked whether there is any custom or practice whereby land is held for the benefit of persons with disabilities responded: 'Yes they have a responsibility. It is given to someone assigned that responsibility in the clan. Clan leaders will bring family members together and see how to distribute equally.' A knowledge bearer stated that clans and families have always protected property from being grabbed. Another knowledge bearer reported that leaders and heads of households have the responsibility to look for food for persons with disabilities so they do not die. The same individual said it is wrong to abandon a child with a disability.

Little else was said that reflected a communitarian ethos. Most customary knowledge bearers were unable to provide examples that spoke to an ethos of caring for or honouring persons with disabilities.

The customary knowledge bearers largely portrayed ubuntu as a foreign concept in Mukono District. There was no indication of any sense of cultural ownership based on the fact that it is a Bantu ethos. Arguably some of the knowledge bearers characterised ubuntu as an African or international version of moral imperialism—a foreign value that they are encouraged to accept as their own. Although such a characterisation has a negative connotation, there was little apparent disdain or resistance amongst the customary knowledge bearers over the source of ubuntu.

I did not detect a local idealised communitarianism where community members are all called recognize the dignity of their fellow person and offer care and support based on an appreciation of common humanity. However, if we see forms of indigenous African communitarianism as expressive of recognition that individual people are essential to the functioning and well-being of a community[719], we can find pertinent examples in Mukono District. For example, guardians care for children with the idea that children may serve valuable purposes to the guardian or the community later on in life. In addition, it is important for clan leaders to have the social skills needed to manage human relationships.

The emphasis on functionality and usefulness can help explain the differences in the treatment of persons with different disabilities in different customary contexts. For persons with disabilities, this pragmatic and consequential form of communitarianism can be a detriment rather than an aid.

---

[719] *S v Makwanyane* 1995 3 SA 391 (CC) para 224 (opinion of J Langa).

Cultural Receptivity to Change

Another cultural factor worth noting is receptiveness to progressive change in the context of disability rights. The customary knowledge bearers spoke favourably about human rights, social progress and cultural advancement. Being 'enlightened', even with all of its neocolonial baggage, is portrayed outwardly in a positive and welcoming manner. Many of the interviewees associated progressive development with improved cultural treatment of persons with disabilities. Moreover, none of the interviewees complained that local improvements in the rights, status and treatment of persons with disabilities are a threat to old ways or treasured traditions.

Two customary knowledge bearers indicated that conduct that protects and benefits persons with disabilities is a recent development and not something that springs from the indigenous culture. One said that the tendency to hold property in trust for persons with disabilities is more now because of more 'enlightened people and sensitising'. The other said that '[i]n some cases enlightened families can hold and manage land on their behalf. Meanwhile families that are not enlightened can try to take away their land'.

The indigenous cultural leaders gave no indication of any opposition to the global advancement of disability rights. Instead they outwardly welcome this advancement. The customary knowledge bearers reflected a collective sense that foreign powers are interested in the furtherance of certain humanitarian causes and that if Ugandans accede to these interests that outside aid and support will follow. There is also a sense of inevitable acceptance of the human rights agenda which includes disability rights.

Confirming the Value of the Semi-Autonomous Social Field

The findings related in this section confirm the value of Moore's semi-autonomous social field. Culture and custom are permeable. Customary legal frameworks are more than the pure product of tradition and indigenous cultural content. The inclusive lens of the semi-autonomous social field allows us to rightly account for the other sources and influences that form and compose the substance, form and operation of customary law.

Although customary law and practices persist in Mukono District regardless of the pronouncements and strictures of domestic and international law, we should account for these formal legal sources if we want to understand the customary legal frameworks and the scenarios that generate customary outcomes. Other legal sources impact and influence customary legal scenarios, despite the continued disregard and non-use of formal legal structures and procedures. Moreover, there are institutions and initiatives that are capable of fostering greater linkage and accountability of custom with formal law and international rights standards. Appreciating relevant cultural content can inform efforts to bridge the gaps between formal law and custom that enable and allow discrimination on the basis of disability in customary legal scenarios. The fieldwork points to the importance of specific knowledge concerning semi-autonomous fields in informing change strategies, the importance of people's beliefs about disabilities in deeply pluralistic environments and the wisdom behind multi-pronged approaches to achieving change.

Assessment of Approaches to Effecting Change through Law and Legal Structures

Chapter 4 canvassed a variety of tools and strategies for bringing about positive changes in the rights, status and treatment of persons with disabilities. This section presents an applied assessment of various change theories. This section is divided into two sub-sections. The first sub-section presents analysis concerning top-down change strategies. The second sub-section presents a critique of bottom-up change strategies.

Top-Down Approaches

The fieldwork indicates that top-down approaches to improving the rights, status and treatment of persons with disabilities have value in customary contexts in Mukono District and they can be leveraged for greater impact.

Domestic formal law

When it comes to domestic formal law in Uganda, the Constitution stands in a place of privilege. People are aware of the Constitution and they know it to be the supreme law of the land. The Constitution is not a lightning rod for resentment. Instead it is revered. Thus sharing knowledge about constitutional details concerning persons with disabilities presents an opportunity for improving status, rights and treatment of persons with disabilities in customary contexts.

The fieldwork speaks to the practical irrelevance of other domestic laws pertaining to disability in Mukono District. Thus it cuts against the perceived utility of legislative reform at the grassroots level. Nonetheless, legislative reform has its place. People's beliefs and perceptions about disabilities influence status, rights and treatment. This is especially true in customary contexts. So there is some social utility in using 'ableist' language when describing disability in all contexts— including legislation—that can form and influence attitudes about disability.

International legal instruments

International human rights instruments are not well known in Mukono District. However, human rights instruments appear to have some level of legal and cultural relevance. In addition, the fieldwork indicates that the content of human rights instruments can disseminated to receptive community members through radio broadcasts and sensitisations.

Despite a lack of name recognition, the fieldwork speaks well of the scope and content of the CRPD. Section IV in this chapter assesses the substance of the CRPD in light of the research findings.

Strategic Litigation

The research offers mixed messages on the issue of litigation based change efforts. There is little indication that strategic litigation seeking legal reform has an impact on customary legal scenarios. However, it appears that the ability of individuals to access formal legal oversight of customary legal decisions is an important means of closing the gap between the formal law and customary legal scenarios.

Bottom-Up Approaches

The fieldwork demonstrates the wisdom and viability of many of the bottom-up strategies presented in Section III of Chapter 4.

Facilitative Change Strategies

The fieldwork offers insights for proponents of facilitative change strategies for human rights development. One facilitative change technique involves identifying local beliefs and practices and then building on them. The research targeted indigenous communitarianism as a local value that could integrate disability rights concepts such as universal human dignity and equality into customary contexts. Yet the research failed to identify an active communitarian ethos aligned with of dignity and equality. Instead the research indicates that people are valued based what they can do for the community rather than their humanity.

Appreciating the cultural importance placed on human functionality and usefulness can benefit disability rights actors. The message that 'disability is not inability' is well crafted to bring about positive results in Mukono District's customary frameworks.

Facilitative approaches also include strategies for leveraging indigenous institutions and practices to broker change. The fieldwork indicates that Buganda institutions have been considerably weakened since independence. Yet both the Kingdom and local leaders are respected in matters of custom and retain cultural authority.

Notably the Kabaka is regarded as the ultimate customary law giver. Thus he has the power to declare practices that discriminate against persons with disabilities improper. Disability rights groups could engage the Kabaka to tell his people that discrimination on the basis on disability in areas such as succession, marriage and guardianships is contrary to Baganda custom. If the Kabaka has limited reach to share his message due to resource limitations, disability rights organisations could use their own resources to share and disseminate the proclamations of the Kabaka.

Acculturation

A key acculturation process in terms of disability rights in Mukono District is the inculcation of human rights standards into the local context. The fieldwork offers encouraging findings for those who advocate for acculturation strategies. Customary knowledge bearers expressed openness to disability rights standards coming from other places. There is a sense that disability rights are just, moral and associated with progress.

Radio broadcasts appear to be an effective means of sharing about disability rights. Messages on the radio are deemed to be authoritative and helpful sources of information.

Direct Engagement

The fieldwork speaks to the potential of direct engagement to effect change. In particular, the apparent success in integrating human rights standards into Islamic succession rites through local formal oversight is an intriguing research finding. If customary legal scenarios could be subjected to similar official and regularly occurring oversight it could help reduce instances of discriminatory conduct. However, the formal illegitimacy of customary succession could make such direct engagement untenable based on rule of law considerations.

Actor-oriented Change Strategies

Actor-oriented change strategies are important in customary contexts. Persons with disabilities must be equipped and empowered to champion their own rights. The willingness of persons with disabilities to assert their rights and to engage formal checks on discrimination are key factors in combatting discrimination in customary legal scenarios. Thus strategies designed to give persons with disabilities the tools and courage they need to self-advocate offer considerable potential for positive change.

Contextual and Research-Based Appraisal of the CRPD

This section provides an appraisal of the substance of the CRPD in light of the research findings. Despite the fact that the CRPD is essentially unknown by the people of Mukono District, the fieldwork speaks well of its content and scope.

The CRPD does not turn a blind eye to customary legal scenarios. It brings out the importance of community and culture to the effective realisation of human rights.[720] In addition, its extensive detail and integrative approach addresses many of the challenges to disability rights in customary contexts. Thus despite its place as a formal international rights instrument adopted by most of the nations of the world, the CPRD is not drafted on the presumption that it can effect change from the top down.

The CRPD contains more than broad prohibitions on discriminatory conduct. It specifically addresses areas where discrimination take place including the pivotal customary legal scenarios identified in the field

---

[720] CRPD arts 3, 19.

research.[721] The CPRD requires State Parties to modify or abolish laws, customs or practices that discriminate against persons with disabilities.[722]

The CPRD confronts the challenge of discrimination in marriage. Article 23(1)(a) provides that all persons with disabilities who are of marriageable age have the right to marry with the free and full consent of the spouse. Cruel and inhuman treatment such as social abuse during wedding introduction services is prohibited by Article 15. Moreover, the scope of the CRPD is broad enough to qualify the prohibition of marriage for impotent men improper discrimination because impotence is a 'long term physical impairment' that hinders 'full and effective participation in society on an equal basis with others'.[723]

With respect to legal personality and inheritance, Article 3(a) provides for 'respect for inherent dignity, individual autonomy including the freedom to make one's own choices, and independence of persons' and for 'full and effective participation and inclusion in society'. Article 12(4) requires that 'States Parties shall ensure that all measures that relate to the exercise of legal capacity provide for appropriate and effective safeguards to prevent abuse in accordance with international human rights law.' Article 12(5) requires states parties to 'take all appropriate and effective measures to ensure the equal right of persons with disabilities to own or inherit property' and to 'ensure that persons with disabilities are not arbitrarily deprived of their property'.[724] Thus paternalistic discrimination in customary inheritance is prohibited. The challenge is making these restrictions operative within semi-autonomous social fields.

---

[721] *Ibid* art 2.

[722] *Ibid* art 4(1)(b).

[723] *Ibid* pre.

[724] A similar provision is found in the Draft Protocol to the African Charter on Human and Peoples' Rights on the Rights of Persons with Disabilities at art 8(3)(f).

In the context of forced guardianships of the children of parents with disabilities, the CRPD provides that 'States Parties shall ensure that a child shall not be separated from his or her parents against their will' and that '[i]n no case shall a child be separated from parents on the basis of a disability of either the child or one or both of the parents.'[725]

One could fairly question whether the scope of the CRPD is broad enough to cover the practice of customary guardianship that is prevalent in Mukono District. Article 23(2) of the CRPD provides that 'States Parties shall ensure the rights and responsibilities of persons with disabilities, with regard to guardianship, wardship, and trusteeship, adoption of children or similar institutions, where these concepts exist in national legislation'. It includes no provision that addresses custodial relationships which are not expressly established by legislation. Regardless, the general application of the CRPD as well as its specific application to cultural matters forbids discrimination in the context of customary guardianship.

In terms of the abuse and mistreatment of children, the CRPD addresses those practices as well. Article 23(3) charges State Parties with ensuring 'that children with disabilities have equal rights with respect to family life' and provides that in order 'to prevent concealment, abandonment, neglect and segregation of children with disabilities States Parties shall undertake to provide early and comprehensive information, services and support to children with disabilities and their families'.

The CPRD's mandates access to information and cultural identity.[726] Thus the CRPD requires States Parties to address the problem of persons with hearing based disabilities not being able to learn customary law through its predominantly oral tradition.

Article 8 on 'Awareness-raising' is strongly validated by the fieldwork. Among other things, this article calls on states parties '[t]o pro-

---

[725] *Ibid* art 23(4).

[726] *Ibid* art 9(2)(f) and 30(4).

mote awareness of the capabilities and contributions of persons with disabilities.'[727] The fieldwork indicates that community attitudes about the capabilities and contributions of persons with disabilities are highly consequential in customary legal scenarios. If fully and effectively implemented, more favourable perceptions about the abilities of persons with disabilities can greatly improve their status, rights and treatment in customary scenarios.

Comparing Gender with Disability in Customary Contexts

This section builds on an earlier discussion about the relationship between disability and gender in customary legal scenarios discussed in some detail in Sections II (Marriage and Divorce) and V (Succession) of Chapter 7. It provides comparative analysis concerning place, study and treatment of disability and gender in customary legal frameworks. It also outlines the cumulative impact of gender-based and disability-based discrimination in customary legal scenarios.

Existing studies and research often focus on gender-based distinctions in customary contexts.[728] This thesis indicates that disability status should also be considered when evaluating customary legal frameworks from a human rights perspective.

One reason why disability is rarely explored in customary contexts is its complexity. In contrast to gender, which presents as a largely fixed

---

[727] *Ibid* art 8(1)(c) and (2)(a)(iii).

[728] See e.g. AM Tripp 'Women's movements, customary law, and land rights in Africa: the case of Uganda (2014) 7.4 *African Studies Quarterly* 1-19; TW Bennett 'The equality clause and customary law (1994) 10 *S Afr J on Human Rights* 122-130; I Yngstrom 'Women, wives and land rights in Africa: Situating gender beyond the household in the debate over land policy and changing tenure systems' (2002) 30(1) *Oxford Development Studies* 21-40; J Bond 'Gender, discourse, and customary law' (2010) 83 *Southern California L Rev* 425-490.

and binary trait[729], disability presents dynamically in diverse ways along continuums. Thus the customary ramifications of disability are not as well established and known through practice and tradition as those associated with gender.

Despite the heightened challenge in discerning customary law pertaining to disability, there are advantages that come with the situational aspect of disability in customary contexts. Importantly, those seeking to advance the interests of person's disabilities could face a more receptive climate for customary legal changes than gender rights advocates. In the case of gender rights there are operational customary structures such as patrilineal land tenure that undergo significant disruption if both genders receive equal treatment. However, the elimination of situational discrimination against persons with disabilities does not portend similar structural destabilisation. Thus disability rights actors in Mukono District can benefit from a positive association with progress without the negative stigma of social angst and cultural upheaval associated with women's rights.

On the negative side, the complexity of disability rights makes for a more intensive acculturation project than gender-based rights. The disability rights movement seeks more than equal treatment. Disability rights entail proactive inclusion, mainstreaming and accommodation. In addition, merely understanding the diverse challenges and experiences of persons with disabilities is a considerable task.

Gender and disability are rightly considered together in both the CPRD[730] and the Draft Protocol to the African Charter on Human and

---

[729] Of course many are challenging the fixed and binary conception of gender in the modern times especially within the scholarship and politics developed nations. See e.g. F Romeo 'Beyond a medical model: Advocating for a new conception of gender identity in the law' (2004-2005) 36 *Columbia Human Rights L Rev* 713; J Lobber 'Beyond the binaries: Depolarizing the Categories of Sex. Sexuality and Gender' (1996) 66(2) *Sociological Inquiry* 143-159.

[730] art 6.

Peoples' Rights on the Rights of Persons with Disabilities in Africa.[731] Female status can exacerbate the impact of disability based discrimination. Women face cultural expectations in marriage that require them to have certain physical abilities. This can present a heightened barrier to marriage for women with disabilities. The tendency of some to view women with disabilities as sexual objects with curative qualities places them in dangerous and exploitive situations. The fact that women are not allowed to be customary heirs prevents them from assuming a key position of power and influence through which they could champion their inheritance rights. The tendency to give women less land through inheritance places women with disabilities in especially precarious circumstances in customary succession.

The harmful combinations of gender-based and disability-based discrimination confirm the wisdom of the CRPD's mandate to 'incorporate a gender perspective in all efforts to promote the full enjoyment of human rights and fundamental freedoms by persons with disabilities'[732] and the necessity of Article 16 of the CPRD which requires State Parties to address gender-based exploitation, violence and abuse.

Conclusion

Formal and informal sources of law interact to impact the status, rights and treatment of persons with disabilities in deeply pluralistic legal settings. The comprehensive lens of the semi-autonomous social field enables us to see a variety of factors at work in legal ecosystems. This chapter demonstrates the necessity of specific contextual research to understand the interaction of various legal sources and cultural influences that form, influence and impact customary legal frameworks.

---

[731] art 22.

[732] CPRD pre (s).

The inclusive consideration of relevant legal and cultural sources in particular contexts presents fertile opportunities for applied analysis. This chapter related informed insights for disability rights strategies in Mukono District, the substance of the CRPD and a comparative treatment of gender and disability. Each of these instances of applied analysis considered the interface of customary legal substance with other legal sources and cultural content. The perspectives presented in these sections confirm the utility and wisdom of Moore's research approach.

9

CONCLUSION

Introduction

This concluding chapter serves three broad purposes. First, it presents the major findings. Second, it proffers selected strategies for improving the status, rights and treatment of persons with disabilities. Third, it offers a reflection on the fieldwork with proposed subjects for further research.

Core Research Findings

This research was motivated by the belief that disability status is likely to be significant and consequential in customary legal scenarios and warrants field-based inquiry. The fieldwork confirms that impairments impact the customary rights, status and treatment of persons with disabilities.

Disability status can have a significant impact in the contexts of customary marriage, clan leadership, customary guardianship, customary succession and land ownership. Although a particular impairment rarely results in rigidly established customary legal treatment[733], disability impacts and influences the actors who discern customary law and carry out customary processes. Often such actors will discriminate on the

---

[733] One clearly established exception is the fact that male impotency disqualifies a person from customary marriage.

basis of disability. This is especially true in the context of land inheritance.

Formal law provides an incomplete picture of the legal content and systems shaping the lives of persons with disabilities in Mukono District. This is particularly the case in the context of succession law and other familial and relational legal scenarios.[734]

Disability is diverse and fluid. There are countless impairment that people experience and these impairments differ widely in severity and impact. Impairments can manifest and increase at various times in life as a result of physical trauma, disease and age. In addition, social contexts and physical environments can significantly heighten the challenges presented by impairments.

The diversity and complexity of disability combine with the attributes of customary law to produce highly situational legal outcomes. Customary law is flexible and situational.[735] Inherently distinctive legal disability scenarios are unlikely to generate the consistent results which can crystallise into established customary law—especially when customary outcomes are localised and unwritten. There is minimal customary legal clarity concerning the status, rights and treatment of person with disabilities in Mukono District.

Customary law and practice pertaining to disability offers little in terms of established precedent. Human disability and its implications are

---

[734] International Justice Mission (IJM) *Property Grabbing from Ugandan Widows and the Justice System: A Mixed-Methods Assessment in Mukono County, Uganda* (2015) at 65 (finding that only 1.3 per cent of widows participated in the formal probate of their husbands' estates).

[735] A Allott 'The judicial ascertainment of customary law in British Africa' 20(3) (1957) *The Modern Law Review* 244-263; TW Bennett & T Vermeulen 'Codification of customary law' (1980) 24(2) *Journal of African Law* 206-219; SF Moore *Social facts and fabrications customary law on Kilimanjaro, 1880-1980* (1986); A Haugerud 'Land tenure and agrarian change in Kenya' (1989) 59(1) *Africa* 61-90.

highly situational. Thus customary legal actors adjudicating and establishing the status and rights of persons with disabilities find themselves exercising human reason and discretion rather than applying firmly established legal consequences.

For the most part, the customary legal frameworks—which entail substantive customary law, procedures, institutions and legal actors—are not inherently discriminatory against persons with disabilities. Instead, customary legal scenarios present opportunities where discrimination can occur. The disability-based discrimination in customary contexts is largely the product of people's attitudes and prejudices as opposed to an adherence to perceived customary rules.

While there is little in terms of established customary law pertaining to disability, there are certain recurring phenomena. First, consequential decisions are made about the legal status, rights, and treatment of persons with disabilities outside of the formal law and with minimal direct checks from formal actors. Key customary decisions are typically made by clan and family members in connection with rites of passage such as marriage and burial. This thesis' field research indicates that discrimination on the basis of disability occurs within customary decision-making scenarios.

Impairments can be consequential factors for decision makers in customary contexts. Notions people hold concerning persons with impairments impact customary legal outcomes. Beliefs and biases about human capacity and functionality are especially impactful. For its part the CPRD expressly addresses the need to inculcate positive beliefs about the capacity and functionality of persons with disabilities.[736] This thesis confirms the wisdom in that mandate.

---

[736] Convention on the Rights of Persons with Disabilities (CRPD), adopted 13 December 2006 by GA Res 61/106, Annex I, UN GAOR, 61st Sess, Supp No 49 at 65, UN Doc A/61/49 (2006), entered into force May 3, 2008, UN Doc A/61/61, art 8(1)(c) requiring state parties to undertake to adopt measures 'to

There is growing awareness in Mukono District that the formal law opposes discrimination on the basis of disability. Interviewees provided examples where knowledge of the formal law helped to combat discrimination in customary contexts. However, in other customary legal scenarios the formal law has little or no impact. Instead, many decision makers render customary legal outcomes based on pragmatic concerns and biases.

I never detected palpable resistance, either in action or word, to the substantive requirements of the formal law. This is especially the case with respect to the Ugandan Constitution which is widely accepted at the supreme law of the land.[737] Also, many of the interviewees with disabilities indicated that they are aware of their power to challenge customary legal processes in formal institutions. Yet, none of the interviewees with disabilities indicated that they proactively challenged the outcome of a customary legal scenario in the formal court system.[738] Moreover, others cited social cost as a factor that discourages the challenging of customary legal outcomes.

---

promote awareness of the capabilities and contributions of persons with disabilities' and art 8(2)(a)(iii) requiring state parties to 'To promote recognition of the skills, merits and abilities of persons with disabilities'.

[737] Constitution of Uganda 1995 (as amended in 2005). Although the fieldwork indicates that the exact content of the Uganda Constitution pertaining to disability is not known. Instead residents of Mukono District have a general sense that the Constitution generally supports the rights of persons with disabilities.

[738] The two interviewees with disabilities reported some engagement with the formal legal system to defend their rights to land. One individual reported being pushed off of his kibanja holding without just cause. Another individual has been involved in litigation a property grabbing case where he was found to be the party in the wrong due to his efforts to remove a widow from land belonging to a deceased relative.

Suggested Strategies

This thesis is not a wholly dispassionate academic pursuit. It is put forward in the hope of encouraging and informing initiatives that improve the status, rights and treatment of persons with disabilities in places where customary legal frameworks are pervasive and consequential. This section presents strategies suggested by this thesis for improving the lives of persons with disabilities in communities in Mukono District. Several of these specific strategies fall within in the categories of bottom-up approaches to effecting human rights development discussed in Section III of Chapter 4. Other strategies discussed below link formal institutions and top down change agents to grassroots actors and contexts.

Legal Sensitization and Community Engagement

This thesis speaks to the viability of acculturation strategies through grassroots sensitisation and community engagement in the promotion of disability rights in customary contexts. Community attitudes and knowledge about disabilities inform and guide customary legal scenarios.

People's attitudes about persons with disabilities are not fixed and rigid. In Mukono District there is a claimed willingness to alter views about disability based on exposure to legal knowledge and other information. Thus purposeful acculturation initiatives appear to be workable strategies for engendering desired changes in the context of disability rights. In this sense, the wisdom of the CRPD's inclusion of content calling for 'awareness-raising'[739] is affirmed by this thesis.

Like the CPRD[740], the findings place beliefs about the capabilities of persons with disabilities at the fulcrum of their status, rights and treatment within customary legal frameworks. Many decisions that impair

---

[739] CRPD art 8.

[740] CRPD art 8 at (1)(c) and (2)(a)(iii).

and diminish the legal status or rights of persons with disabilities are shaped by conceptions about what people can or cannot do. Thus sharing stories and evidence about the functional capabilities of persons with disabilities could positively impact customary actors and their treatment of persons with disabilities.

Many discriminatory customary legal decisions are motivated by the desire and duty to do what is wise and rational. Customary actors apply their own reason and understanding in customary legal scenarios. They make decisions about customary rights and status based on their knowledge, experience and common sense. Customary actors will not simply accept a human rights principle, such as non-discrimination against persons with disabilities, if applying that principle does not make practical sense to them. The findings speak to the wisdom of state obligations to campaign against harmful practices applied to persons with disabilities and to promote positive representations of persons with disabilities as provided for in the Draft Protocol to the African Charter on Human and Peoples' Rights on the Rights of Persons with Disabilities.[741]

Presenting the human rights mandate of non-discrimination as an abstract legal requirement of equality that requires compliance no matter how unworkable is likely to fail in this context. The reason and common sense of customary actors must be engaged regardless of the dominant human rights suppositions that may cause some human rights actors and trainers to go straight to the 'what' of human rights requirements without realistically addressing the 'how'. Community members need to see why adherence to the rights and principles espoused in the CRPD or Ugandan law actually make sense in their lived environment. Grassroots change initiatives should appeal to the practical wisdom of customary actors. Yet sensitization efforts must be careful not to permit the at-

---

[741] Draft Protocol art 2(d) and (e).

tendant legitimization of human rationality as a license to discriminate or disregard legal requirements.

Other potential sensitisation-related challenges include sparking broad interest in disability issues among those that consider themselves to be without disability, determining how to encourage attendance at sensitisation events without turning the event into a mere 'facilitation' handout, and effectively navigating the politically charged nuances flowing from the association the disability movement with other progressive social movements involving gender and sexuality.

Persons with Disabilities

The field research confirms the importance of actor-oriented change strategies in bringing about positive changes. In Mukono District persons with disabilities are crucial actors in the realising and championing of their rights in customary legal scenarios. Thus, persons with disabilities need to be equipped and empowered to leverage formal channels and institutions to hold customary legal actors accountable to the formal law's protections against discrimination.[742]

A foundational area of empowerment is knowledge of the law. There are organisations in Uganda that are dedicated to ensuring that persons with disabilities are aware of formal laws. The fieldwork findings indicate that such initiatives can be highly beneficial. All persons with disabilities, including the blind and those that are kept away from the public, need to be the target of purposeful efforts to overcome particular barriers to accessing legal knowledge. Relatedly, in the customary context this research indicates that special efforts need to be made to ensure that

---

[742] This has been an ongoing point of emphasis in scholarship discussing discriminatory and exploitive treatment of women and children within customary legal frameworks in Uganda. V Bennett, G Faulk, A Kovina et al 'Inheritance law in Uganda: The plight of widows and children' (2006) 7 *Georgetown Journal of Gender & the Law* 451-530.

persons with hearing impairments can learn the customary legal content that is shared orally.

A second key area of empowerment is the capacity and support needed to overcome social pressure. Interviewees with disabilities indicated that they chose not to bring formal challenges against discriminatory customary occurrences because of the cost of social hardship. Several interviewees reported that the prospect of disputes with family and neighbors was so unappealing that they simply choose to relinquish their rights to land inheritance. Building community and support networks among persons with disabilities could help to encourage people to overcome the stifling effects of social pressure.

A third important element is access to justice. Most people in Mukono District do not engage the formal legal justice system. Although there are human rights organisations which offer free legal assistance in the context of human rights abuses, their effective reach is limited. Thus there is a need to ensure that persons with disabilities who are subjected to discrimination in customary legal scenarios can access legal representation that enables them to combat discrimination through formal channels. Here the need for exceptional professional advocacy is heightened because the challenges of access to court locations, structures, systems and content prevent many persons with disabilities from engaging the formal legal process.[743] If other community members understand that the threat of formal legal action is real and available for persons with disabilities, instances of discrimination could be thwarted within customary scenarios. International Justice Mission has adopted a targeted strategy to combat 'property grabbing' of widows and orphans in Mukono District with some success. Perhaps such a targeted strategy

---

[743] For a discussion of challenges to rights access and realisation facing persons with disabilities see DA Young and R Quibell 'Why rights are never enough: Rights, intellectual disability and understanding' 15(5) Disability and Society 758.

could go a long way in bringing human rights standards for persons with disabilities to grassroots customary contexts.

The Need to Facilitate Formal Engagement

Unless a person is willing to pursue formal legal review of discriminatory customary actions, it can be difficult for the requirements of the formal law to check and influence the customary law. However, the formal legal system is alien and largely ignored by most residents of Mukono District. Thus top-down legal change strategies need to be designed to link people at the grassroots to the benefits of formal legal rights and reforms.

The widespread practice of customary succession in Mukono District[744] flies in the face of formal law. According to the formal law there is no such thing as customary succession; it has been fully preempted by longstanding statutory law.[745]

Formal engagement and oversight could address discrimination and other human rights abuses within customary succession. Yet formal courts are ill equipped to conduct engaged review over legal nullities. Adhering to the law requires the more radical approach of ignoring or striking down all instances of customary succession.

The practice of customary guardianship faces a similar disconnects. It is a wholly illegitimate practice in the eyes of the formal law. Thus the formal law largely ignores customary guardianship as oppose providing oversight and guidance.

Customary Institutions

Baganda customary law offers unique opportunities for reception-based change strategies. The Buganda Kingdom has institutions and hierarchies that could be leveraged to advance the status, rights and

---

[744] IJM (note 2).

[745] The Succession Act (Uganda) (Cap 162) (1906); The Administrator's General Act (Uganda) (Cap 157) (1933).

treatment of persons with disabilities in zones where Baganda customary law persists.

The penultimate customary institution in the Buganda Kingdom is the Kabaka. The Baganda people view the Kabaka as the best and truest source of Baganda customary law. The Kabaka has the power to pronounce and alter Baganda customary law. Disability advocates should not overlook the possibility of engaging the assistance of the Kabaka and other Buganda institutions to further the rights and interests of persons with disabilities.

Parents of Children with Disabilities

Another key 'actor' in improving the status, rights and treatment of persons with disabilities in customary frameworks are family members.[746] In particular, parents of persons with disabilities are especially well placed to positively impact the status, rights and treatment of persons with disabilities in Mukono District.

Parents have great influence on the attitudes and beliefs of others about persons with disabilities. As one interviewee noted 'if parents discriminate against their own children with disabilities, why shouldn't society do the same'.

One important way parents can shape the attitudes of others is by educating their children with disabilities. If community members observe these parents investing in their children's education, the community will see that the parents value their children. This social benefit is in addition to the many benefits that come from education itself.

Parents also have significant power to ensure that their children with disabilities are treated justly in customary legal scenarios. The fieldwork speaks to the continuing deference given to both written and unwritten final instructions, whether set forth in wills or otherwise, in customary succession scenarios. Thus if parents proclaim final instructions that

---

[746] CRPD pre (x); art 8(1)(a); and art 23.

their children with disabilities are to be treated the same as their other children, the parents can greatly improve the chances of equitable treatment in matters of succession and clan leadership.

Parents can also see to it that their children with disabilities are aware of their rights and the protections against discrimination provided for them under the formal law. They can ensure that non-disabled siblings are aware of relevant legal and human rights-based requirements so that the siblings can hold themselves and others accountable to non-discrimination in customary legal scenarios.

Thus the purposeful engagement of parents of children with disabilities is key strategic avenue for combatting discrimination within customary legal frameworks. CRPD wisely calls upon States Parties to 'undertake to provide early and comprehensive information, services and support to children with disabilities and their families'.[747]

The Need for Contextually Specific Understanding

This thesis' field research offers valuable insights for effecting positive changes in the lives of persons with disabilities in Mukono District. Crafting change strategies that are informed by these findings will help ensure that the specific cultural barriers and opportunities for positive changes are considered and addressed. The findings would be particularly useful in the case of facilitative bottom-up change strategies such as the framing approach and the soft approach discussed in Section III of Chapter 4.

The value of this thesis' field research to the selection and design of change strategies for advancing the status, rights and treatment of persons with disabilities should encourage similar research initiatives. While there are general lessons that can be gleaned from this thesis, the need for culturally specific knowledge should caution against a broad application of the Mukono-specific and Baganda-specific findings.

---

[747] CRPD art 23(3).

The Need for Future Research

This thesis demonstrates the need for future research. Customary legal systems are diverse. Research findings about customary legal frameworks in Mukono District are necessarily unique. Similar fieldwork should be conducted in other places to learn more about the status, rights and treatment of persons with disabilities within those settings. Such research will offer specific insights for the places studied and help to provide the perspective and depth needed to make broader assertions about disability and customary legal frameworks.

In addition, research in places that are distinct from Mukono District would help to generate content for comparative analysis. For example, in Uganda it would be useful to conduct research in areas where customary landholding systems predominate as opposed to Mailo tenure. Similarly, there would be comparative value in conducting research in areas where the dominant indigenous people groups tend to hold land collectively, where the indigenous people are predominantly cattle herders, or in areas that are more or less urban.

There are research topics pertaining to disability and customary law that were not substantially addressed in the fieldwork. The relationship between mental impairments and customary law remains largely unexplored. This is especially true when it comes to cataloguing the actual experiences of persons with mental disabilities in customary scenarios. Moreover, further research would be useful concerning the use of customary guardianship to strip widows with disabilities of custody of their children, the customary heir selection process, and the impact that disability could have on a husband's ability to recoup bride wealth[748].

Furthermore, the thesis points to the potential of applied research that can assess the viability and potential of various change strategies.

---

[748] Despite the fact that the formal law now prohibits the forced return of bride wealth in *Mifumi (U) Ltd and 12 Others v Attorney General* UgSC Const App No. 2/14 [2015].

Research opportunities can be combined with change strategies. For example, this thesis suggests the possibility of engaging the Kabaka to make human rights compliant pronouncements about the status, rights and treatment of persons with disabilities under customary law in traditional Buganda Kingdom lands. If such pronouncements were made and publicised it would be useful to track the impact and efficacy of such pronouncements within customary legal scenarios.

Historic and cultural research could also be done to catalog all of the acts of present and past Kabakas that concern disability and other rights based issues so that they can be shared with community members. A historic and cultural case could be made for disability rights in the customary law of the Buganda Kingdom that could be used to influence customary legal scenarios. Similar efforts could be made for other people groups especially where there are traditionally respected top-down customary power structures.

This thesis points to the absence of accessible and integrative formal oversight for customary succession processes. The CRPD requires States Parties to 'prohibit all discrimination on the basis of disability and guarantee to persons with disabilities equal and effective legal protection against discrimination on all grounds'.[749] There is a need for pragmatic strategies such as local government oversight initiatives or customary actor trainings designed to ensure that instances of customary succession comply with the formal law's prohibitions against discrimination. These strategies need to be developed, implemented and assessed for effectiveness.

The impact of international instruments on the customary legal level is another topic that warrants additional research. This research indicates that there is a willingness to accept the disability related international human rights standards in Mukono District. Research initiatives could explore the means and methods of inculcating the standards of the

---

[749] CPRD 5(2)

CRPD into customary legal scenarios through various means. Examples include research on the effectiveness of CRPD mandated sensitisation initiatives to impact ideas about customary law and the application of customary law and practices in key areas such as the informal succession of land rights.

Conclusion

Human disability is a consequential factor in customary legal frameworks in Mukono District. Yet disability status does not inevitably lead to established customary legal treatment. The customary ramifications of disability status are discerned on a case by case basis by actors who often seek to do what they think is best for families and clans. The attitudes and beliefs that people hold about various impairments are integral to how the status, rights and treatment of persons with disabilities are meted out in customary legal scenarios.

The research project points to the value of descriptive field research informed with emergent understandings of legal pluralism and customary law. This thesis should encourage others to investigate the status, rights and treatment of persons with disabilities in other highly customary contexts.

BIBLIOGRAPHY

Books

Allot, A The Limits of Law (London: Butterworth, 1980).

An Na'im, AA (ed) Human Rights Under African Constitutions, Realizing the Promise for Ourselves (Philadelphia: University of Pennsylvania Press, 2003).

Arksey, H. and Knight, PT (eds) Interviewing for Social Scientists: An Introductory Resource with Examples (Los Angeles: Sage, 1999).

Behling, O and Law, KS Translating Questionnaires and Other Research Instruments (Los Angeles: Sage, 2000).

Bekker, JC Seymour's Customary Law in Southern Africa (Cape Town: Juta, 1989).

Bekker, JC, Rautenbach, C and Goolam N (eds) Introduction to Legal Pluralism in South Africa 3 ed (Durban: LexisNexis South Africa, 2010).

Benedict, R Patterns of Culture (Boston: Houghton Mifflin Harcourt, 1934).Bennett, TW 1985 The Application of Customary Law in Southern Africa – The Conflict of Personal Laws (Cape Town: Juta, 1985).

Bennett, TW Human Rights and African Customary Law (Cape Town: Juta, 1995).

Bickenbach, JE Physical Disability and Social Policy (Toronto: University of Toronto Press, 1993).

Burke, J Osborn's Concise Law Dictionary (London: Sweet and Maxwell: year and edition unknown).

Charlton, J Nothing About Us Without Us (Berkeley: University of California Press, 1998).

Collins English Dictionary 4th ed (Glasgow: Harper Collins, 1998).

Doyle, BJ Disability Discrimination: Law and Practice 6th ed (Bristol: Jordans, 2008).

Du Plessis Access to work for disabled persons in South Africa: A rights critique (PULP: Pretoria, 2017).

Eade, D Capacity-Building: An Approach to People-Centred Development (Oxford: Oxfam, 1997).

Easterly, W White Man's Burden; Why the West's Efforts to Aid the Rest Have Done so Much Ill and so Little Good (New York: Penguin Press, 2006).

Ehrlich, E The Fundamental Principles of the Sociology of Law (Cambridge, Harvard University Press, 1936).

Elam, Y The Social and Sexual Roles of Hima Women (Manchester: Manchester University Press, 1973).

Ewick, P and Silbey, SP The Common Place of Law: Stories from Everyday Life (Chicago: University of Chicago Press, 1998).

Flynn, RJ & Nitch, KE Normalization, Social Integration, and Community Services (Baltimore: Baltimore University Press, 1980).

Geertz, C Local Knowledge: Further Essays in Interpretive Anthropology (New York: Basic Books, 1983).

Gibson, GD and Larson, TJ and McGurk, CR The Kavango Peoples (Wiesbaden: Studien zur Kulturkunde, 1981).

Glendon, MA Comparative Legal Traditions in a Nutshell (St. Paul: West Academic Publishing, 1982).

Goffman, E Stigma: Notes on the Management of Spoiled Identity (New York: Simon and Schuster, 1963).

Grobbelaar-du Plessis, I and van Reenen, T Aspects of Disability Law in Africa (Pretoria: PULP, 2011).

Habermas, J The Structural Transformation of the Public Sphere: An inquiry into the Category of Bourgeois Society (Cambridge: MIT Press: 1991)

Haugen, G & Boutros, V The Locust Effect (Oxford: Oxford University Press, 2014).

Haydon, ES Law and Justice in Buganda (London: Butterworths, 1960).

Herr, SS, Gostin, LO and Koh, HH (eds) The Human Rights of Persons with Intellectual Disabilities: Different but Equal (Oxford: Oxford University Press, 2003).

Holleman, JF Shona Customary Law (Manchester: Manchester University Press, 1952).

Isser, D (ed) Customary Justice and the Rule of Law in War Torn Societies (Washington DC: United States Institute of Peace, 2011).

Ikuenobe, P Philosophical Perspectives on Communalism and Morality in African Traditions (London: Lexington Books, 2006).

Johnstone, D An Introduction to Disability Studies 2d ed (London: David Fulton, 2001).

Jjuuko, FW and Kibalama, E Culture and Women: The Position of Women in Buganda (Kampala: Fountain, 2011).

Kameri-Mbote, P, Odote, C and Nyamu-Musembi, C et al Ours by Right: Law, Politics and Realities of Community Property in Kenya (Nairobi, Strathmore University Legal Press, 2013).

Keck, M and Sikkink, K Activists Beyond Borders: Advocacy Networks in International Politics (Ithaca: Cornell University Press, 1998).

Knight, P (ed) Small Scale Research Design (Los Angeles: Sage, 2002).

Liamputtong, P Researching the Vulnerable Moral and Ethical Issues in Researching Vulnerable People (Los Angeles: Sage, 2006).

Martin, EA ed Dictionary of Law 4th ed (Oxford: Oxford University Press, 2006)

Marwick, BA The Swazi (London: Frank Cass, 1966).Mead, L Beyond Entitlement: The Social Obligations of Citizenship (New York: Free Press: 1986)

Menski, W Comparative Law in a Global Context: The Legal Systems of Asia and Africa 2d ed (Cambridge: Cambridge University Press, 2006).

Merry, SE Human Rights and Gender Violence: Translating International Law into Local Justice' (Chicago: University of Chicago Press, 2006).

Miller, RL Researching Life Stories and Family Histories, Analysing Life Histories (Los Angeles: Sage, 2000).

Moore, SF Social facts and fabrications customary law on Kilimanjaro, 1880-1980 (Cambridge: Cambridge University Press, 1986)

Moyo, D Dead Aid: Why Aid is not Working and How There is a Better Way for Africa (New York: Farrar, Straus and Giroux, 2009).

Mönning, HO The Pedi (Pretoria: Van Schalk, 1967).

Mutua, M Human Rights: A Political and Cultural Critique (Philadelphia: University of Pennsylvania Press, 2013).

Ntagali, S and Hodgetts, EE More Than One Wife: Polygamy and Grace (Riviera Beach, Florida: Emerge Publishing, 2011).

Oliver, M The Politics of Disablement: A Sociological Approach (London: Palgrave Macmillan, 1990).

Oliver, M Understanding Disability: From Theory to Practice (London: Palgrave Macmillan, 1996).

Ollenuu, N Principles of Customary Land Law in Ghana (London: Sweet and Maxwell, 1962)

Parrinder, EG African Traditional Religion (London: Faber and Faber, 1962).

Priestley, M Disability Politics and Community Care (London: Jessica Kingsley, 1999)

Quinn, G and Degener, T Human Rights and Disability: the Current Use and Future Potential of United Nations Human Rights Instruments in the Context of Disability (New York: United Nations Publications, 2002)

Seppä en, S Possibilities and Challenges of the Human Rights-Based Approach to Development (Helsinki: Hakapaino Oy, 2005).

Schapera, I A Handbook of Tswana Law and Custom 2d ed reissue (London: Frank Cass, 1970).

Schapera, I The Tswana (London: KPI, in association with the International African Institute, 1984).

Schatzman, L and Strauss, AL Strategies for a Natural Sociology (Upper Saddle River: Prentice Hall, 1973).

Scheyvens, R and Storey, D (eds) Development Fieldwork (Los Angeles: Sage, 2003).

Shakespeare, T Disability Rights and Wrongs (Milton Park: Taylor & Francis, 2006).

Smart, J Disability, Society and the Individual (New York: Aspen Publishers, 2000).

Stebbins, RA Exploratory Research in the Social Sciences (Los Angeles: Sage, 2001).

Taylor, JV Primal Vision 2d ed (Nairobi: Acton, 2001).

Tempels, PF La Philosophie Bantoue (Paris: Présence Africaine, 1959).

Tumusiime, J and Bichachi, CO (eds) The People and Culture of Uganda 4th ed (Westport, Connecticut: Greenwood, 2011).

Van Tromp, J Xhosa Law of Persons (Cape Town: Juta, 1947).

Weber, MC Understanding Disability Law (Dayton: Lexis-Nexis, 2007).

Werner, D Nothing About Us Without Us: Developing Innovative Technologies for, by and with Disabled Persons (Palo Alto: HealthWrights, 1998).

West, HW Land Policy in Buganda (London: Cambridge University Press, 1972).

Wilson, RA (ed) Human Rights, Culture and Context: Anthropological Perspectives (London: Pluto Press, 1997).

Wolfensberger, W A Brief Introduction to Social Role Valorization: a High-Order Concept for Addressing the Plight of Societally Devalued People, and for Structuring Human Services (Syracuse: Syracuse University, 1998).

Wolfensberger, WP, Nirje, B, Olshansky, S et al The Principle of Normalization in Human Services (Toronto: National Institute on Mental Retardation, 1972).

Journal Articles and Chapters in Books

Abberley, P 'The concept of oppression and the development of a social theory of disability' (1987) 2(1) Disability, Handicap & Society 5-19.

Adjami, ME 'African courts, international law, and comparative case law: chimera or emerging human rights jurisprudence?' (2002) 24 Michigan Journal of International Law 103-167, at 118

Albert, B 'Briefing note: the social model of disability, human rights and development' (2004) Disability KaR Research Project 1-8.

Allot, A 'Introduction' in E Cotran (ed) (1987) Case Book on Kenya Customary Law.

Allott, A 'The judicial ascertainment of customary law in British Africa' 20(3) (1957) The Modern Law Review 244-263.

An-Na'im, AA 'Toward a cross-cultural approach to defining international standards of human rights: the meaning of cruel, inhuman, or degrading treatment or punishment' in An Na'im, AA (ed) Human Rights in Cross-Cultural Perspectives: A Quest for Consensus (1995) 19-43.

Areheart, BA 'When disability isn't "just right": the entrenchment of the medical model of disability and the Goldilocks dilemma' (2008) 83 Indiana Law Journal 181-232.

Armstrong, A, Beyani, C, Himonga C et al 'Uncovering reality: excavating women's rights in African family law' (1993) 7 International Journal of Law and the Family 314-369.

Armstrong, P 'Beyond (human) rights?' (2009) 29(4) Disabilities Studies Quarterly.

Asante, SKB 'Nation building and human rights emergent African nations' 2 Cornell Int Law Jnl 72-107.

Baffoe, M 'Stigma, discrimination & marginalization: gateways to oppression of persons with disabilities in Ghana, West Africa' (2013) 3(1) Journal of Educational and Social Research 187-198 at 191.

Bagenstos, SR 'Justice Ginsburg and the judicial role in expanding "We the People": the disability rights cases' (2004) 104 Columbia Law Review 49-59.

Banda, F 'Global standards: local values' (2003) 17 International Journal of Law, Policy and the Family 1-27.

Banks, AM 'CEDAW, compliance, and custom: human rights enforcement in Sub-Saharan Africa' (2009) 32 Fordham International Law Journal 781-845.

Bennett, TW and Vermeulen, T 'Codification of customary law' (1980) 24(2) Journal of African Law 206-219.

Bennett, TW 'The compatibility of African customary law and human rights' (1991) Acta Juridica 18.

Bennett, TW 'The equality clause and customary law (1994) 10 S Afr J on Human Rights 122-130.

Bennett, TW 'Human rights and the African cultural tradition' (1993) 22 Transformation: 30-40

Bennett, V, Falk, G, Kovina A et al 'Inheritance law in Uganda: the plight of widows and children' (2006) 7 Georgetown Journal of Gender & the Law 451-530.

Bickenbach, JE and Bickenbach, JE 'Disability, culture and the UN convention' (2009) 31(14) Disability and Rehabilitation 1111-1124.

Borg, J, Bergman, AK and Ostergen, PO 'Is "legal empowerment of the poor" relevant to people with disabilities in developing countries? An empirical and normative review' (2013) 6:22854 Global Health Action.

Bond, J 'Gender, discourse, and customary law' (2010) 83 Southern California L Rev 425-490.

Brinks, D & Gauri, V 'A new policy landscape: legalizing social and economic rights in the developing world' in G Varun & D Brinks (eds)Courting Social Justice: Judicial Enforcement of Social and Economic Rights in the Developing World (2008) 303-352.

Burchardt, T 'Capabilities and disability: the capabilities framework and the social model of disability' (2004) 19(7) Disability & Society 735-751.

Bwengye, F 'Land as a sensitive matter in Uganda in the eyes of the law' (2007) 5(1) Uganda Living Law Journal 1.

Claassens, A and Mnisi, S 'Rural women redefining land rights in the context of living customary law' (2009) 25 SAJHR 491-516

Coldham, S 'Land reform and customary rights: the case of Uganda reviewed' (2000) 44(1) Journal of African Law 65-77.

Combrinck, H 'Regional developments: disability rights in the African regional human rights system during 2011 and 2012' (2013) 1 ADRY 361-368.

Cooper, S, Ssebunnya, J, Kigozi, F et al 'Viewing Uganda's mental health system through a human rights lens' (2010) 22(6) International Review of Psychiatry 578-588.

Cornwall, A and Nyamu-Musembi, C 'Why rights, why now? Reflections on the rise of rights in international development' (2005) 36(1) IDS Bulletin 9.

Corradi, G 'Access to justice in Pemba City: How exploring women's lived realities with plural law uncovers programmatic gaps' (2011) 64 Journal of Legal Pluralism and Unofficial Law 1-31.

Corradi, G 'Advancing human rights in legally plural Africa: the role of development actors in the justice sector' (2013) 26(1) Afrika Focus 89-98.

Cotula, L 'Introduction' in L Cotula (ed) Changes in "Customary" Land Tenure Systems in Africa (2007) 5-13.

Davis, LJ 'The end of identity politics: On disability as an unstable category' in (2013) The Disability Studies Reader 263-277.

De Silva de Alwis, R 'Mining the intersections: advancing the rights of women and children with disabilities within an interrelated

web of human rights' (2009) 18 Pacific Rim Law. & Policy J
293-322.

Degener, T 'Disability in a Human Rights Context' (2016) 5(3) Laws
35.

Degener, T 'International disability law - a new legal subject on
the rise: the Interregional Experts' Meeting in Hong Kong
December 13-17, 1999' (2000) 18 Berkeley J Int'l Law
180-195.

Devlieger, PJ 'From handicap to disability: language use and cultural
meaning in the United States' (1999) 21(7) Disability and
Rehabilitation 346-354.

Devlieger, PJ 'Persons with a physical disability at the interstices of
classification: examples from Africa and the United States'
(1998) 2 Zeitschrift Behinderung und Dritte Welt 45-49.

Devlieger, PJ 'Physical "disability" in Bantu languages: understanding
the relativity of classification and meaning' (1998) 21(1)
International Journal of Rehabilitation Research 51-62.

Devlieger, PJ 'Why disabled? The cultural understanding of physical
disability in an African society' in Susan Reynolds Whyte
& Benedicte Ingstad (Eds) Disability and Culture (1995)
94-106.

Dewsbury, G, Clarke, K, Randall, D et al 'The anti social model of
disability' (2004) 19(2) Disability, Poverty and Development
145-158.

Dinokopila, BR 'The rights of persons with disabilities in Botswana:
policy and institutional framework' in Grobbelaar-du Plessis,
I and van Reenen, T Aspects of Disability Law in Africa
(2011) 261-280.

Donnelly, J 'Cultural relativism and universal human rights' (1984) 6(4) Human Rights Quarterly 400-419.

Engel, DM 'Vertical and horizontal perspectives on rights consciousness' (2012) 19(2) Indiana Journal of Global Legal Studies 423-455.

Fefoame, GO, Walugembe, J and Mpofuat, R 'Building partnerships and alliances in CBR' in Musoke, G and Geiser, P (Eds) Linking CBR, Disability and Rehabilitation (2013) 37-51.

Fenrich, J, Galizzi, P and Higgins, T 'Introduction' in Fenrich, J, Galizzi, P and Higgins, T (Eds) The Future of African Customary Law (2011) 1-8.

Gabel, S and Peters, S 'Presage of a paradigm shift? Beyond the social model of disability toward resistance theories of disability' (2004) 19(6) Disability & Society 585-600.

Gä̈ber, B 'Women's land rights and tenure security in Uganda: experiences from Mbale, Apac and Ntungamo' (2013) 13(24) Stichproben, Wiener Zeitschrift für kritische Afrikastudien 1-32.

Geiser, P and Boersma, M 'The role of the community in CBR' in Musoke, G and Geiser, P (eds) Linking CBR, Disability and Rehabilitation (2013) 24-36

Goodman, R and Jinks, D 'How to influence states: socialization and international human rights law' (2004) 54 Duke Law Journal 621-703.

Goodman, R and Jinks, D 'Toward an institutional theory of sovereignty' (2003) 55 Stanford Law Review 1749-1788.

Grant, E 'Human rights, cultural diversity and customary Law in South Africa' (2006) 50(01) Journal of African Law 2-23.

Grech, S 'Disability, poverty and development: Critical reflections on the majority world debate' (2009) 24(6) Disability & Society 771-784.

Griffiths, A 'Using ethnography as a tool in legal research: an anthropological perspective' in R Banakar and M Travers (eds) Theory and Method in Socio-Legal Research (2005) 113-31, at 115.

Griffiths, J 'Is law important?' (1979) 54 New York University Law Review 339-374.

Griffiths, J 'The social working of legal rules' (2003) 48 Journal of Legal Pluralism and Unofficial Law 1-84.

Griffiths, J 'What is legal pluralism?' (1986) 24 Journal of Legal Pluralism and Unofficial Law 1-55.

Groce, NE and Trani, JF 'Millennium development goals and persons with disabilities' (2009) 374(9704) The Lancet 1800-1801.

Hahn, H 'The political implications of disability definitions and data' (1993) 4(2) Journal of Disability Policy Studies 41-52.

Harknett, SG 'Cultural factors in the definition of disability: a community study in Nyankunde, Zaire' 1 African Journal of Special Needs Education 18-24.

Harpur, P 'Embracing the new disability rights paradigm: the importance of the Convention on the Rights of Persons with Disabilities' (2012) 27(1) Disability & Society 1-14.

Harpur, P 'From disability to ability: changing the phrasing of the debate' (2012) 27(3) Disability & Society 325-337.

Harpur, P 'Time to be heard: how advocates can use the Convention on the Rights of Persons with Disabilities to drive change (2011) 45(3) Valparaiso Univ LR 1271-1296.

Haugerud, A 'Land tenure and agrarian change in Kenya' (1989) 59(1) Africa 61-90.

Himonga, C 'Exploring the concept of ubuntu in the South African legal system" (2011) 15(17) Ideologie und Weltanschauung im Recht 1-22.

Himonga, C 'Constitutional rights of women under customary law in Southern Africa' in Baines, B, Barak-Erez, D and Kahana, T (Eds) Feminist Constitutionalism: Global Perspectives (2012) 317-335.

Himonga, C 'The future of living customary law in African legal systems in the twenty-first century and beyond, with special reference to South Africa' in Fenrich, J, Galizzi, P and Higgins, T (eds) The Future of African Customary Law (2011) 31-53.

Himonga, C, Taylor, M and Pope, A 'Reflections on judicial views of ubuntu' (2013) 16(5) PER/PELJ 1-61.

Hinz, MO 'Justice for justice and justice for peace: legal anthropological observations on traditional and informal justice systems' in Hinz, MO and Mapaure, C (eds) (2010) In Search of Justice and Peace, Traditional and Informal Justice Systems in Africa 3-23.

Hughes, B and Patterson, K 'The social model of disability and the disappearing body: towards a sociology of impairment' (1997) 12(3) Disability & Society 325-340.

Ibhawoh, B 'Between culture and constitution: Evaluating the cultural legitimacy of human rights in the African State' 22(3) Human Rights Quarterly 838-860.

Ibhawoh, B 'Cultural relativism and human rights: reconsidering the Africanist discourse' (2001) 1 Netherlands Quarterly of Human Rights 43-62.

Inksaterm K 'Transformative juricultural pluralism: indigenous justice systems in Latin America and international human rights' (2010) 60 Journal of Legal Pluralism 105-142.

Kakooza, JMN 'The application of customary law in Uganda' (2003) 1(1) The Uganda Living Law Journal 23-42.

Kalaluka, L 'Towards an effective litigation strategy of disability rights: The Zambia experience' (2013) 1 ADRY 165-189.

Kamundia, E 'Choice, support and inclusion: implementing Article 19 of the Convention on the Rights of Persons with Disabilities in Kenya' (2013) 1 ADRY 49-72.

Katsui, H and Kumpuvuori, J 'Human rights based approach to disability in development in Uganda: a way to fill the gap between political and social spaces?' (2008) 10(4) Scandinavian Journal of Disability Research 227-236.

Kent, AD 'Custody, maintenance, and succession: the internalization of women's and children's rights under customary law in Africa' (2007) 28 Michigan Journal of International Law 507-538

Khadiagala, L 'Negotiating law and custom: judicial doctrine and women's property rights in Uganda' (2002) 46 Journal of African Law 1-13.

Kiyaga, NB and Moores, DF 'Deafness in sub-Saharan Africa' (2003) 18 American Annals of the Deaf 18-24.

Kiani, S 'Women with disabilities in the North West province of Cameroon: resilient and deserving of greater attention' (2009) 24(4) Disability & Society 517-531.

Kisanji, J 'Interface between culture and disability in the Tanzanian context: Part II' (1995) 42(2) International Journal of Disability, Development and Education 109-118.

Kobusingye, DN, Van Leeuwen, M and Van Dijk, H 'Where do I report my land dispute? The impact of institutional proliferation on land governance in post-conflict Northern Uganda' (2016) 48(2) The Journal of Legal Pluralism and Unofficial Law 238-255.

Kyed, HM 'Introduction to the special issue: legal pluralism and international development interventions' (2011) 63 Journal of Legal Pluralism and Unofficial Law 1-23.

Kyed, HM 'The politics of legal pluralism: state policies on legal pluralism and their local dynamics in Mozambique' (2009) 59 Journal of Legal Pluralism and Unofficial Law 87-120.

Lang, R 'A critique of the disability movement' (1998) 9(1) Asia Pacific Disability Rehabilitation Journal 1-9.

Leonardi, C, Isser, LD, Moro, N et al 'The politics of customary law ascertainment in South Sudan' (2011) 63 Journal of Legal Pluralism and Unofficial Law 111-142.

Link, BG, Yang, LH and Collins, PY 'Measuring mental illness stigma' (2004) 30(3) Schizophrenia Bulletin 511-541.

Lobber, J 'Beyond the binaries: Depolarizing the Categories of Sex. Sexuality and Gender' (1996) 66(2) Sociological Inquiry 143-159.

Lord, JE and Stein, MA 'The domestic incorporation of human rights law and the United Nations Convention on the Rights of Persons with Disabilities' (2008) 83 Washington LR 449-479.

Lord, JE and Stein, MA 'Prospects and practices for CRPD implementation in Africa' (2013) 1 ADRY 97-114.

Maboreke, M 'Understanding law in Zimbabwe' in Ann Stewart (Ed) Gender, Law & Social Justice (2000) 101-116.

Macfarlane, LJ 'Marxist theory and human rights' (1982) 17(4) Government and Opposition 414-428.

Masasa, T, Irwin-Carruthers, S and Faure, M 'Knowledge of, beliefs about and attitudes to disability: implications for health professionals' (2005) 47(7) South African Family Practice 40-44.

McKnight, GH 'Land, politics, and Buganda's "indigenous" colonial state' (2000) 28(1) The Journal of Imperial and Commonwealth History 65-89.

Meekosha, H 'Decolonising disability: thinking and acting globally' (2011) 26(6) Disability and Society 667 682, at 670.

Méon, PG, Mersland, R, Szafarz, A and Labie, M. 'Discrimination by microcredit officers: theory and evidence on disability in Uganda' (2011) 11(06) ULB--Universite Libre de Bruxelles.

Merry, SE 'Changing rights, changing culture' in Cowan, JK, Dembour, MB and Wilson, RA (Eds) Culture and Rights, Anthropological Perspectives (2001) 31-55.

Merry, SE 'Transnational human rights and local activism: mapping the middle' (2006) 108 American Anthropologist 38-51.

Mitra, S, Posarac, A and Vick, B 'Disability and poverty in developing countries: a multidimensional study'(2012) 41 World Development 1-18.

Mokgoro, JY 'Ubuntu and the law in South Africa' (1998) PELJ at 2-3.

Mollow, A 'Identity politics and disability studies: a critique of recent theory (2004) 43(2) Michigan Quarterly Review 269-296.

Moore, SF 'Certainties undone: fifty turbulent years of legal anthropology' (2001) 7 Journal of the Royal Anthropology Institute 95-116.

Moore. SF 'Changing African land tenure: reflections on the incapacities of the state' (1998) 10(2) European Journal of Development Research 33-49.

Moore, SF 'Law and social change: the semi-autonomous social field as an appropriate subject of study (1973) 7(4) Law & Society Review 719-746.

Mostert, MP 'Stigma as barrier to the implementation of the Convention on the Rights of Persons with Disabilities in Africa' (2016) 4 ADRY 3-24.

Mpofu, E 'Enhancing social acceptance of early adolescents with physical disabilities: effects of role salience, peer interaction, and academic support interventions' (2003) 50(4) International Journal of Disability, Development and Education 435-454.

Muller, G 'On considering alternative accommodation and the rights and needs of vulnerable people' (2014) 30 SAJHR 41-62.

Mureriwa, J 'Some reflections on the draft African Disability Protocol and socio-economic justice for persons with disability' (2011) 12:3 ESR Rev 3-6.

Mute, L 'Moving from the norm to practice: Towards ensuring legal capacity for persons with disabilities in Kenya' (2012) 9 Equal Rights Rev 138-148, at 139.

Mwendwa, TN, Murangira, A and Lang, R 'Mainstreaming the rights of persons with disabilities in national development frameworks' (2009) 21 J Int'l Dev 662-672.

Ngwena, C 'The new disability convention: Implications for disability equality norms in the South African workplace in OC Dupper & C Garbers (eds) (2010) Equality in the workplace: Reflections from South Africa and beyond181-203.

Nhlapo, TR 'The African family and women's rights: friends or foes?' (1991) Acta Juridica 135-146.

Nhlapo, T 'Cultural diversity, human rights and the family in contemporary Africa: lessons from the South African constitutional debate' (1995) 9 International Journal of Law and the Family 208-225.

Nickel, JW 'Cultural diversity in human rights' in Nelson, JL and Green, VM (eds) International Human Rights Contemporary Issues (1980) 43-56.

Nyamu-Musembi, C 'An actor oriented approach to rights development' (2009) 36(1) IDS Bulletin 36 (2009) 41-51.

Nyamu-Musembi, C 'Are local norms and practices fences or pathways? The example of women's property rights' in AA An-Na'im (Ed) Cultural Transformation and Human Rights in Africa (2002) 126-150.

Nyamu-Musembi, C 'Local norms, institutions, and women's property rights in rural Kenya' (2003) 9(2) East African Journal of Peace & Human Rights 255-289.

Nyamu-Musembi, C 'Ruling out gender equality? The post-cold war rule of law agenda in Sub-Saharan Africa' 27(7) Third World Quarterly 1193-1207.

Nyamu-Musembi, C 'Towards an actor-oriented perspective on human rights' in Kabeer, N (cd) Inclusive citizenship: Meanings and expressions (2005) 31-49.

Oba, AA 'The future of customary law in Africa' in Fenrich, J, Galizzi, P and Higgins, T (Eds) The Future of African Customary Law (2011) 58-82.

Ochich, GO 'The withering province of customary law in Kenya' in Fenrich, J, Galizzi, P and Higgins, T (Eds) The Future of African Customary Law (2011) 103-128.

Oliver, M 'Defining impairment and disability: issues at stake' in C Barnes and G Mercer (Eds) Exploring the Divide (1996) 29-54.

Odgaard, R & Benton, AW 'The interplay between collective rights and obligations and individual rights' (1998) 10(2) European Journal of Development Research 105-16.

Ogechi, NO and Ruto, SJ 'Portrayal of disability through personal names and proverbs in Kenya; evidence from Ekegusii and Nandi' (2002) 2(3) Vienna Journal of African Studies 63-82.

Oyaro, LO 'Country report: Uganda' (2014) 2 ADRY 247-266.

Perju, V 'Impairment, Discrimination, and the Legal Construction of Disability in the European Union and the United States' (2011) 44 Cornell Int'l L J 279-348.

Priestley, M 'Constructions and creations: Idealism, materialism and disability theory' (1998) 13 (1) Disability and Society 79-94.

Preiswerk, R 'The place of intercultural relations in the study of international relations' in D Hunt (ed) (1978) The Yearbook of World Affairs 251-67.

Putnam, M 'Conceptualizing disability developing a framework for political disability identity' (2005) 16(3) Journal of Disability Policy Studies 188-198.

Raday, F 'Culture, religion and gender' (2004) 1(4) International Journal of Constitutional Law 663-715, at 665-66.

Ranger, T 'The invention of tradition in colonial Africa' in Hobsbawm, E and Ranger, T The Invention of Tradition (1983) 211-263.

Rwezaura, BA Traditionalism and Law Reform in Africa (5 July 1983) Lecture before the European Institute of the University of Saarland, Saarbrücken.

Rioux, M and Carbert, A 'Human rights and disability: The international context' (2003) 10(2) Journal on Developmental Disabilities 1-13.

Romeo, F 'Beyond a medical model: Advocating for a new conception of gender identity in the law' (2004-2005) 36 Columbia Human Rights L Rev 713.

Roy, O and Annichino, P 'Human rights between religions, cultures and universality' in Vrdoljak, AF (ed) Cultural Dimension of Human Rights (2013) 14-25.

Ruppel, OC and Ruppel-Schilichting, K 'Legal and judicial pluralism in Namibia and beyond: A modern approach to African legal architecture' (2011) 64 Journal of Legal Pluralism 33-63.

Petracco, CK and Pender, J 'Evaluating the impact of land tenure and titling on access to credit in Uganda' (2009), IFPRI Discussion Paper 00853.

Pfeiffer, D 'Overview of the disability movement: history, legislative record, and political implications' (1993) 21 Policy Studies Journal 724-734.

Philpott, S 'Too little, too late? The CRPD as a standard to evaluate South African legislation and policies for early childhood development' (2014) 2 ADRY 51-74.

Quinn , G 'Disability and human rights: a new field in the United Nations' in Krause, C and Scheinin, M (eds) International Protection of Human Rights, A Textbook (2009) 247-271.

Selway, D and Ashman, AF 'Disability, religion and health: A literature review in search of the spiritual dimensions of disability' 13(3) (1998) Disability & Society 429-439.

Sezgin, Y 'How to integrate universal human rights into customary and religious legal systems' (2010) 60 Journal of Legal Pluralism 5-40.

Sezgin, Y 'Theorizing formal pluralism: quantification of legal pluralism for spatio-temporal analysis' (2004) 50 Journal of Legal Pluralism 101-118

Shakespeare, T 'Disabled people's self-organisation: a new social movement' (1993) 8(3) Disability, Handicap and Society 249-264, at 254.

Srem-Sai, J 'The hugger-mugger of enforcing socio-economic rights in Ghana: A threat to the rights of persons with disabilities' (2015)135 ADRY 135-159.

Ssenyonjo, M 'Culture and the human rights of women in Africa: between light and shadow' (2007) 51(01) Journal of African Law 39-67.

Stein, MA and Lord, JE 'Future prospects for the United Nations Convention on the Rights of Persons with Disabilities' in Quinn, G and Arnardotti, OM (eds) The United Nations

Convention on the Rights of Persons with Disabilities: European and Scandinavian Perspectives (2009) 17-40

Stern, C 'Human rights or the rule of law—the choice for East Africa?' (2015) 24 Michigan State Int'l L Rev 45-78.

Swain, J and French, S 'Towards an affirmation model of disability' (2000) 15(4) Disability & Society 569-582.

Stone-MacDonald, A and Butera, G 'Cultural beliefs and attitudes about disability in East Africa' (2012) 8(1) Review of Disability Studies: An International Journal 62-77.

Swidler, A 'Culture in action: symbols and strategies' (1986) 51(2) American Sociological Review 273-286.

Talle, A 'A child is a child: disability and equality among the Kenya Maasai' in Ingstad, B and Whyte, SR (eds) Disability and Culture (1995) 56-72.

Tamanaha, BZ 'Understanding legal pluralism: past to present, local to global' (2008) 30 Sydney Law Review 375-411.

TenBroek, J and Matson, F 'The disabled and the law of welfare' (1966) 54 California L Rev 809-840.

Tesemma, ST 'Economic discourses of disability in Africa: An overview of lay and legislative narratives' (2014) 2 ADRY 121-147.

Tripp, AM 'Women's movements, customary law, and land rights in Africa: the case of Uganda (2014) 7.4 African Studies Quarterly 1-19.

Turmusani M, A Vreede and SL Wirz 'Some ethical issues in community-based rehabilitation initiatives in developing countries' (2002) 24(10) Disability Rehabilitation 558-64

Tushnet, M 'The critique of rights' (1994) 47 SMU L Rev 23-34.

Twining, W 'Diffusion of law: a global perspective' (2004) 49 Journal of Legal Pluralism and Unofficial Law 1-45.

Twinomugisha, BK 'African customary law and women's human rights in Uganda' in Fenrich, J, Galizzi, P and Higgins, T (Eds) The Future of African Customary Law (2011) 446-466

Van Reenen, T and Combrinck, H 'International financial institutions and the attainment of the UN Millennium Development Goals in Africa – with specific reference to persons with disabilities' in Grobbelaar-du Plessis, I and van Reenen, T (eds) (2011) Introduction to Aspects of Disability Law in Africa 197-230.

Van Reenen, T and Combrinck, H 'The UN Convention on the Rights of Persons with Disabilities in Africa: Progress after 5 years' (2011) 14 SUR-Int'l Journal on Human Rights 133-165.

VanRooym G, Amadhila, E and Mannan, H et al 'Core concepts of human rights and inclusion of vulnerable groups in the disability and rehabilitation policies of Malawi, Namibia, Sudan, and South Africa' (2012) 23 Journal of Disability Policy Studies 67-81.

Von Benda-Beckmann, F 'Citizens, strangers and indigenous peoples: conceptual politics and legal pluralism' (1997) 9 Law and Anthropology 1-42.

von Benda-Beckmann, F, Benda-Beckmann, K and Eckert, J 'Rules of law and laws of ruling; law and government between past and future' in von Benda-Beckmann, F, von Benda-Beckmann, K and Eckert, J (eds) Rules of Law and Laws of Ruling; On Governance and Law (2009) 1-30.

Von Benda-Beckmann, F 'Scape-goat and magic charm: Law in development theory and practice' (1989) 28 Journal of Legal Pluralism and Unofficial Law 129-148,

Von Benda-Beckmann, F 'Who's afraid of legal pluralism' (2002) 47 Journal of Legal Pluralism 37-82.

Von Benda-Beckmann, K 'Legal pluralism' (2001) 6 Thai Culture 18-40.

Ubink, J 'The quest for customary law in African state courts' in Fenrich, J, Galizzi, P and Higgins, T (eds) The Future of African Customary Law (2011) 83-128.

Vanderlinden, J 'Le Pluralisme Juridique: Essai de Synthèse' in Gilissen, J (ed) Le Pluralisme Juridique (1971) 19-56.

Vrdoljak, AF 'Liberty, equality, diversity: states, cultures, and international law' in Ana Filipa Vrdoljak Ed Cultural Dimension of Human Rights (2013) 26-70.

Wa-Mungai, M '"For I name thee...": disability onomastics in Kenyan folklore and popular music' (2009) 29(4) Disabilities Studies Quarterly.

Wickenden, M, Mulligan, D et al 'Stakeholder consultations on community-based rehabilitation guidelines in Ghana and Uganda' (2012) 1(1) African Journal of Disability 1-10.

Wiessner, S 'Culture and the rights of indigenous peoples' in Vrdoljak, AF (ed) Cultural Dimension of Human Rights (2013) 117-156.

Woodman, GR 'Legal pluralism and the search for justice' (1996) 40(2) Journal of African Law 152-167.

Woodman, GR 'The limits of law' (1983) 21 Journal of Legal Pluralism and Unofficial Law 129-153.

Woodman, GR 'A survey of customary laws in Africa in search of lessons for the future' in Fenrich, J, Galizzi, P and Higgins, T (eds) The Future of African Customary Law (2011) 9-30.

Yngstrom, I 'Women, wives and land rights in Africa: Situating gender beyond the household in the debate over land policy and changing tenure systems' (2002) 30(1) Oxford Development Studies 21-40.

Zola, IK 'Developing new self images and interdependence' in Crewe, NM and Zola, IK (eds) Independent Living for Physically Disabled People (1993) 49-59.

Zwart, T 'Using local culture to further the implementation of international human rights: the receptor approach' (2012) 34(2) Human Rights Quarterly 546-569.

Reports, Theses, Monographs and Papers

Adoku, J and Akin J Understanding and Strengthening Women's Land Rights under Customary Tenure in Uganda Land Equity Uganda Working Paper (April 2011) available at <http://landportal.info/sites/landportal.info/files/2._understanding_and_strengthening_womens_land_rights_under_customary_tenure_in_uganda_lemu_ug.pdf> last accessed 1 December 2016.

Afadameh-Adeyemi, A Indigenous Peoples and the Right to Culture: An International Law Analysis (2009) PhD dissertation University of Cape Town.

Berghs MJ, et al 'Implications for public health research of models and theories of disability: a scoping study and evidence synthesis' (2016).

BI Bruhns, A Murray, T Kanguehi et al NEPRU Research Project
No. 9: Disability and Rehabilitation in Namibia; A National
Survey (1995).

Central Intelligence Agency (USA) World Fact Book of the United
States Central Intelligence Agency (2015).

Clark, L and Marsh, S 'Patriarchy in the UK: The language of disability' (2002) 2nd Draft available at <http://pf7d7vi404s1dxh27
mla5569.wpengine.netdna-cdn.com/files/library/Clark-
Laurence-language.pdf> accessed on 25 September 2017.

Committee on the Rights of Persons with Disabilities 'Consideration
of reports submitted by States parties under article 35 of the
Convention: Initial Report of Uganda' (received 22 January
2013; distributed 10 March 2015).

Corradi, G Advancing Human Rights in Legally Plural Africa:
The Role of Development Actors in the Justice Sector (2013)
unpublished PhD thesis Ghent University.

Cousins, B 'Potentials and pitfalls of communal land reform: experience in Africa and implications for South Africa' Paper presented at the World Bank Conference on Land Governance in
Support of the MGDs: Responding to New Challenges (2009).

Dube, AK Participation of Disabled People in the PRSP/PEAP Process
in Uganda (2005) available at <http://r4d.dfid.gov.uk/PDF/
Outputs/Disability/PolicyProject_uganda_prsp.pdf> accessed
on 26 October 2015.

Einos Iteso Kopiteny and Land Equity Movement in Uganda
Principles, Practices, Rights and Responsibilities (PPRR)
of Customary Land Management in Teso Region (2009).

Gloppen, S 'Social movement activism and the courts' in Mobilizing Ideas (February 2013) available at https://mobilizingideas. wordpress.com/2013/02/04/social-movement-activism-and-the-courts/ accessed on 7 October 2017.

Harrington, A 'Key issues in customary justice: a comparative study' USIP Research Report (2010).

Human Rights Watch 'As if We Weren't Human': Discrimination and Violence against Women with Disabilities in Northern Uganda (2010).

International Justice Mission Property Grabbing from Ugandan Widows and the Justice System: A Mixed-Methods Assessment in Mukono County, Uganda (2014).

Kane, M, Oloka-Onyango, J and Tejan-Cole, A 'Reassessing customary law systems as a vehicle for providing equitable access to justice for the poor' (2005) Arusha Conference 'New Frontiers of Social Policy'.

Katsui, H 'Ugandan disability movement: political achievements and social challenges of WWD' (2008) available at <disability-uganda.blogspot.com> accessed on 27 October 2015.

Keogh, M, Fox, N and Flynn, E 'How far towards equality, a vulnerabilities approach to the rights of disabled people' Research Paper No 29/2010 (5 July 2010) UCD Working Papers in Law, Criminology & Socio-Legal Studies available at <http://dx.doi.org/10.2139/ssrn.1634806> last visited on 12 December 2016.

Ker Kwaro Acholi and Land Equity Movement in Uganda Principles and Practices of Customary Tenure in Acholiland (2008).

Kress-White, M The Quest of Inclusion: Understandings of Albeism, Pedagogy and the Right to Belong (2009) thesis University of Saskatchewan.

Kuman Elder's Forum and Land Equity Movement in Uganda Kumam Principles, Practices, Rights and Responsibilities (PPRR) for Customary Land Tenure Management (2011).

Jok, AA, Leitch, R and Vandewint, C A Study of Customary Law in Contemporary Southern Sudan (2004).

Lango Cultural Foundation and Land Equity Movement in Uganda Principles, Practices, Rights and Responsibilities (PPRR) of Customary Land Tenure in Lango Region - No. 1 (2009).

Legal Action for People with Disabilities 'Violation of rights for the disabled woman: draft baseline study report' (2011).

Lwanga-Ntale, C 'Chronic poverty and disability in Uganda' paper presented at Staying Poor Chronic Poverty and Disability Policy Manchester, United Kingdom (April 2003) at 4 available at <http://digitalcommons.ilr.cornell.edu/ gladnetcollect/320> last accessed 28 October 2015.

Marriott, A and Gooding, K Social Assistance and Disability in Developing Countries (2007) Position paper supported by DFID and Sightsavers International.

Mbazira, C 'Enforcing rights of persons with disabilities to have access to barrier-free physical environment in Uganda: is litigation an option' (2009) A position paper written for Legal Action for Persons with Disabilities.

Moyo, DS Ensuring Sexual and Reproductive Health Rights of Women with Disabilities: A Study of Policies, Actions and Commitments in Uganda and Zimbabwe (2010) unpublished dissertation, Reading University.

Mulumba, M Mainstreaming Disability into the Poverty Reduction Processes in Uganda: The Role of the Human Rights-Based Approach to the National Development Plan (2011) unpublished LLM thesis Stellenbosch University.

National Union of Disabled Persons of Uganda Implementation of the UN Convention on the Rights of Persons with Disabilities in Uganda: Submission of National Union of Disabled Persons of Uganda (NUDIPU) in response to the List of issues of the Committee on the Rights of Persons with Disabilities for the initial review of the Republic of Uganda on the implementation of the Convention on the Rights of Persons with Disabilities (January 2016).

Norwegian Agency for Development Cooperation Mainstreaming Disability in the New Development Paradigm, Evaluation of Norwegian Support to Promote the Rights of Persons with Disabilities: Uganda Country Study—summary (2012).

Nyamu-Musembi, C 'Review of experiences in engaging with 'non-state' justice systems in East Africa' (2003) Department for International Development (DfID) UK.

Nyombi, C and Mulimira, MW Mental Health Laws in Uganda: A Critical Review (Part 1) (2012) at 5, available at<http://www.researchgate.net/publication/228124324_Menta l_Health_Laws_in_Uganda_A_Critical_Review_(Part_1)> accessed on 15 June 2015.

Obaikol, E 'Women's land rights and the law' (2009) Uganda Land Alliance policy paper.

Obi, NC The Customary Law Manueal: A Manual of Customary Laws
Obtaining in the Anambra and Imo States in Nigeria (1977).

Office of the High Commissioner for Human Rights 'Working paper,
a review of the Ugandan legal framework relevant to persons
with disabilities: comparative analysis to the Convention on
the Rights of Persons with Disabilities' (2008).

Oliver, M 'Capitalism, disability and ideology: Materialist critique of
the normalization principal' (1999) in R Flynn and R Lemay
A Quarterly. A Quarter-Century of Normalization and Social
Role Valorization: Evolution and Impact available at
<http://www.independentliving.org/docs3/oliver99.pdf> last
accessed 24 September 2017.

Olanya, DR 'Colonial legacy, access political economy of land, and
legal pluralism in Uganda: 1900-2010' Gulu University
(2011).

Oloka-Onyango, J 'The problematique of economic, social and
cultural rights in globalized Uganda: a conceptual review'
HURIPEC Working Paper No 3 (March 2007).

Pew Forum on Religion and Public Life Tolerance and Tension: Islam
and Christianity in Sub-Saharan Africa (2010).

Rawls, AC Policy Proposals for Justice in Liberia: Opportunities
Under the Current Legal Framework to Expand Access
to Justice (2011).

Rugadya, MA 'Escalating land conflicts in Uganda: A review
of evidence from recent studies and surveys' (2009) A paper
commissioned by the International Republican Institute
available at <http://mokoro.co.uk/wp-content/uploads/
escalating_Uganda_landconflicts.pdf> last accessed on 15
June 2015.

Rugadya, MA Women's Land Rights in Uganda: Status of Implementation of Policy and Law on Women's Land Rights for ECA a paper offered at ACGS Addis Adaba (June 2010).

Special Olympics Press Release 'Anniversary of first Special Olympics celebrates legacy of recent World Games in Greece' available at <http://www.specialolympics.org/RegionsPages/content.aspx?id=17727&LangType=1036> accessed on 26 October 2015.

Tukahirwa, JMB 'Policies, people and land use change in Uganda: case study in Ntungamo, Lake Mburo and Sango Bay sites, LUCID working Paper Series No. 17 (2002).

Uganda Bureau of Statistics The National Population and Housing Census (2014).

Union of the Physically Impaired against Segregation Fundamental Principles of Disability (1976).

Uganda National Action on Physical Disability's 'Publication of selected legal provisions in domestic and international laws on physical accessibility' (2010) available at <http://www.medbox.org/ug-disability/publication-of-selected-legal-provisions-in-domestic-and-international-laws-on-physical-accessibility/preview?> last accessed 28 October 2015.

United Nations Disability and the Millennium Development Goals (2011) available at <http://www.un.org/disabilities/documents/review_of_disability_and_the_mdgs.pdf> last accessed 17 December 2016.

United Nations 'From exclusion to equality: realizing the rights of persons with disabilities' (2007).

United Nations World Youth Report 2007: Young People's Transition to Adulthood: Progress and Challenges.

United Nations Commission for Social Development Mainstreaming Disability in the Development Agenda (2008) available at <www.un.org/disabilities/default.asp?id=708> last accessed on 27 October 2015.

UN World Health Organization (WHO) World Report on Disabilities available at <http://www.who.int/disabilities/world_report/2011/report.pdf> last accessed 9 October 2017.

United States Institute of Peace & the Rift Valley Institute Local Justice in Southern Sudan (2010).

Weigand, C and Grosh, M Levels and Patterns of Safety Net Spending in Developing and Transition Countries (2008) available at <http://siteresources.worldbank.org/SOCIALPROTECTION/Resources/SP-Discussion-papers/Safety-Nets-DP/0817.pdf > last accessed 27 October 2015.

World Health Organization The International Classification of Functioning, Disability and Health (2014).

World Intellectual Property Organization Customary Law, Traditional Knowledge and Intellectual Property: An Outline of the Issues (2013).

Periodical and Newspaper Articles

'Disability: Who Counts? Defining disability is tricky—and measuring it is even harder' The Economist (14 December 2013) 56.

Ruth First 'Uganda: The latest coup d'état in Africa' (1971) 27(3) The World Today 131-138.

H Lubwama 'Accessibility law bites Centenary Bank' (Sept.-Oct.
2008) 6(4) UNAPD Update available at
<http://www.unapd.org/userfiles/September_october_
2008.pdf> last accessed 12 November 2015.

'United Nations enable Convention and Optional Protocol signatures
and ratifications' United Nations web-based article available
at <http://www.un.org/disabilities/countries.asp?id=166>
last accessed 19 December 2015.

Websites

Website of the Office of the Hight Commissioner of Human Rights
'Delcaration on the Rights of Mentaly Retarded Persons'
<http://www.ohchr.org/EN/ProfessionalInterest/Pages/Rights
OfMentallyRetardedPersons.aspx> last accessed on
26 February 2017.

Website of the United Nations 'United Nations Decade of Disabled
Persons' <http://www.un.org/esa/socdev/enable/
disunddp.htm> last accessed on 26 October 2015.

International Treaties, Instruments and Protocols

Convention on the Rights of Persons with Disabilities (CRPD), adopted 13 December 2006 by GA Res 61/106 Annex I UN GAOR
61st Sess Supp No 49 at 65 UN Doc A/61/49 (2006) entered
into force 3 May 2008 UN Doc A/61/61; signed by Uganda on
30 March 2007 and ratified by Uganda on 25 September 2008.

International Covenant on Civil and Political Rights (ICCPR), adopted
16 December 1996, GA Res 2200A (XX1), 21 UN GAOR
Supp (No. 16) at 52, UN Doc A/6316 (1966), 999 UNTS 171,
entered into force 23 March 1976, acceded to by Uganda 21
June 1995.

International Covenant on Economic, Social and Cultural Rights, GA res 2200A (XXI), UN Doc A/6316 (1966), entered into force 3 January 1976, acceded to by Uganda 21 January 1987.

Convention on the Elimination of Discrimination Against Women (CEDAW), adopted 18 December 1979 by GA resolution 34/180, entered into force on 3 September 1981, ratified by Uganda 22 July 22 1985.

Convention on the Rights of the Child, GA res 44/25, annex, 44 UN GAOR Supp (No. 49) at 167, UN Doc.= A/44/49 (1989), entered into force 2 September 1990, ratified by Uganda 17 August 1990.

Regional Treaties, Instruments, Protocols and Resolutions

African [Banjul] Charter on Human and Peoples' Rights, adopted 27 June 1981, OAU Doc. CAB/LEG/67/3 rev 5, 21 ILM 58 (1982), entered into force 21 October 1986, ratified by Uganda 10 May 1986.

Organization of African Unity (OAU), African Charter on the Rights and Welfare of the Child, 11 July 1990, CAB/LEG/24.9/49 (1990).

Protocol to the African Charter on Human and Peoples' Rights on the Rights of Women in Africa (the Maputo Protocol), adopted 11 July 2003, entered into force November 2005, signed by Uganda, 18 December 2003, ratified by Uganda, 22 July 2010.

Draft Protocol to the African Charter on Human and Peoples' Rights on the Rights of Persons with Disabilities in Africa, adopted at the 19th Extra-Ordinary Session of the African Commission on Human and Peoples' Rights, 16-25 February 2016, in the Islamic Republic of the Gambia.

OAU Doc CAB LEG/24.9/49 adopted on 11 July 1990 and entered into
force on 29 November 1999; AU Executive Council Resolution EX.CL/477 (XIV), adopted during the 14th ordinary
session of the African Heads of State and Government, 26–30
January 2009.

Ugandan Cases

Centre for Health Human Rights and Development (CEHURD)
& Three others v Attorney General UGSC Constitutional
Appeal No. 01 of 2013 [2015].

Mifumi (U) Ltd and 12 Others v Attorney General UgSC Const App
No. 2/14 [2015].

Centre for Health Human Rights and Development (CEHURD)
& Three others v Attorney General, Constitutional Petition
No. 16 of 2011, UGCC 4 [2012].

Centre for Health Human Rights and Development (CEHURD)
and Iga Daniel v the Attorney General UGCC Const Pet
No 64 of 2011 [2015].

Mifumi (U) Ltd and 12 Others v Attorney General UGCC 2 Const
Petition No. 12/07 [2010].

Kampala District Land Board and George Mitala v. Venansio
Babweyaka et al UCSC App 2 of 2007 [2008].

Bruno Kiwuwa v Ivan Serunkuma & Juliet Namazzi HCUg Suit No. 52
of 2006.

Legal Action for People with Disabilities v. Attorney General and
Another [2014] UGHC 42.

Mustafa Kadala Nsubuga v. Mawandu Balumu and Others, High Court
of Uganda at Kampala, Civil Suit No. 1086 of 2000.

Santo Dwoka & Anor v Centenary Rural Development Bank Ltd
HCUg [2008]

Foreign Cases

Republic of South Africa

Bhe v Magistrate Khayelitsha 2005 (1) SA 580 (CC).

S v Makwanyane 1995 3 SA 391 (CC).

MEC for Education: Kwazulu-Natal v Pillay 2008 1 SA 474 (CC).

Shilubana and Others v Nwamitwa and Other 2009 (2) SA 66 (CC).

S v Shiluban 2008 1 SACR 295 (T); Mabena v Letsoala 1998 (2) SA
1068.

Alexkor Ltd. and Another v Richtersveld Community and Others 2004
(5) SA 460.

United States of America

Sutton v United Airlines Inc [1999] 527 US 471.

Ugandan Statutes

Constitution of Uganda 1995 (as amended in 2005).

The Administrator's General Act (Uganda) (Cap 157) (1933).

Business, Technical, Vocational Education and Training Act of 2008
(cap 130).

The Children Act of 2003 (cap 59). The Civil Procedure Act 2002
(cap 71).

The Employment Act of 2006 (cap 219). The Equal Opportunities
Commission Act of 2007.

The Evidence Act of 1909 (cap 6).

Hindu Marriage and Divorce Act of 1961 (cap 250).

The Judicature Act of 1996 (cap 13).

The Land Act of 1998 (cap 227).

The Land (Amendment) Act 2010.

The Local Governments Act 1997 (cap 243).

The Marriage Act of 1904 (cap 251).

The Parliamentary Elections Act of 2005 (cap 140).

The Persons with Disabilities Act of 2006. Magistrates Courts Act of 1971 (cap 16).

The Movement Act 1998 (cap 261).

The National Council for Disability Act of 2003, amended in 2010. Registration of Titles Act of 1924 (cap 230).

Succession Act (cap 162) (1906).

The Traffic and Road Safety Act of 1998 (cap 361).

The Uganda Communications Act of 1998 (cap 106).

The Universities and Tertiary Institutions Act of 2001, amended 2006 (cap 59).

The Workers Compensation Act of 2000 (cap 225)

Ugandan Draft Bills

The Persons with Disabilities Bill, 2014, Bills Supplement No. 5 to the Uganda Gazette, 9 May 2014

Colonial Era Agreements and Orders

Buganda Agreement of 1900.

The Succession Order of 1926 (Buganda Kingdom).

Foreign Statutes

United States of America

Americans With Disabilities Act of 1990, Pub L No 101-336, 104 Stat 328 (1990).

Ugandan Policies

Ministry of Gender, Labour and Social Development National Policy on Disability in Uganda (2006).

Ministry of Lands, Housing and Urban Development Uganda Land Policy (2013).

Ministry of Finance, Planning and Economic DevelopmentUganda Vision 2045 (2013).

APPENDIX

Interview Consent Forms

Information Sheet & Consent Form for Stage One and Stage Three Field Interviews with Persons with Disabilities

(1) Hello, my name is Brian Dennison and I am conducting research towards a doctoral degree in law from the University of Cape Town. I am researching about the status, rights and treatment of persons with disabilities in Mukono District and would like to invite you to participate in the project. The name of my research project is *The Status, Rights and Treatment of Persons with Disabilities within Customary Legal Frameworks in Uganda: A Study of Mukono District.*

(2) My research is about how community practices and customary law in Mukono District impact persons with disabilities. I hope my research will provide a roadmap for how local customs can be engaged to improve the rights, status and treatment of persons with disabilities in Mukono District.

(3) I am looking for information about how persons with disabilities are treated at the family and community level in Mukono District. I want to know how the rights, status and treatment of persons with disabilities compare with other people in Mukono District. I am particularly interested in hearing stories about how persons with disabilities are treated and the rights they have in your community. I want to interview people who can tell stories that shed light on those areas of interest.

(4) Your participation is voluntary. The choice to participate is yours alone. If you choose not to participate, nothing bad will happen. If you choose to participate, but wish to stop at any time, you will be free to do so. You also have the right to refuse to answer any questions.

(5) I want to meet with you for some period of time and give you the opportunity to talk. The conversation could be as short at 10 minutes or as long as 3 hours. It really depends on the stories that you have to share. The interview may be recorded. However, the interview will not be recorded if you would prefer that no recording be made. All recordings will be kept securely. I will not share the recordings with the public.

(6) You will be paid a modest honorarium for taking part in this research. This will be provided to you regardless of the answers that you give. In addition, transport reimbursements will be provided when necessary. There will be no other direct benefit to you for your participation.

(7) You should not expose yourself to any risk through your participation in this research. We will have our discussions in a confidential setting. You might experience some discomfort in the story telling process as it might cause you to think of painful and difficult personal experiences.

(8) I will preserve your anonymity. I will do this by keeping any written or recorded records of our conversation confidential and secure. When reporting on the stories provided in my research I will not reveal names or other personally identifiable information. Given that your story might be somewhat unique it is possible that someone will be able to connect your story to you. However, to protect confidentiality I will report stories in my research in a way that will

prevent people from knowing that the story is about any particular person.

(9) I plan on having an interpreter with me during the interview in case the interview needs to be conducted in Luganda. The interpreter will also respect your anonymity and strive to preserve confidentiality.

(10) I would like to record our interview in order to insure that I accurately transcribe and report the feedback that you provide. I will ask you for permission to record. These recordings will be kept confidential.

(11) *If you have concerns about the research, its risks and benefits or about your rights as a research participant in this study, you may contact the Law Faculty Research Ethics Committee Administrator, Mrs Lamize Viljoen, at 021 650 3080 or at lamize.viljoen @uct.ac.za. Alternatively, you may write to the Law Faculty Research Ethics Committee Administrator, Room 6.28 Kramer Law Building, Law Faculty, UCT, Private Bag, Rondebosch 7701. South Africa.*

Uganda Translation of Information & Consent Form for Stage One and Three Interviews of Persons with Disabilities:

Enyinnyonnyola ne ffoomu esaba olukusa (emboozi ez'eby'obulemu)

> *(1)* Nkulamusizza, erinnya lyange nze Brian Dennison era nkola okunoonyereza okulubirira okufuna ddiguli yange ey'okusatu mu mateeka okuva mu Ssetendekero ly'e Cape Town. Nkola okunoonyereza ku mbeera, eddembe, n'engeri abantu abalina obulemu mu Bbeendobeendo (District) ly'e Mukono gye bayisibwamu era nga nkusaba onegatteko mu kunoonyereza kuno. Omulamwa gw'okuunoonyereza kuno gutuumiddwa *"Embeera, Eddembe, n'Enkwaata y'Abantu*

Abalina Obulemu Okusiinziira ku Mateeka g'Eby'obuwangwa n'Ennono mu Uganda: Okunoonyereza nga kwesigamiziddwa ku Bbeendobeendo ly'e Mukono."

(2) Okunoonyereza kwange kukwata ku ngeri obulombolombo bw'ekitundu, n'amateeka g'eby'obuwangwa n'ennono gye biyisaamu abantu abalina obulemu mu Bbeendobeendo ly'e Mukono. Nina esuubi nti okunoonyereza kwange kuno kujja kuluŋŋamya engeri z'eby'obuwangwa eby'ekinnansi gyebiyinza okukozesebwamu okutumbula eddembe, embeera n'empisa abantu abalina obulemu gye bayisibwaamu mu Bbeendobeendo ly'e Mukono.

(3) Nnoonyereza ku ngeri abantu abalina obulemu gye bayisibwaamu ku mutendera gw'amaka n'ogw'ekitundu mu Bbeendobeendo ly'e Mukono. Njagala okumanya engeri eddembe, embeera n'empisa y'abantu abalina obulemu gye bayisibwaamu bwe biri nga obigerageranyizza n'abantu abalala mu Bbeendobeendo ly'e Mukono. Okusingira ddala njagala okuwulira emboozi ezikwaata ku bantu abalina obulemu gye bayisibwaamu, n'eddembe lye balina mu kitundu kyo. Njagala okubuuza abantu bannyinyonnyole okuyita mu mboozi ezongera ekitangaala ku mulamwa guno gwe noonyerezaako.

(4) Okweetaba kwo mu kunoonyereza kuno si kwa buwaze; kiri gy'oli okukweetabamu oba n'edda. Tovunaanibwa, singa tokweetabamu. Naye ne bw'osiima okukweetabamu, oky'alina eddembe okukuvaamu wonna w'onooba oyagalidde. Era oli wa ddembe okugaana okuddamu ekibuuzo kyonna.

(5) Njagala nkusisinkane mu kiseera ekigere ombuulire ky'olowooza ku nsonga eno. Ekitono ennyo, kino kiyinza

okutwaala eddakiika nga 10, oba ekinene ennyo okumala essaawa 3. Kinasiinziira ku mboozi z'olina okunyumya. Emboozi yaffe eyinza okukwaatibwa ku katambi. Naye ne kino tekijja kuba kya buwaze singa nga t'okisiimye. Obutambi bwonna bujja kukuumibwa butiribiri. Ssijja kubuwa muntu yenna.

(6) On'oweebwaayo akasiimo olw'okweetaba mu kunoonyere-za kuno. Akasiimo kano tekaliiko bukwakkulizo ku ngeri gy'onooba ozeemu bibuuzo. Bwe kinaaba nti entambula gy'okozesezza ogisasulidde, omutemwa ogwo gunakuddiz-ibwa. Kyokka, tewajja kuba mutemwa mulala gunakuweebwa ogutagwa mu ttuluba eryo.

(7) Kikulu nnyo obutateeka bulamu bwo mu katyabaaga nga kwe kuusa ku kweetabakwo ku kunoonyereza kuno. Em-boozi zaffe zigyakuba nekusifu. Wakati mu mboozi yaffe, wandyesanga nga okalubiriziddwa okunyumya kw'ebyo ebiyinza okukuleetera obulumi olw'ebyo by'oyiseemu.

(8) Erinnya lyo ligya kukuumiibwa nga lya kyaama. Kino nja kukikola nga nkuuma butiribiri ebiwandiiko n'obutambi bw'emboozi zaffe bwonna. Amannya n'engeri yonna ey'ekuusa ku binaampeebwa, nkakasa nga be naaba mbigambyeeko tebamanya wa gye mbijje oba ani gwe byogeerako. Kisaana kitegeerekeke nti newankubadde nga by'onombuulira byandiba eby'enjawulo ku by'abalala, kisooboka omuntu okubikwaanaaganya naawe. Wabula, olw'okukuuma ebikukwaatako nga bya kyaama nja kwogeranga mu ngeri en'eremesanga abalala okumanya nti emboozi zino zikwaata ku muntu gwe bamanyi.

(9) Nina enteegeka okuba n'omuvvuunuzi mu mboozi yaffe singa onooba onyumiza mu Luganda. Wabula,

n'omuvvuunuzi; erinnya lyo, n'ebikufaako wa ku bikuuma nga bya kyaama.

(10) Nnaandyagaadde nnyo emboozi yaffe nsinge ku gikwaata ku katambi kinsobozese okuwandiika ebyo bye nnyini by'oŋŋaambye. Kye nva nkusaba olukusa okubikwaata ku katambi. Obutambi buno bwa kukuumibwa butiribiri.

(11) Wetegereze: Singa olina okwekengera kwonna ku kunoonyereza kuno, oba obulabe bwe kuyinza okukutu- usaako, oba okuganyulwa kw'oyinza okukufunamu, oba eddembe lyo ng'eyeetabye mu kunoonyereza kuno, oky'ayinza okutuukirira Law Faculty Research Ethics Committee Administrator, Mrs. Lamize Viljoen, ku 021 650 3080 oba lamize.viljoen@uct.ac.za. Oba oyinza oku- wandiikira Law Faculty Research Ethics Committee Admin- istrator, Room 6.28 Kramer Law Building, Law Faculty, UCT, Private Bag, Rondebosch 7701. South Africa.

Information Sheet & Consent Form for Stage Two Interviews (Customary Law and Practice Interviews)

(1) Hello, my name is Brian Dennison and I am conducting research towards a doctoral degree in law from the University of Cape Town. I am researching about the status, rights and treatment of persons with disabilities in Mukono District and would like to in- vite you to participate in the project. The name of my research project is The Status, Rights and Treatment of Persons with Disa- bilities within Customary Legal Frameworks in Uganda: A Study of Mukono District.

(2) My research concerns how community practices and customary law in Mukono District impact persons with disabilities. I hope my re- search will provide helpful information as to how indigenous cus-

toms can be engaged to improve the rights, status and treatment of persons with disabilities in Mukono District.

(3) I am approaching you because you have been identified as someone who knows about matters of custom and culture in Mukono District.

(4) I am interested in knowing about the status, rights and treatment of persons with disabilities in matters of succession, land, marriage, leadership, personal accountability and legal authority. I have created a set of questions regarding such matters. I would like to meet with you for some time and go through the questions I have prepared. If you would like to see these questions prior to deciding whether to take part in this interview I am happy to share them with you.

(5) Please understand that your participation is voluntary. The choice to participate is yours alone. If you choose not to participate, there will be no negative consequence. If you choose to participate, but wish to withdraw at any time, you will be free to do so without negative consequence. You also have the right to refuse to answer any questions. I would be most grateful if you would assist me by allowing me to interview you.

(6) The interview process is likely to take one to two hours. You will be paid a reasonable honorarium for your participation in the interview process as well as reimbursement for transport as necessary. The honorarium and any transport reimbursment will be provided to you regardless of the answers that you give. There will be no other direct benefit to you outside of these payments.

(7) You should not be exposed to any risk through your participation in this research. I am not seeking personal or sensitive information in these interviews. Instead I will be asked you to provide your

knowledge and opinion as to the relevant laws, customs and culture as you know them to exist.

(8) I will preserve your anonymity. I will keep track of certain information such as your sex, age, disability status and level of education. However, those that read my research paper will not be able to connect you individually to the answers that you provide. I would like to record our interview in order to insure that I accurately transcribe and report the feedback that you provide. I will ask you for permission to record. These recordings will be kept confidential.

(9) If you have concerns about the research, its risks and benefits or about your rights as a research participant in this study, you may contact the Law Faculty Research Ethics Committee Administrator, Mrs Lamize Viljoen, at 021 650 3080 or at lamize.viljoen@uct.ac.za. Alternatively, you may write to the Law Faculty Research Ethics Committee Administrator, Room 6.28 Kramer Law Building, Law Faculty, UCT, Private Bag, Rondebosch 7701. South Africa.

Luganda Translation of Information & Consent Form for Stage Two Interviews (Customary Law and Practice Interviews):

Enyinnyonnyola ne ffoomu esaba olukusa (emboozi ez'ebyamateeka g'obuwangwa, ennono n'obulombolombo)

(1) Nkulamusizza, erinnya lyange nze Brian Dennison era nkola okunoonyereza okulubirira okufuna ddiguli yange ey'okusatu mu mateeka okuva mu Ssetendekero wa Cape Town. Nkola okunoonyereza ku mbeera, eddembe, n'engeri abantu abalina obulemu mu Bbeendobeendo (District) ly'e Mukono gye bayisibwamu era nga nkusaba onegatteko mu kunoonyereza kuno. Omulamwa gw'okuunoonyereza kuno gutuumiddwa *"Embeera, Eddembe, n'Enkwaata y'Abantu Abalina Obulemu Okusiinziira ku Matee-*

ka g'Eby'obuwangwa n'Ennono mu Uganda: Okunoonyereza nga kwesigamiziddwa ku Bbeendobeendo ly'e Mukono."

(2) Okunoonyereza kwange kukwata ku ngeri obulombolombo bw'ekitundu, n'amateeka g'eby'obuwangwa n'ennono gye biyisaamu abantu abalina obulemu mu Bbeendobeendo ly'e Mukono. Nina esuubi nti okunoonyereza kwange kuno kujja kuluŋŋamya engeri z'eby'obuwangwa eby'ekinnansi gyebiyinza okukozesebwamu okutumbula eddembe, embeera n'empisa abantu abalina obulemu gye bayisibwaamu mu Bbeendobeendo ly'e Mukono.

(3) Nkutuukiridde kubanga olowoozebwa okubaako ne ky'omanyi ku by'obuwangwa n'ennono mu Bbeendobeendo lino ery'e Mukono.

(4) Njagala okumanya engeri eddembe, embeera n'empisa y'abantu abalina obulemu gye bayisibwaamu naddala ku nsonga ez'obusika, ettaka, obufumbo, obukulembeze, obweerufu obwa ssekinnomu, n'ebyobuyinza obw'amateeka. Nina ebibuuzo ebikwaata ku nsonga zino. Nnaandyagadde okukusisinkana okumala akabanga tusobole okuyita mu bibuuzo byentegese. Bw'oba nga waandyagadde okulaba ebibuuzo ebyo nga tonasalawo kweetaba mu mboozi eno, nnina essanyu okubigabana naawe.

(5) Okweetaba kwo mu kunoonyereza kuno si kwa buwaze; kiri gy'oli okukweetabamu oba n'edda. Tovunaanibwa, singa tokweetabamu. Naye ne bw'osiima okukweetabamu, oky'alina eddembe okukuvaamu wonna w'onooba oyagalidde. Era oli wa ddembe okugaana okuddamu ekibuuzo kyonna. N'assanyuka nnyo bw'ononzikkiriza okukubuuzaayo ebibuuzo ebitonotono.

(6) Emboozi yaffe yaanditwaala wakati w'essaawa emu n'ebbiri. On'oweebwaayo akasiimo olw'okweetaba mu kunoonyereza kuno. Akasiimo kano tekaliiko bukwakkulizo ku ngeri gy'onooba ozeemu bibuuzo. Bwe kinaaba nti entambula gy'okozesezza ogisasulidde,

omutemwa ogwo gunakuddizibwa. Kyokka, tewajja kuba mutemwa mulala gunakuweebwa ogutagwa mu ttuluba eryo.

(7) Kikulu nnyo obutateeka bulamu bwo mu katyabaaga nga kwe kuusa ku kweetabakwo mu kunoonyereza kuno. Mu mboozi zino ssinoonya kumanya bikukwaatako oba ekintu kyonna ekyekusifu. Naye nja kukusaba ombuulire by'omanyi n'endowooza yo ku mateeka, ennono n'eby'obuwangwa nga bwebirambikiddwa.

(8) Erinnya lyo ligya kukuumiibwa nga lya kyaama. Nja kwagala okumanya ekikula kyo, emyaka gyo, obanga olina obulemu, n'eddaala ly'okusoma kwo. Wabula, abanaaba basoma okunoonye- reza kwange tebajja kusobola kukukwanaaganya bibuuzo by'onooba ozeemu naawe ng'omuntu. Wabula, abo ab'anasoma ku kunoonyereza kwange tebajja kusobola kubikwaanaganya naawe.

(9) Nnaandyagaadde nnyo emboozi yaffe nsinge ku gikwaata ku katambi kinsobozese okuwandiika ebyo bye nnyini by'oŋŋaambye. Kye nva nkusaba olukusa okubikwaata ku katambi. Obutambi buno bwa kukuumibwa butiribiri.

(10) *Wetegereze: Singa olina okwekengera kwonna ku kunoonyereza kuno, oba obulabe bwe kuyinza okukutuusaako, oba okuganyulwa kw'oyinza okukufunamu, oba eddembe lyo ng'eyeetabye mu kunoonyereza kuno, oky'ayinza okutuukirira Law Faculty Research Ethics Committee Administrator, Mrs. Lamize Viljoen, ku 021 650 3080 oba lamize.viljoen@uct.ac.za. Oba oyinza okuwandiikira Law Faculty Research Ethics Committee Administrator, Room 6.28 Kramer Law Building, Law Faculty, UCT, Private Bag, Ron- debosch 7701. South Africa.*

Fieldwork Survey Instruments

Field Interview Scripts

The following are the interview scripts used for the three phases of fieldwork for this thesis. (Note that prior to each interview basis demographic information was collected about each interviewee.)

I. Semi-Structured Interview Script for Persons with Disabilities in Mukono District for the Stage One Interviews in English and Luganda:

- What is a disability?

  Obulemu kye ki?

- What sort of conditions do you consider a disability?

  Mbeera za ngeri ki z'olowooza nti obwo bulemu?

- Do you know people with disabilities?

  Olinayo abantu b'omannyi nga balina obulemu?

- How are people with disabilities treated in your society?

  Abantu abalina obulemu mu kitundu kyo bayisibwa batya?

- Can you tell us some stories that can teach us something about how persons with disabilities are treated in your community?

  Oyinza okutunyumizaayo emboozi eziriko kye zituyigiriza ku ngeri abantu abalina obulemu mu kitundu kyo gye bayis-ibwaamu?

- Are persons with disabilities permitted by society to do all the things people without disabilities are permitted to do? (With follow up based on answers)

Abantu abalina obulemu mu kitundu kyo tebakugirwa kwennyigira oba kukola ebyo byonna abatalina bulemu bye bakola? (Ka nkikase okusinziira ku biddiddwamu).

o   Do you have any stories that support your views?

Olina eby'okulabirako ebikakasa ky'ogamba?

o   Are all people with disabilities permitted to own land? (With follow up asking for relevant stories)

Bonna   abalina   obulemu   b'akkirizibwa   okuba n'obwannanyini ku ttaka? (Musabe akuwe obukakafu ku nsonga eyo).

o   Are there special provisions that are made to make sure that persons with disabilities have access to land? (With follow up asking for relevant stories)

Waliwo enkizo eweebwa abalina obulemu ebasobozesa okufuna ettaka? (Musabe akuwe obukakafu ku nsonga eyo)

o   Do all people with disabilities have the same rights to inherent property as all other people? (With follow up asking for relevant stories)

Bonna abalina obulemu balina eddembe ly'okusikira ebintu ng'abalala bonna? (Musabe akuwe obukakafu ku nsonga eyo)

o   Are all people with disabilities permitted to marry? (With follow up asking for relevant stories)

Bonna   abalina   obulemu   bakirizibwa   okuwasa   oba okufumbirwa? (Musabe akuwe obukakafu ku nsonga eyo)

o   Does your community take special care of persons with disabilities?

Abantu b'omu kitundu kyo balina engeri yonna ey'enjawulo gye bafaayo ku abo abalina obulemu?

o   If so how? (With follow up asking for relevant stories)

Bwe kiba bwe kityo, bakikola batya?

o   (Interviewees were also asked customary about guardianship and were asked if there was anything else that they would like to add to help us understand the rights, status and treatment of persons with disabilities at the conclusion of the interview.)

II Semi-Structured Interview Script for Customary Knowledge Bearers for Stage 2 Interviews in English with Luganda Translations

The following is the semi-structured interview template used for customary knowledge bearers in the second stage of field interviews in English with Luganda translations:

1. Questions to Establish Authority to Speak on Matters of Custom

o   Are you considered by members of your community to knowledgeable about the customary laws and practices of the Buganda people living in Mukono District?

Omanyi ebikwaata ku by'obuwangwa, ennono, n'obulombolombo by'abantu ba Buganda abali mu Bbeendobeendo ly'e Mukono?

o   Why do you say this?

Lwaki ogambye bw'otyo?

o   Are you knowledgeable about the customary laws and practices of the Buganda people living in Mukono District?

Olina kyomanyi ku Tteeka lye nnono/etteeka erifuga obuwangwa ne nneeyisa ya Baganda ababeera mu mukono?

o   Why do you say this?

Lwaki ogambye bw'otyo?

2. Questions About Beliefs About Persons with Disabilities

o   Who are persons with disabilities?

Bantu ki abalina obulemu?

o   List the disabilities you are aware of.

Wa obulemu bwomayi obubeera ku bantu?

o   What do you believe is the cause of disabilities?

Kiki kyomanyo ekireeta obulemu/

o   What are some of the traditional beliefs among the people of Mukono District about the cause of disabilities?

Bintu ki ebyobuwangwa abantu bye ba kkirirzaamu mu Mukono ebivaako obulemu?

o   What do religions practiced in Mukono District teach us about the cause of disabilities?

Eddini eziri mu mokono ziyigiriza ki ku bivaako abantu okuba nobulemu?

o   What words exist in Luganda for disabilities and for persons with disabilities?

Bigambo ki oba njogera ki eziri mu luganda nga zitegeeza bulemu oba nga ebigambo bitegeeza muntu alina obulemu

o   Are persons with disabilities given any particular names in your culture as a matter of custom or tradition? If so what names are they given?

Kyabuwangwa abantu abalina obulemu okutuumibwa amannya agenjawulo ? Bwekiba nga kituufu mannya nga ki agabatuumibwa?

- For each name provided --- what does that word mean? Are there any other meanings or uses for that word?

   Amannya ago gategeeza ki mubulambulukufu?

3. Questions about Personal Knowledge and Relationships

- Do you know people with disabilities?

   Olinayo bomanyi abalina obulemu?

- (If Yes) Are these individuals treated the same as other individuals in the community?

   Abantu abo bogambye bayisibwa mu ngeri yemu nga abatalina bulemu?

- Explain your answer.

   Nnyonnyola okuddamu kwo.

4. Questions Regarding Laws and Customs

4.1 General Initial Questions about Customary Law and Persons with Disabilities

- Are there any customs or practices in this community that protect persons with disabilities?

   Waliwo enkola yonna etangira oba eranirira eddembe lyabo abalina obulemu mu kitundu kino?

- (if Yes) Explain your answer and describe the customs or practices:

   Bwekiba nga kituufu, nnynnyola bwe bakikola?

- o (if Yes) Of these customs and practices are any existing from time immemorial?

  Enkpla eno ebadde wo kuva dda oba yakajja?

- o (if Yes) Of these customs and practices are any based on current community standards and practices?

  Ku nkola eno waliwo emu ku zzo ekolebwa nga basinziira ku mbeera eriwo akakyo kano?

- o Are there any customs in this community that tend to harm or lessen the social or legal status of persons with disabilities?

  Waliwo enkola yonna eyobuwangwa etyooboola eddembe lyabo abalina obulemu?

- o (if Yes) Explain your answer and describe the customs or practices:

  Bwekiba nga kituufu; Nnyonnyola enkola eyo?

- o (if Yes) Of these customs and practices are any existing from time immemorial?

  Enkola eyo ebadde wo kuva dda oba yakajja?

- o (if Yes) Of these customs and practices are any based on current community standards and practices?

  Enkola eyo ekolebwa nga basinziira ku ngeri ebintu gyebitambulamu ensangi zino?

4.2 Land Holding

- o Can a person with disabilities own land?

  Omuntu alina obulemu asobola okuba nannyini Ttaka?

o Can someone's disability have an impact on their status as a kibanja holder?

Obulemu obuli ku muntu bulina kyebukola oba okuyamba ku ngeri omuntu alina ekibanja gyayisibwaamu?

o Could persons with disabilities always be kibanja holders from time immemorial?

Abantu abalina obulemu basobola okubeerera ddala be ba nannyini kibanja kuva mu ntandikwa?

o Are there cases where property is held in trust for or on the behalf of a person with a disability who is not otherwise permitted to own or inherit land?

Singa omuntu aliko abulemu takkirizibwa kuba nabintu oba okuba omusika, asobola okweyimirirwa mu musango?

o Is you answer based on customary practice as it has existed from time immemorial or is it based on current community standards and practices?

Kiba kyabuwangwa oba basinziira ku mbeera eriwo?

o Do heads of household, clans or clan leaders have any special responsibilities in terms of land management for persons with disabilities?

Abakulebeze mu maka, abakulu b'ekika balina obuvunany-izibwa obenjawulo okulabilira ebyabo abalina obulemu?

o Is you answer based on customary practice as it has existed from time immemorial or is it based on current community standards and practices?

Kyabuwangwa bbo okukikola oba basinziira ku mbeera eriwo?

4.3. Laws of Succession

- o Can a person with disabilities inherit land under the traditional laws of succession of the Buganda people?

  Mu Buganda abantu abaliko obuleme basobola okusikira ettaka?

- o Is you answer based on customary practice as it has existed from time immemorial or is it based on current community standards and practices?

  Ekyo kyabuwangwa oba kisinziira ku mbeera eriwo?

- o Does your answer above apply to all persons with disabilities or are people with different disabilities treated differently depending on the type of disability or the extent of the disability?

  Okuddamu kwo okwo waggulu kusinziira ku kika kya bulemu oba buli alina obulemu ayisibwa kyekimu?

- o Can all people with disabilities inherit property other than land from the estate of a deceased?

  Nga ojjeeko ettaka, abantu abalina obulemu basobola okusikira ebintu ebirara eby'omugenzi.?

- o Is you answer based on customary practice as it has existed from time immemorial or is it based on current community standards and practices?

  Ekyo kyabuwangwa oba kisinsiira ku mbeera eriwo?

- o Can a person with a disability be a customary heir?

  Omuntu aliko obulemu asobola okuba omusika?

o   Is you answer based on customary practice as it has existed from time immemorial or is it based on current community standards and practices?

Kyabuwangwa oba kisinziiral ku mbeera eriwo mu kitundi ekyo?

o   What attributes and qualities do families and clans look for when naming a customary heir when no heir has been named by a will?

Bintu ki bye batunuulira okufuula omuntu omusika ssinga ekiramo tekimwogerako?

o   Are there special protections in the context of succession rights for persons with disabilities under the customary law and practices of the Buganda people in Mukono District? If your answer is "Yes" please describe these special protections.

Waliwo okukugira kwonna oba obukuumi mu tteeka lye nsikirano okuyamba abao abaliko obulemu mu mukono? Nnyonnyola... ...

o   Is you answer based on customary practice as it has existed from time immemorial or is it based on current community standards and practices?

Okuddamu kwo osinzidde ku bya buwangwa oba kisinziira ku mbeera eriwo?

o   Can persons with a disability make a willwills under the customary law of the Buganda?

Abantu abaliko obulemu bawandiika ekiraamo mu mu Buganda?

- o Is you answer based on customary practice as it has existed from time immemorial or is it based on current community standards and practices?

  Ekyo kya buwangwa oba kisinziira ku mbeera eriwo?

- o Are there some persons with a disability who would not be permitted to make a will under the customary law of the Buganda?

  Eriyo abantu abatakkiribwa kuwandiika kiraamo olwobulemu bwebalina okusinziira ku buwangwa oba kisinziira ku mbeera eriwo.?

- o Is you answer based on customary practice as it has existed from time immemorial or is it based on current community standards and practices?

  Okuddamu kwo kusinzidde ku buwangwa oba ku mbeera ebaawo nandi ki omutido ogubaawo?

4.4 Marriage, Family and Sexual Relations

- o Can all people with disabilities marry?

  Abantu abaliko obulemu bakkirizibwa okuwasa oba okufumbirwa?

- o (if Yes) Of these customs and practices have any existing from time immemorial?

  Ekyo Kyava dda ?

- o (if Yes) Of these customs and practices are any based on current community standards and practices?

  Ekyo kyakatandika kakyo kano?

o   If not, which persons with disabilities do not have the right to marry?

Bwekiba nga sikituufu, Bantu kika ki abaliko obulemu abatakkirizibwa kuwasa oba kufumbirwa?

o   (if any) For each type of person who does not have the right to marry is this a tradition that has existed from time immemorial?

Abantu abaliko obulemu butakkirizibwa kuwas oba kufumbirwa kyabuwangwa?

o   (if any) For each type of person who does not have the right to marry, is this a custom based on current community standards and practices.

Oba basinziira ku mbeera eriwo?

o   Are men with disabilities who are seeking to marry someone's daughter ever charged a higher or lower bride price based on their disability?

Omusajja alina obulemu basobola okumukenderezaako ku mutwaalo gwatwaala eri abazadde bo'muwala?

o   Are there certain people who may not participate in sexual relations based on their disabilities?

Waliwo abantu abatasobola kweggata na mukazi oba musajja lwa bulemu?

o   *Is you answer based on customary practice as it has existed from time immemorial or is it based on current community standards and practices?*

Ekyo kyabuwangwa oba kisinziira ku mbeera eriwo?

o   If a spouse becomes disabled, can that be grounds for divorce in a customary marriage in Mukono District?

Singa omu ku bafumbo afuna obulemu, eyo esobola okuba ensongs erimu eggumba omuntu okwawukan ne munne ousinziira ku buwangwa mu mukono?

o   *Is you answer based on customary practice as it has existed from time immemorial or is it based on current community standards and practices?*

Okuddamu kwo kusinzidde ku buwangwa oba kisinziira ku mbeera eriwo?

o   If a wife gives birth to a child with a disability, can that be grounds for divorce in a customary marriage in Mukono District?

Ssinga omukyaala azaala omwana aliko obulemu, esobola okuba ensonga rimu eggumba abafumbo bano okwawukana okusinziira ku buwangwa mu mukono?

o   Is you answer based on customary practice as it has existed from time immemorial or is it based on current community standards and practices?

Okuddamu kwabuwangwa oba kisinziira ku mbeera eriwo?

o   Please describe the process of getting a divorce under the customary law of the Baganda as practiced in Mukono District.

Tunnyonnyole emitendera egiyitibwaamu ssinga abantu bagala kwawukana mu mateeka mu Buganda era nga bekikolebwa mu mukono disitulikiti?

4.5 Questions Regarding Guardianship

- *Please describe the process by which guardians are appointed under customary law.*

  Mietendera ki egiyitibwaamu okulndaomukuza w' abaana b'omugenzi okusinziira ku buwangwa mu Buganda?

- *Can a person with a disability be appointed or named as a guardian under customary law in Mukono District?*

  Omuntu aliko obuleme asobola okulndebwa nga omukuza okusinziira ku buwangwa mu mukono disiturikiti?

- What are the expected benefits or rewards that would come from serving as a guardian?

  Omuntu alondebwa okuba omukuza afuniramu wa oba aganyirwamu atya?

- Are there any customs or practices existing in Mukono district whereby adults with disabilities are placed in guardianships?

  Waliwo emikolomegikolebwa mu mukono distulikiti ssinga omuntu alina obulemu alondebwa okuba omukuza?

- *If yes, please describe them and please indicate whether the desires and will of the disabled person are considered in the process.*

  Bwekiba nga kituufe nnyonnyola,ate olage oba omuntu aliko abulemu byateesa bissibwaamu ekitiibwa?

4.6 Questions Regarding Clan Leadership

- Can a person with a disability become a clan leader in Mukono District?

Omuntu aliko obulemu asobola okuba omukulu w'ekiga mu ggombolola y'emukono?

o   Are there some forms of disability that would prevent a person from being a clan leader in Mukono District?

Eriyo ekika ky'obulemu ekitinza okulemesa omuntu okufuuka omukulu w'ekika mu distrikiti ye mukono/

o   Please describe the process of selecting a clan leader as practiced among the clans in Mukono District.

Nnyonnyola emitendera egiyitibwaamu okulonda omukulu w'ekika mu disitulikiti ye mukono?

5 Questions Regarding the Uganda Constitution and International Human Rights Instruments

o   Do you know what the Uganda Constitution says about persons with disabilities?

Omanyi Ssemateeka wa Uganda kya yogera ku bantu abalina obulemu

o   Does the Uganda Constitution have any impact on how persons with disabilities are treated within their communities in Mukono District?

Ssemateeka oyo alina kyayamba ku ngeri abantu abalina obulemu gyebayisibwama mu Ggombolola ye mukono?

o   (If yes) Describe the impact.

Eyamba etya?

o   Do you think that the customary law practiced in Mukono District should change to be consistent with any rights and protections for persons with disability stated in the Uganda Constitution?

Olowooza waliwo ebyetagisa okukyusibwa mu ngeri abantu abaliko obulemu gye bakwatibwamu okusobola okutuukana nekyo ekilagibwa Ssemateeka wa Uganda nda eddembe lyabwe?

o Do you know about any International Human Rights Instruments that concern the rights of persons with disabilities?

Olina yo etteeka lyensi yonna lyomanyi erilwanirira eddembe lyabo abalina obulemu?

o Do international human rights instruments have any impact on how persons with disabilities are treated within their communities in Mukono District?

Amateeka ago gomanyi agensi yonna galina kye gayamba ku ngeri abntu abalina obulemu gye bayisibwamu mu bitundu byabwe mu ggobolola ye mukono?

o (If yes) Describe the impact.

Nnyonnyola engeri gyegayambye mu?

o Do you think that the customary law practiced in Mukono District should change to account for the rights of persons with disabilities provided in international human rights instruments?

Olowooza nti etteeka erifuga ebyobuwangwa mu ggombolola ye mukono lisaanye likyusibwe lituukane n'omutindo gwago a'ensi yonna?

6. Questions Regarding Ubuntu

o What is Ubuntu?

Ubuntu kyekki?

- How does Ubuntu impact the customs and cultures of people in Mukono District?

  Guyamba ki mu byobuwangwa my ggombolola ye mukono

- Does Ubuntu have any effect on the customs and rights of the people in your community?

  Ububtu alina engeri gyakosaamu ebyobuwangwa?

- Is Ubuntu relevant to the treatment and rights of persons with disabilities in your community?

  Ubuntu ya mugaso mu kulwanirira eddembe lyabo abaliko obulemu?

- If "yes", how?

  Atya?

- If "no", why not?

  Lwaki nedda?

III Interview Script for Stage 3 Interviews of Persons with Disabilities to Check and Validate Findings from the Stage 3 Customary Knowledge Bearer Interviews:

(Note: Questions were translated directly into Luganda by the translator present for the interviews.)

- Who poses the biggest problem for persons with disabilities within Buganda Culture:

- Current Buganda society or Buganda traditions?

- Buganda society, families in Buganda or individual Muganda?

- Is discrimination against PWDs more attributable to hatred/dislike of PWDs or more attributable to a belief that a PWD cannot do things? (give land inheritance example)

- Are deaf and mute people given less rights and status in Buganda culture that other PWDs?

- Has the NRM government been the most effective change agent for PWDs in Mukono District?

- Have foreign nations and foreign individuals in Uganda been effective change agents for PWDs in Mukono District?

- Do you need a reason to get divorced under customary law?

- Is there any procedure that one must follow to get a divorce in a Baganda customary marriage?

- Do the cultural institutions of the Buganda (Ministers, the Court in Mengo) have any positive impact on the lives of PWDs in Mukono District?

- Are the cultural institutions of the Buganda weak because of a lack of financial resources?

- Can PWDs with knowledge of formal law (court law) use that knowledge to prevent discrimination and mistreatment at the customary level?

- Do you agree with the statement "At the end of the day the law will prevail?"

- Do you believe that someone can get a disability from witchcraft? Do you know other people that believe this?

- Do you believe that someone can get a disability from failing to meet cultural obligations? Do you know other people that believe this?

- o Do you believe that someone can get a disability from failing to appease gods like Wanema, Magobew and Musoke? Do you know other people that believe this?

- o Is the amount of bride price paid up to the groom or the father-in-law?

- o Do PWDs tend to avoid Kwanjulas?

- o Over the past 30 years have there been changes within Baganda culture or are things the same as they have been from time immemorial with respect to:

- o The possibility and practice of PWDs serving as clan leaders

- o The possibility of PWDs serving as customary heirs

- o The possibility of PWDs serving as guardians

- o The ability of PWDs to marry

Interviewee Data Set Tables

Table A

PARTICIPANT GENDER	NUMBER
Men (green)	44
Women (blue)	19

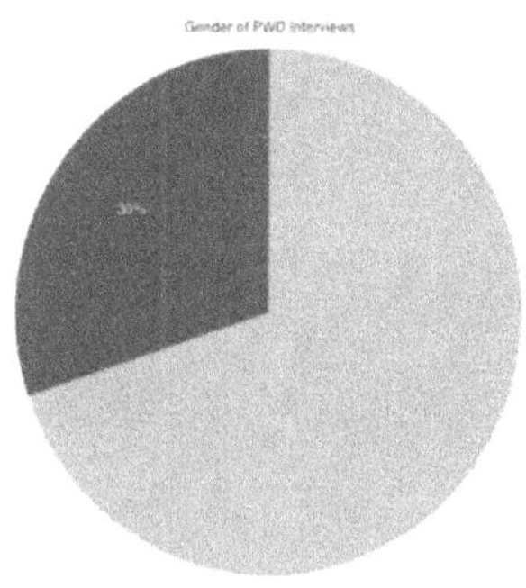

Table B

IMPAIRMENT		NUMBER
Physical Limb Disabilities		51
Vision Impairments		6
Hearing Impairments		4
Speech Impediment only		1
Albinism		1
Acid Burn Survivor		1

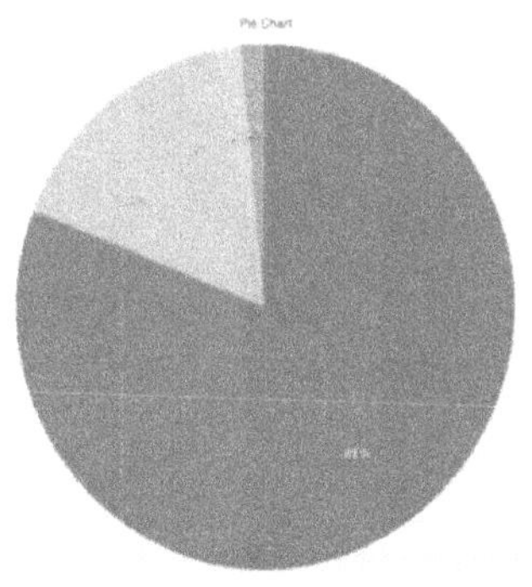

Table C
People Groups of Interviewees with Disabilities (Bantu)

PARTICIPANT GENDER		UNITS SOLD
Buganda (Bantu) (green)		39
Other Bantu (blue)		12
Non-Bantu		12

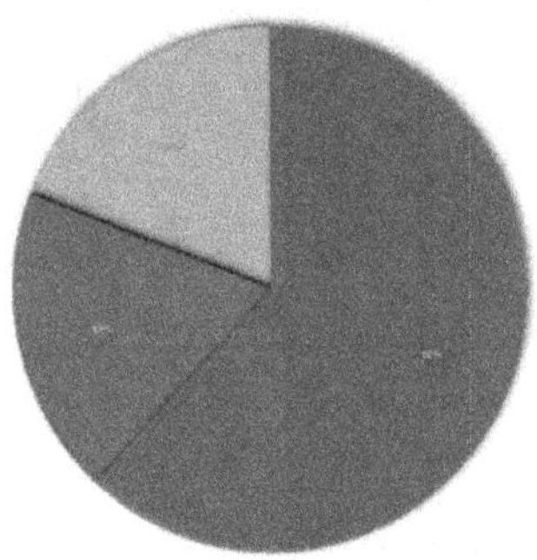

Table D

Religious Afiliation of Interviewees with Disabilities

PARTICIPANT	RELIGIOUS AFFILIATION
Protestant	30
Catholic	17
Mormon	1
Jehovah's Witness	1
Muslim	14

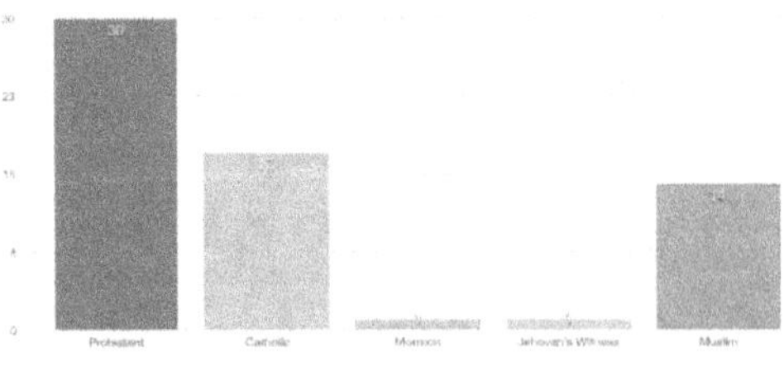

Table E

Formal Educational Background of Interviewees with Disabilities

PARTICIPANT	NUMBER
None	3
Primary	19
Secondary	23
Tertiary	17
Islamic Studies Only	1

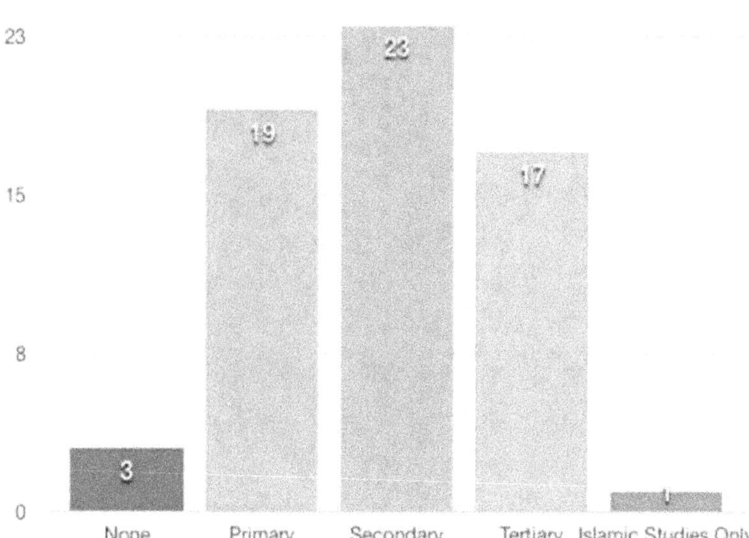

Formal Educational Background of Interviewees with Disabilities

Table F

Employment Categories of Interviewees with Disabilities

PARTICIPANT	NUMBER
Agriculture	19
Service & Trade	21
Disability Advocacy	5
Teachers & Counselors	3
Administrative	4
Homemaker	3
Electrical Engineer	1
Student	3
Unemployed or Retired	4

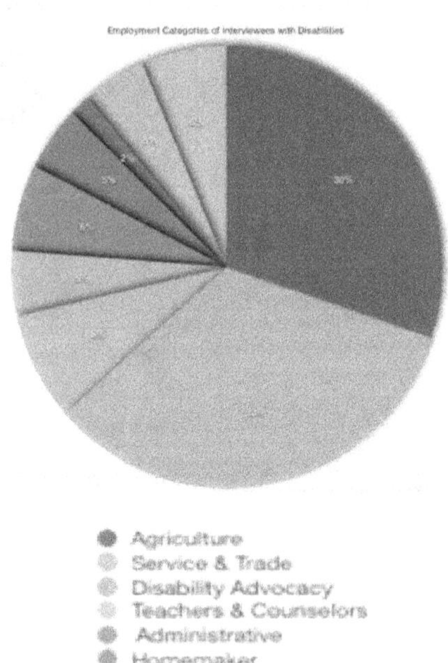

Table G

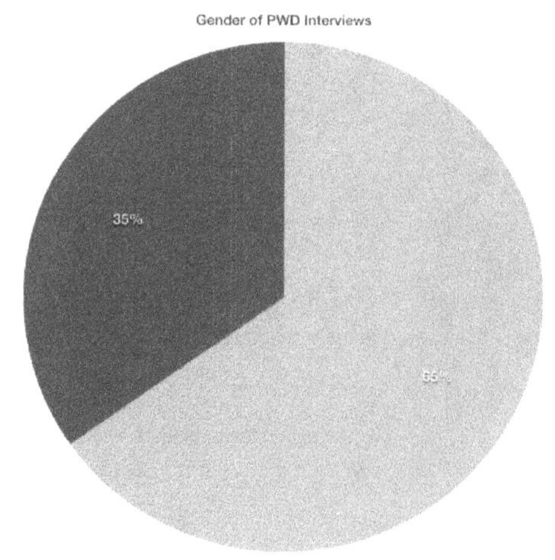

Table H

Religious Affiliation of Interviewees with Disabilities

PARTICIPANT	RELIGIOUS AFFILIATION
Protestant	8
Catholic	5
Muslim	10

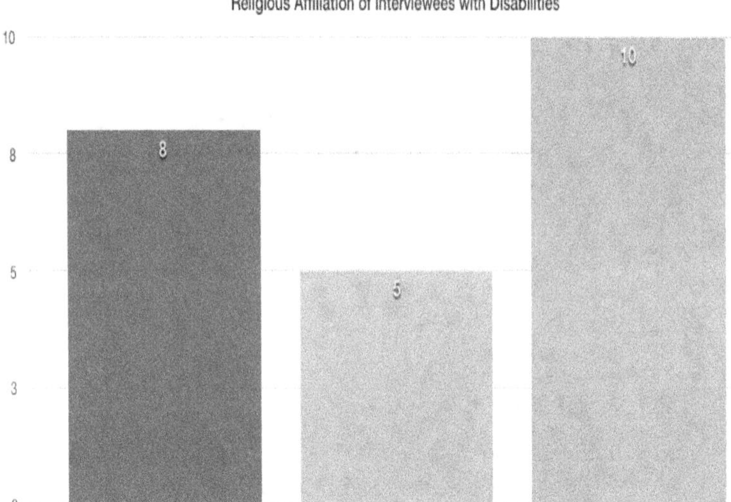

Religious Affiliation of Interviewees with Disabilities
10
8
5
3
0
8
5
10
Protestant
Catholic
Muslim

Stage One Interviewee Redacted Matrix

Reference code	A	B	C
Can PWDs own land?	Yes	Yes	Yes
Do PWDs who are with Kibanja land rights encounter greater problems retaining their land rights?	Yes	Yes	NA
Are there special customs or practices that enable PWDs to access land?	Nothing done to help assess.	Unaware	Permitted to own. Kibanja not a problem.
Education Level	P?	S3	S1
Religion	RC	Mus	Mus
Tribe	Myrwanda	Muganda	Muganda
Disability	Blind in one eye. Limb based impairment	Polio Survivor, Both legs impaired	Polio survivor with bad leg
Sex	M	M	M
Age	59	23	50

D	E	F	G	H
Yes	Yes	No	Yes	Do not know
Yes	Yes	Yes bc the land lord knows you are weak.	PWDs are teated inequality by land lords.	Land lords may not take advantage of pwd kibanja.
Yes, but maybe not permitted to inherit land.	No special help.	No	No	In other places.
P6	P5	None	P6	No
Mus	RC	Protestant (Pentecostal)	RC	Mus
Muganda	Muganda	Muganda	Muganda	Muganda
Polio Survivor	Polio survivor	Polio Survivor	Polio Survivor	Says that his joints stiffened due to witchcraft
M	F	F	F	M
52	30	34	36	30

I	J	K	L	M
Yes	Yes, with money.	Yes	Yes	Yes
Landlords always try to take advantage of PWDs. Especially if you have no documents.	NA	NA	Yes	Land lords will despise and take advantage of PWDs who do not have self esteem.
No	No	No	No	No
P4	S3	P7	S4	P7
RC	Protestant (Pentecostal)	Mus	Protestant	Protestant
Busia/Samyier	Munyoro	Muganda	Muganda	Muganda
Polio survivor	Partial paralyzation from malaria	Polio Survivor	Polio Survivor	Polio Survivor
M	F	M	M	M
37	34	43	56	50

N	O	P	Q	R
Yes, with money.	Yes, with money.	Yes	Yes	Yes, with money.
No, as long as busuulu is paid a PWD is treated the same.	No, pwd kibanja holders are treated the same as others.	It is possible to evict a PWD bc of the disability.	Yes, there is often mischief bc PWD seen as defense-les.	Landlords treat PWDs the same.
No, just the community hospital.	No	In other places.	No	No
S4	P4	S2	No	S1
Protestant	Protestant	Protestant	Protestant	Protestant
Muganda	Muganda	Musoga	Musanyia	Muganda
Bone disease in legs	Acid Burn survivor	Polio Survivor	Polio Survivor	Polio Survivor
M	F	F	F	F
26	38	30	45	30

S	T	U	V	W
Yes	Yes	Yes, with money.	Yes	Yes, with money.
If you are intelligent they cannot chase you. If you pay busuulu they cannot chase you.	PWDs can be treated un-fairly by Kibanja land lords.	No, all long as they pay their busuulu	A PWD will always be mistreated and taken ad-vantage of by the landlord	No, as long as busuulu is paid PWD is treated fairly
There is a place called Bubiiro were they raise crops & animals.	No	No indigenous programs.	No, because they do not think PWDs can do the work.	Never seen it.
P4	S2	Diploma	P7	P4
Protestant (Pentecostal)	Protestant (Pentecostal)	RC	RC	Mus
Munyole,	Muganda	Muganda	Eteso	Muganda
Knee problem	Left leg injury	Shortened leg	Partial paralyzation from injection	Polio Survivor
F	M	M	M	M
28	46	67	57	49

X	Y	Z	AA	AB
Yes, with money.	Yes	Yes	They can, but they are despised.	Yes
A PWD can be easily by mistreated by a kibanja land lord.	NA: did not discuss with interviewee	NA	NA	Na
No	Not there	Never seen that.	Not there.	No
S4	Certificate in Islamic stud-ies	P3	S2	S3
Protestant	Mus	Protestant	Protestant	Protestant
Muganda	Muganda	Lubaara	Muganda	Muganda
Polio Survivor	Atrophic arm. Birth Defect	Leg paralysis	Polio Survivor	Polio Survivor
M	M	F	M	F
42	70	35	41	38

AC	AD	AE	AF	AG
Yes, you can buy or get from your father.	Yes, he does.	Yes	Yes	Yes, you cannot take away the land.
NA	NA	NA	NA	NA
No, but there are in Seeta town (NGOs only).	No	No	In other places.	No
P2	S?	P4	S4	P1
Mus	Mus	Mus	RC	Mus
Muganda	Muganda	Muganda	Muganda	Japadohla
Polio Survivor	Blind	Paralysis	Injury to arm and leg	Blind and physical disability
M	M	M	M	M
51	60	21	55	73

AH	AI	AJ	AK	
Yes, any denial to own land would be very un-common.	Yes	Yes, with money.	Yes, even in Tesoland.	You can, but it is very hard-especially in urban areas due to high cost of land.
Maybe it is a bit easier to push PWDs around a bit, but that is all.	NA	NA	NA	NA
No	No	No	She thinks there are but she does not know about them specifically.	No
Bachelors Degree	Bachelors Degree	P7	S4	Masters Degree
Protestant (Pentecostal)	Protestant	RC	Protestant	RC
Muganda	Eteso	Muganda	Eteso	Bahima
Polio Survivor	Polio Survivor	Amputee	Polio Survivor	Cerebral Palsy
M	M	M	F	M
48	29	30	19	39

AL	AM	AN	AO	AP
Yes, with money.	Yes, with money.	Yes	Yes, if you buy with money.	yes
NA	NA	NA	NA	NA
No	No	No	No.	No other that a gov't animal husbandry project.
S6	None	Diploma	Bachelors Degree	S6
Protestant	RC	Protestant	Protestant	RC
Muganda	Rwandese	Muganda	Mutoro	Acholi
Leg injury	Injury to leg	Albinism	Little Person	Polio Survivor
F	M	F	M	M
38	68	24	34	20

AQ	AR	AS	AT	AU
Yes	Yes	No, bc they are denied their right to inheritance.	Yes, they can buy. But people will try to defraud PWDs as perceived vulnerable people.	Not at all.
NA	NA	NA	NA	NA
No	No	Some CBRs try but they do not help.	Not in her district. In Kampala the municipal government there had a special program.	No
S3	S1	Bachelors Degree	P7	S6
Protestant	Protestant	Protestant	RC	Jehovah's Witness
Muganda	Muganda	Samyier	Mutoro	Langi
Polio Survivor	Leg injury	Partial deafness, but can speak	Polio Survivor	Deaf
M	F	F	F	F
33	40	24	37	23

AV	AW	AX	AY	AZ
Yes, with money.	Yes, if you are sane.	Yes, although there can be problems with inheritance.	Yes	Yes
NA	NA	NA	NA	NA
"Not really. It is money that saves you."	Misunderstood the question	No	Not aware.	He thinks there may be some programs out there but people are not aware.
Graduate school studies	S4	Diploma	Bachelors Degree	Bachelors Degree
Protestant	Mus	RC	RC	RC
Muganda	Muganda	Muganda	Munyankole	Muganda
Limb amputations	Deaf	Blind	Speech impediment	Cerebral Palsy
M	M	M	M	M
24	23	59	28	27

BA	BC	BD	BE	BF
Yes, if you purchase it.	Yes, with money.	Yes per the law.	Yes	Yes, with money.
NA	Landlords do take advantage of PWD kibanja holders. They are vulnerable.	NA	NA	NA
Aware of a government program.	No	Organizations like NIDIPU are working for progress on this front.	No	No
S3	P7	Bachelors Degree	Post Graduate studies	P7
Mus	RC	Protestant	Protestant	Protestant
Mugisu	Muganda	Mugisu	Muganda	Muganda
Polio Survivor	Polio Survivor	Bone disease in legs	Blindness	Deaf
M	M	M	M	M
27	46	27	35	37

BG	BH	BI	BJ	BK
Yes, with money.	Yes, in fact there are no problems—PWDS are treated like everyone else.	You are not refused the right to own land, but others want to exploit you.	Yes, if you are empowered and have money..	It depends on the community. In the urban areas of Mukono it is very difficult
NA	NA	NA	NA	NA
Nothing	Nothing special for or against them.	No	No, but the Kabaka gave land to people with vision impairment.	The local council members are supposed to work with courts and land boards to limit abuse. But instead there is a good bit of conniving and corruption that goes on.
S4	Bachelors Degree	Bachelors Degree	Bachelors Degree	Cerificate
Mus	LDS	Protestant	Protestant	RC
Muganda	Samyier	Muganda	Mugisu	Eteso
Polio Survivor	Partial paralyzation from injection	Amputee	Poor vision	Leg injury
M	M	F	M	M
62	63	30	56	38

Reference code	A	B
Can a PWD become a clan leader?	NA	Yes. if the man with a disability is of same line as the clan leader.
Is there a customary practice for the care of adult wards?	Yes, this can be done for close family members.	NA
Can a PWD serve as a customary guardian?	Yes	Y, as long as pwd is friend of deceased
If a woman has a child with a disability is is grounds for divorce or termination of marriage?	Not asked	Used to be
Will Men with Disabilities be charged a Higher Bride Price?	Never heard of the practice.	Yes. In fact he himself was charged a higher bride price
Can PWD Marry?	Yes, but the marriages are not stable.	Yes, but PWDs who marry are "despised."
Are there any customs that are beneficial or helpful to PWDs?	No	No
Can PWDs Inherit land?	Yes, culture permits inheritance by PWDs, but it is grabbed by others.	Inheritance by PWDs is not allowed. The problem lies with family and clan.

C	D	E
Yes, if knowledgable/trustworthy/integrity (merit based)	NA	This is impossible, There is nothing you can do. It comes down to the perceived uselessness of PWDs by clan members
NA	NA	It is possible, but most likely it will not happen.
Y, he is a guardian for four children. Reputation and status are key to appointment.	Y, if you have money they will consider you.	Yes, in fact she is.
Used to be	Not asked	It is possible that a man will run away
Never seen it. His father and law told him to "bring what he could"	It can happen per stories he has heard	Not aware if this happens or not.
Yes	Yes, but women who marry men with disabilities are "condemned."	Yes, but man will despise and make fun of you
No	No	None
Yes, they do. He inherited and got the same thanks to the involvement of Islamic clerics in the inheritance process.	Yes by the law, but you can get less, especially when it comes to land. This happen to him.	No, it is not possible. They will not get the same rights. People think PWDs are useless.

F	G	H
No, it is very difficult for a man with a disability to become a clan leader.	Yes, she has seen it in the case of her younger brother.	Does not know, the interviewee has never seen it.
NA	NA	Yes, even a man with children can.
It is difficult bc people think you cannot take care of children.	Yes	Yes, if the PWD is accepted as trustworthy.
Yes, a man could 'chase' a woman from a marriage or say she is cursed.	Its possible.	No, there is no difference in treatment.
This is sometimes done to discourage men with disabilities bc they are seen as useless.	Don't know.	Depends, some families may let you pay less.
Yes,	Yes	Yes
No	No. They are all suffering mistreatment.	Yes, people give money to PWDs without the without the PWDs asking
She has not seen PWDs inherit. However, there could be some clans and families that treat people equally. "it would depend on someone's heart."	Don't know	If people in the clan accept and trust a PWD then that person can inherit land.

I	J	K
No	NA	NA
This rarely happens.	NA	Never seen it happen, but it is possible.
No, because how can one care for others who requires care themselves?	Yes, depends on the hearts of people.	It is possible depending on the friendship the deceased had.
Yes, for some. The man can just leave her in the hospital	NA	Yes
Requiring a higher bride price from persons with disabilities is very common.	Never heard of that practice.	He has heard of charging men with disabilities a higher bride price.
Yes	Yes, but they are despised and dis-advantaged.	Yes, but some think PWDs are not supposed to.
No	No	No
Yes, but limited. Usually parents prefer to give land to non-disabled children. The clan is more fair.	Yes,	Depends on the bias of the clan. However if there is a will they will follow the will

L	M	N
NA	It is possible. It can be done at clan meetings and also through a will.	Does not know. Usually the first born sons of clan leaders.
NA	It can happen in families and through religious leaders.	Yes
Yes, if PWD is responsible Clan members can select that PWD to be a customary guardian.	Yes, as long as the PWD is respected.	It is Possible.
NA	Men will deny the child is theirs and make the wife raise the child alone.	It is seen as an act of God, not grounds for divorce.
NA	No, in fact families are usually sympathetic and reduce the bride price for men with disabilities.	Yes, it is very common.
Yes, in fact PWDs do not usually find difficulty marrying these days.	Yes, and most are.	Yes
No, other than double standard treatment in criminal contexts where PWDs tend to receive lesser or no punishment	No	No
It depends, Greedy people will not allow. It depends on the good hearts of the deceased, the clan leaders and heirs.	Yes, he inherited uncle's property equally with other beneficiaries. However, usually PWDs will be given unequally smaller shares.	Yes, but it can be challenging.

O	P	Q
Yes, as long as people trust you and you are rich. Typically the clan votes.	Yes, they will select someone with a good heart or is a good mobilize.r	"By chance" (rarely) it could happen. If the father declares the clan leadership to the oldest son who has disabilities in a will the clan will have no choice but to name the son a clan leader..
Very difficult, people will say that person is not useful.	Yes	Yes. if a person cannot help themselves.
It is possible, as long as guardian has financial capacity to provide.	Possible	Possible
A man might leave. He will say 'for our clan we do not have these ones' (i.e. children with disabilities).	The man can divorce you for that.	It would not.
They might actually ask for less for a male suit- or with a disability.	No, PWDs are treated as "normal" in the this context.	Does not know, but it should not be lower for woman with disabilities.
Yes	Yes	Yes
no	Just the provision of political offices under the formal law.	No
No, They cannot. People will say "how can this person manage land?"	Yes, families and clans treat people equally.	Only a by a small chance or miracle can a PWD inherit. It only can happen bc of families.

R	S	T
Never seen it	Never seen it.	Yes, usually you must be educated and have some intelligence. It depends on family and sometimes on the male clan leaders. Usually PWDs are not permitted to come to clan meetings bc leaders are very corrupt.
It is possible when the ward's parents are dead.	It is possible if a person cannot care for themselves.	Yes (but based on the response it is possible that the interviewee did not understand the question)
Not possible. People say you cannot even take care of yourself.	Yes, even she is a guardian	Never seen it.
Yes it can bring divorce.	Her father did not. Only if a man does not think well bc all children are gifts from God.	Yes, it is.
Some will to keep a man with disabilities from marrying their daughter.	No	Sometimes
Yes	Yes	Yes, as long as the PWD has some financial capability and wife's family is wiling.
No	Local gov't says they will, but they do not.	Yes, some community members provide food and clothing.
"Usually able-bodied people inherit land instead." This problem begins with family.	PWDs are not treated equaliy bc people believe PWDs cannot manage property.	Yes, PWDs have same rights when it come to inheritance, but clans and families do not treat equally bc they do not think that PWDs will make proper use of the lard.

U	V	W
Yes, he is in fact a clan leader. And you can become the heir as well	Yes, the key is having money.	Yes, if well mannered and mentored to be clan leader. The clan leadersh p Usually goes to the oldest son.
No	Perhaps if the ward can be useful. Otherwise this will only happen if the family will care for him.	Never heard of such a practice.
Yes	Yes, he was a guardian for his own nephews.	Yes, in fact he is a guardian
It used to be something that would happen, but now it is reducing. If the child has a big head (macrocephaly) men will say that is not mine.	Yes, it is possible	No, bc it is an Act of God.
No. Dowery is done at the discretion of the father and is set to a lesser degree by culture.	Yes, they are charged higher dowery.	No
Yes, although there may be challenges.	Yes, if they have money.	Yes
No	No (laughing at the thought of this) All you get from the community is pity.	None identified.
Yes. PWDs have the same rights because of the Culture.	Yes, Officially the government has emphasized this, but PWDs will get less bc families and clans think they cannot utilise the land.	Yes, he himself inherited.

X	Y	Z
Not possible. Such a person will always be despised. They cannot respect him.	NA	NA
Yes.	Yes	It is possible.
No, because people believe that such a person cannot even take care of themselves.	Yes, as long as not the PWD is not unable to speak.	Not possible
Yes, because the man will say we do not have disabled blood in our clan	NA	NA
Yes, it happened to him.	NA	NA
Yes, if you have financial security.	Yes.	Yes, but it is more challenging for women bc people do not think she can perform womanly duties. (i.e. cleaning, gardening and cooking)
None identified.	No. PWDs get invited to events like everyone else	No
It depends. They cannot allow children with disabilities to inherit, but a PWD child can inherit if the only child.	Yes, in fact he has never heard of PWDs being treated differently in matters of inheritance.	Yes, she has never heard of PWDs being treated differently in matters of inheritance

AA	AB	AC
NA	NA	NA
Not easy bc potential guardians would resist taking on such a responsibility.	Yes, this can be done for those with no feet, those who cannot speak, and those in wheel-chair.	NA
Yes, if you have financial resources.	It can happen, but it is not easy.	It is up to the family. Usually the person needs to have property.
Yes, that usually happens.	NA	NA
No, Fathers of brides do not add to the dowery demand, but they look at it as a disgrace.	NA	NA
Yes, but they are usually despised.	Yes, like herself. She got married in a Muslim ceremony.	Yes, although sometimes there are difficulties with the father.
No	No	No, it is only the family that helps.
It can happen, but the chances are very low.	It depends on the level of disability. It is "very impossible" for people who are blind/deaf/mute. But in general PWDs can inherit.	Yes PWDs can inherit if they are trusted by the clan.

AD	AE	AF
NA	NA	NA
NA	Yes	Yes, it is possible.
Only if they have financial stability.	Not possible.	Yes
NA	NA	Yes, that can happen sometimes. But usually they stay together.
Never heard of this practice.	Yes it can happen, but a man with a disability must have financial capability to be charged a higher amount.	No, actually it is reduced for male suitors with disabilities.
Yes, they can struggle. Family members can help you pay dowery.	Yes	Yes
No. Only you and your family will help. Fellow Muslims sometimes help.	To a very small extent.	No
Yes, wills giving inheritance to PWDs are honored. If there is no will he (as a blind man) would not be permitted to be an heir by the clan.	It is not possible, any able-bodied person will stop you.	Yes PWDs can inherit land but sometimes they are challenged by clans.

AG	AH	AI
NA	NA	NA
It is possible. This is just done for older people.	NA	NA
Yes, in fact he is.	You can, although many people view PWDs as useless. The key is proving yourself as useful.	Yes, but you need to be deemed successful.
NA	NA	NA
NA	It can happen.	NA
Yes, most PWDs are married. It is not hard for them.	Yes. They may be denied for family reasons. People might say you are bewitched.	Yes, but women are more concerned about money these days so they tend to despise male suiters with disabilities.
No	Not really, but advocacy organizations have helped to improve things somewhat.	No. (This interviewee listed the allocation of political offices to PWDs as something special that is done)
Yes. They can inherit through a will. He has not seen PWDs treated differently in matters of inheritance.	They are not prevented by govt policy or custom. It is only some families that do not permit PWDS to inherit property.	This depends on the education level of the family/clan the more education the less like to discriminate over inheritance.

AJ		AK
NA	NA	NA
This is difficult to do.	NA	Not aware of this practice. Guardianships are just for children.
Yes, but he must be trustworthy (not about $ or income; it is about whether they have a good heart.	Yes	NA
NA	NA	It happens, some men will flee and say that our clan does not produce children with disabilities.
NA	NA	NA
Yes, but many have low self-esteem. Men always despise women with disabilities	Yes	Yes, but very few do.
No	Only mentioned that at COMBRA (a CBR center in Seeta) they give out crutches .	It depends on community. Help for PWDs usually comes from family.
Yes, he was made heir of father's estate even though he has older brothers. But others may try to snatch and rob from him.	She thinks so, but does not know about any stories.	"It is not easy, the treatment you get is a lot like women" (i.e. it is discriminatory). "It is very hard."

AL	AM	AN
NA	NA	NA
This is a very normal practice, especially for the elderly	NA	Never seen it occur.
Yes, it depends on ability. She is a guardian of 4 children.	When clan accepts it is possible.	Never seen it.
NA	No	NA
NA	NA	Have not heard of such a practice.
Yes, and it is not more difficult.	Yes, even if the kwanjula fails you can stay together.	Yes, but the probability of marrying is less.
Maybe family members will help.	None identified.	No
Yes you can. There is no discrimination in Seeta currently.	Yes, if there is a will they will follow it. If no will the clan decides and few clans discriminate.	It depends on the family. It is the same in towns and rural areas.

AO	AP	AQ
NA	NA	NA
NA	NA	NA
He has not seen it. it is done informally by families.	Yes	Did not understand concept
Yes, bc people think it happens due to witch-craft.	NA	NA
NA	NA	NA
Yes, but convincing the family can be very hard especially depending on the disability.	Yes, it is easy.	Yes
No	Yes, they take people to hospital	No
He has not seen PWDs permitted to inherit land. This has been the case everywhere he has lived.	PWDs are treated the same but all property goes to oldest brother.	He thinks that he will be treated the same. He cannot speak for others.

AR	AS	AT
NA	Na	NA
NA	NA	NA
Yes they can	Yes, if the PWD has money.	Yes they can. Her sick brother made her guardian for his children, older brother resisted, but later they agreed.
NA	NA	NA
NA	NA	NA
Yes	Yes, if you marry someone with the same disability it is acceptable. Otherwise it can be hard.	In the past you could not. But today you can. But there can still be a good bit of family pressure.
No	Depends on the community. Some parents just leave you.	People help carry things for her. Some start circles or give you money for transport.
She has not heard that it is more difficult	No, people say you cannot support yourself so you do not need land.	Yes, and she was even named heir.. This was for land in Fort Portal not Mukono. Under Toro custom women can be heirs.

AU	AV	AW
NA	NA	NA
NA	Someone with a mental disability might be put in the care of their children.	NA
NA	Depends on whether or not you have money.	It is very hard under the customs of the Buganda to be a guardian if you are a PWD
NA	NA	NA
NA	NA	NA
They are allowed but for some people it is very hard. Especially women.	Yes, but people can pressure against it. Introductions can be difficult.	Some may, others no. When you do not have money, you may not.
No	You could be given a special seat at a funeral. However, people will not let you help by cooking or getting water.	He has never seen it in Uganda—only in outside communities. Here there is special care at the family level only.
Never heard of it ever happening.	PWDs are sometimes treated differently. He was not permitted to inherit his father's land in Masaka.	Their customary rights are not exactly the same, but "if they are not stupid" they will defend themselves and not allow relatives to take advantage of them.

	AX	AY	AZ
	NA	NA	NA
	It can be OK, depends on the reasons and the disability. e.g. deaf and bling need such care	The interview is aware of that happening.	NA
	Yes, if they have $	PWD cannot be guardians	Yes, if you have established the ability to provide care-economic capacity being the most important factor
	NA	NA	NA
	He has not heard of higher dowries for maie suitors with disabilities.	It depends on the culture. Traditionally for the Baganda the bride price is about what you can pay.	NA
	Men with resources can. It is hard for women. Many are impregnated out of wedlock.	It is a challenge bc of social pressures.	Yes, if the PWD seeking marriage has financial resources. If family does not consent to marriage people just cohabit. It is harder for woman with disabilities to get married than a many with
	None mentioned.	None mentioned.	No
	This depends on the families. Some refuse to give PWDs land. This applies to all levels of society.	They are treated equally bc they have that right.	NA

BA	BC	BD
NA	NA	NA
Has never seen this.	It is rare for an adult to be taken care of. Adults are supposed to hake care of themselves.	NA
A person can be a guardian as long as they have resources. He became a guardian for an 8 year old boy who came to him.	Yes, if you have established the ability to provide care. Economic capacity is the most important factor.	Yes, but typically you need to be able to prove that you have resources.
NA	Usually this will make the men run away. Some women just give the child to a grandmother or aunt.	NA
NA	Yes, that usually happens.	Has not heard of such a practice. In fact, actually others often help to see dowery paid by a man with a disability.
Yes, this is easy if you have resources.	Yes, but it depends on the level of disability.	Yes
Some families help.	Just at the family level. There is also some discrete acts of kindness like pushing people in wheelchairs up hills	None mentioned.
Yes, if they have property that they own themselves in order to prove they can be responsible. If you do not have property, you are unlikely to be made an heir.	Some parents allow if it is a boy and even a girl from the aunt. The gov't has a big role to play here to see that property is distributed consistently with the law	Some people view PWDs as "useless" so they do not let PWDs inherit land. Whether intestate or testate. "Give them my land, for what?"

BE	BF	BG
NA	NA	It is very difficult for a man with disabilities to become a clan leader and to be permitted to perform ceremonial functions.
It does happen. Guardians for persons with mental disabilities are rare. Typically families are the care givers.	NA	He is not aware of this happening. Iif it does occur, it is only because people are kind.
Yes ,they can.	Yes, by proving their capability through actions.	No. He was not even permitted to stand as a surety in a formal court.
Men will usually leave women because of this.	NA	NA
NA	NA	NA
Yes, although it might take some time for the family to accept. It can be very difficult for women, bc for women it is essential that they can do household functions.	Yes	It used to be very difficult, but now things are improving. It is easier for men (especially men who have money) than it is for women bc people think women with disabilities cannot do their strenuous
Discrete and random acts of kindness only. For example he gave was giving space to sit at a pew at church. Other people provide helping hands.	No	Not a all. You must do things for yourself.
Under the law you do, but attitudes and traditions can prevent. PWDs don't own the family property and rarely can become the heir. Sometimes the only family land you get is the burial plot.	They have the same rights and there is no oppression at all.	It is very difficult to get an equal share. It is a matter of attitude in families, clans and communities—most family members think disability is a curse.

BH	BI	BJ
NA	NA	NA
NA	NA	This used to happen when family bonds were strong but the family is changing and such
NA	NA	Only if you have performed with outstanding success.
NA	NA	NA
NA	NA	They may charge you double the dowery.
There are social challenges, but they can always get married if they want.	You can but there are many cases where the community applies negative social pressure.	For women it is very hard bc men's families will not let them.
People do little nice things like given up seats on the taxi.	No	Kabaka gave land. People are nice, give care, invite to functions.
Never noted any different treatment	Normally "they" do not consider them.	PWDs are not permitted to inherit land. The cultures are very traditional and they oppose it. In some ways it it better to get your own land and avoid conflict and drama that comes from land inheritance.

BK

NA

In most cases pwd are not provided with basic needs. It is done some time in the rural setting.

He needs to have resources and sometimes other family members will still reject the appointment of a PWD as guardian.

NA

NA

Yes they can. However, the community sees you as abnormal if you marry someone with a disability.

No, they are not supportive.

Family members think you cannot make use of the land so they are often unwilling to give it to you. If you receive land the heir will try to take it from you.

Globethics.net Publications

The list below is only a selection of our publications. To view the full collection, please visit our website.

All products are provided free of charge and can be downloaded in PDF form from the Globethics.net library and at www.globethics.net/publications. Bulk print copies can be ordered from *publictions@globethics.net* at special rates for those from the Global South.
Paid products not provided free of charge are indicated[*].
The Editor of the different Series of Globethics.net Publications is Prof. Dr Obiora Ike, Executive Director of Globethics.net in Geneva and Professor of Ethics at the Godfrey Okoye University Enugu/Nigeria.

Contact for manuscripts and suggestions: *publications@globethics.net*

African Law Series

Ghislain Patrick Lessène, *Code international de la détention en Afrique*, 2013, 620pp. ISBN: 978-2-940428-70-0

D. Brian Dennison/ Pamela Tibihikirra-Kalyegira (eds.), *Legal Ethics and Professionalism. A Handbook for Uganda*, 2014, 400pp. ISBN 978–2–88931–011–1

Pascale Mukonde Musulay, *Droit des affaires en Afrique subsaharienne et économie planétaire*, 2015, 164pp. ISBN: 978–2–88931–044–9

Pascal Mukonde Musulay, *Démocratie électorale en Afrique subsaharienne: Entre droit, pouvoir et argent*, 2016, 209pp. ISBN 978–2–88931–156–9

Pascal Mukonde Musulay, *Droits, libertés et devoirs de la personne et des peuples en droit international africain Tome I Promotion et protection*, 282pp. 2021, ISBN 978-2-88931-397-6

Pascal Mukonde Musulay, *Droits, libertés et devoirs de la personne et des peuples en droit international africain Tome II Libertés, droits et obligations démocratiques*, 332pp. 2021, ISBN 978-2-88931-399-0

Ambroise Katambu Bulambo, *Règlement judiciaire des conflits électoraux. Précis de droit comparé africain*, 2021, 672pp., ISBN 978-2-88931-403-4

David Brian Dennison, *The Status, Rights and Treatment of Persons with Disabilities within Customary Legal Frameworks in Uganda: A Study of Mukono District*, 2021, 355pp. ISBN 978-2-88931-409-6

Focus Series

Bosco Muchukiwa Rukakiza, *Résilience et transformation des conflits dans les États des Grands Lacs africains: Théorie, démarches et applications*, 2021, 126pp. ISBN 978-2-88931-405-8

Global Series

Ariane Hentsch Cisneros / Shanta Premawardhana (eds.), *Sharing Values. A Hermeneutics for Global Ethics*, 2010, 418pp.
ISBN: 978–2–940428–25–0.

Deon Rossouw / Christoph Stückelberger (eds.), *Global Survey of Business Ethics in Training, Teaching and Research*, 2012, 404pp.
ISBN: 978–2–940428–39–7

Carol Cosgrove Sacks/ Paul H. Dembinski (eds.), *Trust and Ethics in Finance. Innovative Ideas from the Robin Cosgrove Prize*, 2012, 380pp.
ISBN: 978–2–940428–41–0

Nicolae Irina / Christoph Stückelberger (eds.), *Mining, Ethics and Sustainability*, 2014, 198pp. ISBN: 978–2–88931–020–3

Philip Lee and Dafne Sabanes Plou (eds), *More or Less Equal: How Digital Platforms Can Help Advance Communication Rights*, 2014, 158pp.
ISBN 978–2–88931–009–8

Sanjoy Mukherjee and Christoph Stückelberger (eds.) *Sustainability Ethics. Ecology, Economy, Ethics. International Conference SusCon III, Shillong/India*, 2015, 353pp. ISBN: 978–2–88931–068–5

Amélie Vallotton Preisig / Hermann Rösch / Christoph Stückelberger (eds.) *Ethical Dilemmas in the Information Society. Codes of Ethics for Librarians and Archivists*, 2014, 224pp. ISBN: 978–288931–024–1.

Prospects and Challenges for the Ecumenical Movement in the 21st Century. Insights from the Global Ecumenical Theological Institute, David Field / Jutta Koslowski, 256pp. 2016, ISBN: 978–2–88931–097–5

Christoph Stückelberger, Walter Fust, Obiora Ike (eds.), *Global Ethics for Leadership. Values and Virtues for Life*, 2016, 444pp.
ISBN: 978–2–88931–123–1

Dietrich Werner / Elisabeth Jeglitzka (eds.), *Eco-Theology, Climate Justice and Food Security: Theological Education and Christian Leadership Development*, 316pp. 2016, ISBN 978–2–88931–145–3

Obiora Ike, Andrea Grieder and Ignace Haaz (Eds.), *Poetry and Ethics: Inventing Possibilities in Which We Are Moved to Action and How We Live Together*, 271pp. 2018, ISBN 978–2–88931–242–9

Christoph Stückelberger / Pavan Duggal (Eds.), *Cyber Ethics 4.0: Serving Humanity with Values*, 503pp. 2018, ISBN 978–2–88931–264-1

Texts Series

Principles on Sharing Values across Cultures and Religions, 2012, 20pp. Available in English, French, Spanish, German and Chinese. Other languages in preparation. ISBN: 978–2–940428–09–0

Ethics in Politics. Why it Matters More than Ever and How it Can Make a Difference. A Declaration, 8pp, 2012. Available in English and French. ISBN: 978–2–940428–35–9

Religions for Climate Justice: International Interfaith Statements 2008–2014, 2014, 45pp. Available in English. ISBN 978–2–88931–006–7

Ethics in the Information Society: The Nine 'P's. A Discussion Paper for the WSIS+10 Process 2013–2015, 2013, 32pp. ISBN: 978–2–940428–063–2

Principles on Equality and Inequality for a Sustainable Economy. Endorsed by the Global Ethics Forum 2014 with Results from Ben Africa Conference 2014, 2015, 41pp. ISBN: 978–2–88931–025–8

Water Ethics: Principles and Guidelines, 2019, 41pp. ISBN 978–2–88931-313-6, available in three languages.

Theses Series

Sabina Kavutha Mutisya, *The Experience of Being a Divorced or Separated Single Mother: A Phenomenological Study*, 2019, 168pp. ISBN: 978-2-88931-274-0

Florence Muia, *Sustainable Peacebuilding Strategies. Sustainable Peacebuilding Operations in Nakuru County, Kenya: Contribution to the Catholic Justice and Peace Commission (CJPC)*, 2020, 195pp. ISBN: 978-2-88931-331-0

Mary Rose-Claret Ogbuehi, *The Struggle for Women Empowerment Through Education*, 2020, 410pp. ISBN: 978-2-88931-363-1

Nestor Engone Elloué, *La justice climatique restaurative: Réparer les inégalités Nord/Sud*, 2020, 198pp. ISBN 978-2-88931-379-2

Hilary C. Ike, *Organizational Improvement of Nigerian Catholic Chaplaincy in Central Ohio*, 2021, 154pp. ISBN 978-2-88931-385-3

Education Ethics Series

Divya Singh / Christoph Stückelberger (Eds.), *Ethics in Higher Education Values-driven Leaders for the Future*, 2017, 367pp. ISBN: 978–2–88931–165–1

Obiora Ike / Chidiebere Onyia (Eds.) *Ethics in Higher Education, Foundation for Sustainable Development*, 2018, 645pp. IBSN: 978-2-88931-217-7

Obiora Ike / Chidiebere Onyia (Eds.) *Ethics in Higher Education, Religions and Traditions in Nigeria* 2018, 198pp. IBSN: 978-2-88931-219-1

Obiora F. Ike, Justus Mbae, Chidiebere Onyia (Eds.), *Mainstreaming Ethics in Higher Education: Research Ethics in Administration, Finance, Education, Environment and Law Vol. 1*, 2019, 779pp. ISBN 978-2-88931-300-6

Ikechukwu J. Ani/Obiora F. Ike (Eds.), *Higher Education in Crisis Sustaining Quality Assurance and Innovation in Research through Applied Ethics*, 2019, 214pp. ISBN 978-2-88931-323-5

Deivit Montealegre / María Eugenia Barroso (Eds.), *Ethics in Higher Education, a Transversal Dimension: Challenges for Latin America. Ética en educación superior, una dimensión transversal: Desafíos para América Latina*, 2020, 148pp. ISBN 978-2-88931-359-4

Obiora Ike, Justus Mbae, Chidiebere Onyia, Herbert Makinda (Eds.), *Mainstreaming Ethics in Higher Education Vol. 2*, 2021, 420pp. ISBN: 978-2-88931-383-9

Christoph Stückelberger/ Joseph Galgalo/ Samuel Kobia (Eds.), *Leadership with Integrity. Higher Education from Vocation to Funding*, 2021, 288pp. ISBN 978-2-88931-389-1

Co-publications & Other

Kenneth R. Ross, *Mission Rediscovered: Transforming Disciples*, 2020, 138pp. ISBN 978-2-88931-369-3

Obiora Ike, Amélé Adamavi-Aho Ekué, Anja Andriamay, Lucy Howe López (Eds.), *Who Cares About Ethics?* 2020, 352pp. ISBN 978-2-88931-381-5

This is only selection of our latest publications, to view our full collection please visit:

www.globethics.net/publications